THE PENGUIN CLASSICS

FOUNDER EDITOR (1944–64): E. V. RIEU

Editor: Betty Radice

GAIUS JULIUS CAESAR was born in 100 B.C. into an ancient patrician family. He was an adolescent during the period of the proscription of Marius (his father's brother-in-law), the dictatorship of Sulla and the early career of Pompey. His family were traditionally against the patrician senatorial oligarchy and Caesar followed suit. He was imprisoned for a short time by Sulla, but managed to maintain good relations with the nobles for ten years after his release; he was even co-opted into the college of priests (73 B.C.). However he came out openly for Pompey in 71 B.C., and Caesar, Pompey and Crassus (whom the senate had also alienated) formed the 'first triumvirate'. For the next nine years Caesar was away on campaigns, returning in 60 B.C. from his service as governor of Further Spain to be elected consul. He was then created governor of Transalpine Gaul, a task which was to occupy him for nine years. He had left the two triumvirs to safeguard his interests in Rome but they had many differences and met in Luca (56 B.C.) in an attempt to solve them. Pompey was appointed sole consul in 52 B.C. after the death of Crassus, which resulted in civil war and the defeat of the Pompeian faction in Spain (45 B.C.). Caesar came back to Rome as dictator. He tried to improve conditions for the Roman citizen and increase the honesty and efficiency of the government. His dictatorship was declared perpetual in February 44 B.C., but his many bitter enemies hatched a conspiracy and assassinated him in March 44 B.C.

S. A. HANDFORD was born at Manchester in 1898 and educated at Bradford Grammar School and at Balliol College, Oxford, where he took a 'double first' in classics. He has been a lecturer in Swansea, and Lecturer and Reader at King's College, London. He has published several books on classical subjects, and has translated Caesar, Sallust and Aesop for the Penguin Classics.

CAESAR
THE CONQUEST
OF GAUL

TRANSLATED BY
S. A. HANDFORD

PENGUIN BOOKS

Penguin Books Ltd, Harmondsworth, Middlesex, England
Penguin Books, 625 Madison Avenue, New York, New York 10022, U.S.A.
Penguin Books Australia Ltd, Ringwood, Victoria, Australia
Penguin Books Canada Ltd, 2801 John Street, Markham, Ontario, Canada L3R 1B4
Penguin Books (N.Z.) Ltd, 182–190 Wairau Road, Auckland 10, New Zealand

—

This translation first published 1951
Reprinted 1953, 1956, 1958, 1960, 1963, 1965, 1967, 1970, 1972, 1974, 1976, 1978

—

—

Made and printed in Great Britain
by Richard Clay (The Chaucer Press) Ltd,
Bungay, Suffolk
Set in Monotype Bembo

CONTENTS

The medallion on the title page shows a coin of about 48 B.C. portraying a Gallic prisoner, in all probability Vercingetorix, who was then imprisoned in Rome.

INTRODUCTION

ROMAN POLITICS IN THE
FIRST CENTURY B.C.

JULIUS CAESAR'S conquest of Gaul – the last war of conquest fought by Republican Rome – occupied the years 58–50 B.C. For centuries the Roman state had been governed by a system which depended largely for its success upon a division of functions and control. Electoral and legislative power lay with various Assemblies of the citizen body. Executive duties were carried out partly by magistrates elected in the Assemblies – the most important being two consuls, a varying number of praetors, and ten tribunes of the commons, who had a special power of preventing by veto the transaction of business by any official body or any other magistrate except a dictator – and partly by the Senate, into which all ex-magistrates were normally drafted.

During the long period of conquest which made Rome first the mistress of Italy, then the ruler of an empire stretching from the Straits of Gibraltar to the Euphrates, the governmental system had worked fairly well. But by the time of Caesar's birth (between 102 and 100 B.C.) it was beginning to break down. The possession of a large empire had brought immense wealth, which demoralized the ruling class. The right of that class, and in particular the right of the Senate, to something like a monopoly of administrative control was being challenged by democratic leaders. Before Caesar was twenty years of age, party strife had led not merely to rioting but to civil war. Lucius Cornelius Sulla was the first to show, in 88 B.C., that Roman legions would follow a popular general against their own country as well as against its enemies. Still worse bloodshed and massacres of political opponents followed his return to Italy in 83 B.C. after a war against Mithridates, king of Pontus in Asia Minor. Reforms which Sulla carried through as dictator restored to some extent the ascendancy of the Senatorial nobles, but did nothing to correct their selfish and short-sighted exclusiveness, which made political stability impossible and further usurpations of military power inevitable. Roman citizenship had recently been extended to nearly the whole of Italy; but these new citizens scattered through the townships and countryside were not the steadying influence that they might have been, because – owing to the lack of a representative system, either for law-making or for electing magistrates – their voting rights were largely ineffective. Since legislative and electoral power still lay mainly in the hands of citizens resident in or near Rome, the rest of Italy had comparatively little interest in the working of the governmental machine.

The twenty years intervening between the resignation of Sulla and the beginning of the Gallic war were marked by the emergence of several able and ambitious men. The consulships of 70 B.C. fell to two candidates who had been active partisans of Sulla and since his death had gained some military distinction: Marcus Licinius Crassus, an immensely rich financier, and Gnaeus Pompeius Magnus – Pompey the Great. Together they carried certain measures which destroyed the ascendancy secured to the Senate by Sulla's legislation. But Pompey's energy and military genius soon enabled him to outstrip Crassus in the competition for power. In 67 B.C. he was endowed with an extraordinary proconsular command over the whole of the Mediterranean and its coasts, in order to clear the sea of the pirates who by infesting it threatened Italy with famine, and discharged his task in three months. The next year he received a general commission to regulate the affairs of Rome in Asia Minor, where a general of the Senate's choice, Lucius Licinius Lucullus, had been campaigning for eight years in another war against Mithridates. Pompey not only won more than his fair share of credit by completing the victory of which Lucullus had laid the foundation, but effected a comprehensive settlement of the Near East. One new Roman province (Syria) was created, two existing provinces were enlarged, and the revenue of the state enormously increased.

Meanwhile Crassus, who was jealous of Pompey's success and suspicious of what his intentions might be on his return to Rome, made various attempts to increase the strength of his own position. For a time he encouraged the ambitions of Lucius Sergius Catilina, an impoverished and dissolute patrician who was determined to obtain a consulship and quite prepared to use lawless force to further either his own aims or the aims of anyone who would buy his services. But after Catiline's rejection at the election held in 64 B.C., when Marcus Tullius Cicero the orator was a successful candidate, Crassus discarded him; and after a further defeat in 63 Catiline embarked on a violent revolutionary plot, which was crushed by Cicero as consul and ended in the death of Catiline and his chief accomplices.

In 62 B.C. (in which year Caesar held the office of praetor) Pompey returned from the East. Cicero, elated by the glory of his consulship and his firm handling of the Catilinarian crisis, conceived the idea of ensuring against further political disturbances by rallying all loyal citizens in defence of the constitution. In particular he sought to secure political co-operation between the Senatorial nobility and the 'Equestrian Order', which consisted of men with capital invested in land, finance, commerce, or the business of tax-collecting.[1] Pompey inspired the hope that he would play the role of leader of such a coalition by at once disbanding his troops and treating the Senate with due deference. But the Senate, with blind perversity, rebuffed him by deliberately postponing the ratification of his Eastern settlement and the grant of land to pension off his veterans. Pompey accepted the situation for the moment. But this only meant that he did not intend to employ the method of a military coup d'état in his pursuit of power. Power, and more power, he meant to have, and though he did not choose to use naked force he had small respect for constitutional restraints.

In 60 B.C. Caesar returned from a year as provincial governor in

1. The term 'Equestrian Order' originally meant men whose means qualified them for service in the army as cavalrymen (equites). But by this time it had come to denote all citizens possessing a capital of some £4000 and not belonging to the Senatorial nobility – i.e. men of substance who had not held a magistracy entitling them to membership of the Senate.

Spain to stand for a consulship. Although he had not yet shown
his hand openly in politics, the conservative Senators must have
known that he was both an exceptionally able man and a poten-
tially dangerous man. What they failed to understand was that the
surest way of making the danger actual was to frustrate him in the
same high-handed way as they frustrated Pompey. Not only did
they allow the obstinate and narrow-minded Marcus Porcius Cato
to thwart Caesar's desire for a triumph in celebration of some military successes in Spain. They went farther. Anticipating his election as consul, they used against him the Senate's right of deter-
mining the 'provinces' or spheres of duty which the consuls about
to be elected should undertake, according to custom, after their
year of office at Rome. Instead of the usual provincial governorships – carrying with them the certainty of obtaining personal gain
and the chance of winning military glory – these particular consuls were assigned the superintendence of the forests and cattle-
tracks of Italy! That was enough. Caesar persuaded Pompey and
Crassus, to whom he owed a huge sum of money, to form with
him the unofficial coalition known as the First Triumvirate, for
the furtherance of their personal aims by forcing the Senate's hand
and obtaining control of the state. The alliance was cemented by a
marriage between Pompey and Caesar's only child Julia.

Caesar was duly elected consul – with a colleague, however,
who was determined to do his best to hinder his designs, one Marcus Calpurnius Bibulus. When Caesar submitted to the Assembly
a bill to provide land for Pompey's veterans, Bibulus and others
employed every means of obstruction, until Caesar brought in a
band of soldiers to turn them out of the forum and got the bill
through by force. Other measures followed, including the ratification of Pompey's Eastern settlement, and finally Caesar's appointment, by a law passed in the Assembly, to a provincial command
for the extraordinary period of five years (1st March, 59–1st
March, 54 B.C.). The province originally voted to him was Cisalpine Gaul (northern Italy between the Alps and the Apennines[1]),

1. Cisalpine Gaul means Gaul on the Italian side of the Alps. Northern
Italy had been peopled for centuries by Gallic tribes; but by Caesar's time
it had been largely Romanized, and most of its inhabitants possessed either

with Illyria (on the east of the Adriatic). A few weeks later the Senate added Transalpine Gaul, which consisted of the Mediterranean coast of France, the lower Rhone valley, and a part of the western Alpine district.[1] These provinces, for the government of which Caesar was assigned four legions, formed a combination that gave him exactly what he wanted. He could spend most of his winters in northern Italy, where it was easy to keep in touch with affairs in Rome through friends and agents. Since Cisalpine Gaul was one of the chief recruiting grounds for the Roman armies, he could raise additional legions whenever he needed them. The inclusion of the Transalpine province provided both a convenient opportunity for embarking on a war of conquest (for the unsettled condition of Gaul beyond the Provincial frontier invited military intervention), and an excellent base from which to conduct it. At the end of eight years he was at the head of a large veteran army experienced in many hard-fought campaigns and entirely devoted to its commander, he had added a large and rich province to the empire, and he had made an enormous fortune for himself.

During all this time the state continued to be under the control of the triumvirs, though the bond of union between them was weakened as time went on, and finally broken. The alliance depended only on their usefulness to one another, and both moderates like Cicero and conservative nobles like Cato were eager to take advantage of the jealousies and suspicions which arose between the big three. The coalition was already in danger of collapse in 56 B.C. But in the spring of that year the partners met at Lucca, in Caesar's Cisalpine province, and made up their differences for the time being. It was agreed that Pompey and Crassus should be consuls again in 55 B.C.; Caesar's provincial command was to be extended (probably until 13th November, 50 B.C.);

full Roman citizenship or at least some of the privileges of Roman citizens. For reasons of security, however, it was administered as a province by a governor. (In this translation, 'northern Italy' or 'Italy' means this province of Cisalpine Gaul.)

1. Provence – though it covers only a part of the area which formed the Roman province – derives its name from the Latin *provincia*. (In this translation, 'the Province' means the province of Transalpine Gaul.)

Pompey was to have the command of the two Spanish provinces, with special leave to exercise it by deputy and to remain himself in Italy; and Crassus was to have the province of Syria, where by provoking a war against Parthia he hoped to win his own share of military glory. In 54 and 53 B.C. the state drifted into something approaching anarchy. Elections were repeatedly prevented by abuse of the tribunes' veto, and, when they were held, were decided either by shameless bribery or by armed rioting. Eventually, in 52 B.C., the Senate recommended the appointment of Pompey to a consulship without a colleague – which meant something not far removed from a dictatorship – on the plea of enabling him to enforce order.

Ever since Caesar's consulship in 59 B.C. a group of aristocrats led by Cato had been scheming to punish him for his defiance of the Senate and the constitution, and they hoped now to be able to use Pompey for their purpose. These plans were helped by the death of Julia (54 B.C.), which removed the strongest personal tie uniting Caesar and Pompey, and the death of Crassus in Parthia (53 B.C.), which left them to face each other alone. Cato and his supporters intended to prosecute Caesar for treason or extortion as soon as he became a private citizen again, on the expiry of his Gallic command. If they could induce Pompey to back such a prosecution, they had little doubt that they could secure Caesar's conviction and so put an end to his career. He was safe as long as he held his governorship and the command of his army. After that, he would again be safe if he could manage to be elected consul, since a man elected to a magistracy was exempt from prosecution. He had been excused, by a special law, from the ordinary rule requiring candidates to attend the elections in person. But since a clear ten years' interval had to elapse between two tenures of the office, the earliest election at which he was legally entitled to stand would be that held in the summer of 49 B.C., by which time his governorship, unless again extended, would have expired and a successor might be appointed. There would thus be an interval of some months during which he would be exposed to the attacks of his enemies.

The years 51 and 50 B.C. were spent in endless negotiations and

intrigues. Caesar expected Pompey and the Senate to let the constitutional rules be strained in his favour, as they had formerly been
strained in Pompey's favour. Cato and his party put great pressure
on Pompey to deliver Caesar into their hands by insisting on the
strict letter of the law. Pompey hesitated and manoeuvred to avoid
coming to a final decision. At last Cato won. Against the will of
all but a small clique of Senatorial aristocrats, Pompey consented
to measures which presented Caesar with a choice between civil
war and his own political extinction. He chose war. Eighteen
months later Pompey was dead, murdered by a soldier in Egypt
after suffering defeat at Caesar's hands. By the spring of 45 B.C.
the Republican cause was lost and Caesar was master of the Roman world. During the brief intervals between campaigns, and in
the one year that remained to him after the conclusion of the war,
he carried out an extensive programme of financial and economic
reconstruction, which included agrarian protection for Italy. But
many of his fellow-citizens, including some of his oldest supporters, had by this time come to look upon him as a tyrant, and
their view was confirmed by his assumption in February, 44 B.C.,
of a dictatorship for life, which precluded any hope of a return to
constitutional government. A month later he lay dying from the
three and twenty dagger-thrusts of his murderers.

§ 2

CAESAR THE MAN

GAIUS JULIUS CAESAR was a member of a patrician family
which had recently emerged from a long period of obscurity.
The instincts of a Roman aristocrat were strongly marked in him.
The word 'honour' was often on his lips. 'Honour' required that
he should be intensely loyal to his friends and supporters, even to
the humblest and least deserving who rendered him service,[1] and
on the other hand that his own claims to high preferment and even

1. If a set of bandits and cut-throats helped him to defend his honour, he
said, he would reward them in the same way as any others.

to unconstitutional privilege should be recognized by his fellow-citizens. He was urbane in social intercourse, a man of easy and polished manners and impressive personality, and except as regards women not intemperate in his personal tastes.

His abilities, considered singly, were such as were not uncommon among his countrymen. Rome produced many able politicians, administrators, generals, orators, and authors. But Caesar's genius was almost unique in its versatility. No other Roman – few men, indeed, of any age or country – was at the same time so astute a politician, so resourceful an administrator, so successful a general, so brilliant an orator, and so gifted an author. Such a career is proof of an extraordinary endowment of qualities. Perhaps the most outstanding are, first, the combination of daemonic energy and level-headed judgement which inspired all he did, both in the early days when he was pushing his way to the top in politics, and in his maturity as soldier and statesman; and, secondly, the almost terrifying determination with which he pursued his aims. 'No man' it has been said 'has ever been so determined to impose his will on others and no man has ever been so gifted by nature for the achievement of his purpose.' He was not naturally a cruel man; on the contrary, his clemency towards fellow-countrymen whom he had defeated was famous, and even in his foreign wars he was not cruel for cruelty's sake. But booty had to be provided for his troops; so towns must be sacked and populations sold into slavery. In order to bring the war to an end before his term as proconsul expired, the Gauls must have their spirit broken and be taught not to keep on rebelling; if repeated defeats would not do it, then recourse must be had to frightfulness – witness the execution of the councillors of the Veneti, the massacre of the Germans, man, woman, and child, in the Rhineland, and the bloody hands at Uxellodunum. His political advancement required the services of great armies and of a multitude of supporters; accordingly, troops and henchmen of every class, including some men of notorious profligacy, were hired with cash obtained by forced loans, confiscation, and pillage. As soon as his schemes brought him into collision with the constitution, he did not hesitate to throw legal restraints to the winds and to enter upon a course which – though he himself

14

may have had no deliberate intention of effecting a revolution – led in the end to civil war and the destruction of the Republic.

Very divergent views have been taken of Caesar's actions and aims in the last years of his life. Shakespeare, enlarging upon hints supplied by the Greek biographer Plutarch, represents him as a great man who has degenerated into a petty and boastful tyrant with a touch of megalomania. This picture is certainly overdrawn. Years of military command had doubtless made him somewhat imperious in word and manner, and he would have been hardly human if such unbroken success had not made him vain. But he had none of the instincts of a vulgar despot. He had concentrated all the power of the state in his own person and clearly meant to retain it. But it is fairly certain that he had no intention of abandoning Roman traditions by the assumption of divine honours or the trappings of a conventional absolute monarch – as witness his ostentatious refusal of the diadem offered him by Mark Antony. Nor did he make any plans for founding a hereditary dynasty. The accounts of the extravagant honours, divine and secular, assigned to him in his last years are probably much exaggerated; and, in so far as they are historical, they appear to have proceeded rather from the excessive adulation of a subservient Senate than from any deliberate choice on Caesar's part. It is not surprising that they insisted on treating as more than human a man who, besides enhancing the imperial power of Rome, had subdued them all to his will and held practically every office of state in his personal gift and patronage. They showered compliments and titles upon him, and he, chiefly it may be as a matter of policy, did not refuse them. At the time of his death he was preparing for a great campaign against Parthia. What plans he had for the permanent government of the state on his return, no one can say. He may have had considered and matured plans for making Rome a totalitarian state; or he may have remained an opportunist, waiting on events and taking action to deal with situations as they arose. Only it seems clear that he regarded the Republic as dead and showed little regret for its demise. As he put it, the Republic had become a mere name without substance. Events proved his judgement correct.

§ 3

GAUL AND ITS INHABITANTS

THE GAUL which Caesar conquered included France, except the part in the south which was already a Roman province, southern Holland, Belgium, the strip of Germany lying west of the Rhine, and most of Switzerland. The greater part of this area, as well as most of Britain, was occupied several centuries before Caesar's time by Celts who came from central Europe. Their racial connexions are uncertain; many ancient writers speak of them as containing, like the Germans, a large proportion of tall, fair-haired men and women. Probably about 200 B.C., a fresh horde of immigrants – the Belgae, a Celtic people with an admixture of German blood – overran the part of Gaul lying north of the Seine and the Marne, and a century or so later some of them crossed the Channel and took possession of south-eastern Britain. Celts and Belgae, both in Gaul and in Britain, spoke dialects of the same language – the language from which Welsh, Gaelic, Irish, and Breton are descended.

The Gauls were fairly prosperous and civilized in a material sense, though politically backward. The wealthier citizens had well-built houses in villages or walled towns connected by good carriage roads and river bridges. The people were skilled in agriculture and grew corn on a big scale. There was a considerable manufacture of swords and other metal-work. Imitations of Greek and Roman coins, as well as native types, were in circulation; some exist bearing the name of the great Gallic leader Vercingetorix. The maritime tribes had fleets of large though clumsy ships and kept up a busy trade with Britain. Writing, however, was apparently not in general use, although the Druids and their pupils used an alphabet of Greek letters.

The political organization of Gaul is described in Chapter I. In that passage and in others Caesar shows how the ambitious intrigues of wealthy and powerful men, including sometimes dethroned kings or their descendants, kept many of the tribes in a chronic state of political instability, and how the bitterness of their rivalries led some of them to make common cause with German or Roman invaders and prevented the development of any effective sense of national unity. The impression which he formed of the Gallic character – brave and impetuous, but completely lacking in steadiness and perseverance – is also clearly brought out in his narrative.

The first encounter of the Romans with Gauls was with the tribes which had settled in the part of northern Italy that the Romans called Cisalpine Gaul (p. 10). In 390 B.C. they overran half Italy and even sacked the capital. There were intermittent conflicts during the next two centuries with these Cisalpine Gauls, but by 190 B.C. the whole area had been conquered by the Romans. Their earliest recorded contact with Gaul beyond the Alps was in 123 B.C., when the Aedui sought Roman support against rival tribes and were recognized as 'Friends and Allies of the Roman People'. Two years later the Romans made themselves masters of the lower Rhone by defeating the Arverni, who had extended their power over the whole of central Gaul; and it was then that the province of Transalpine Gaul (p. 11) was formed. This secured for the first time a land route to the much older Spanish provinces, and opened up southern Gaul to the spread of Roman civilization, language, and trade. A few years later, however, the new province was in danger of being wrested from Rome by invaders who had migrated into central Europe from their homes on the North Sea coast. The German tribes of the Cimbri and Teutoni crossed the Rhine, overran all Celtic Gaul (only the Belgae were able to resist them), and in the years 109–105 B.C. defeated three Roman armies in the Province and seriously threatened Italy. Eventually the Teutoni were routed by Gaius Marius at Aix-en-Provence; the Cimbri went over the Brenner pass and were defeated in northern Italy by Marius and his colleague Quintus Lutatius Catulus.

In 77 B.C. the tribes of the Transalpine province rose in sympathy with the rebellion of Quintus Sertorius[1] in Spain. In 61 B.C. the powerful tribe of the Allobroges was goaded into revolt by the oppressive exactions of the Roman tax collectors. Meanwhile

1. See the Glossary.

danger was threatening from Germany again, where a confederacy of tribes known as the Suebi was gradually pressing westwards. At some time between 70 and 65 B.C. the Arverni and Sequani hired the help of a Suebic army, under its able king Ariovistus, to fight against their ancient rivals the Aedui. Ariovistus helped the Sequani to defeat the Aedui and then, retaining a part of the Sequani's territory in Alsace as the reward of his services, proceeded to call in fresh hordes of Germans, evidently meaning to found a German kingdom in Gaul. Eventually his harsh treatment of the Sequani seems to have made them turn against him, and he defeated them and the Aedui and their allies in a great battle fought in 61 B.C. The Aeduan Druid Diviciacus laid an appeal for protection before the Roman Senate, but received only a vague general undertaking. Ariovistus also applied for Roman recognition, and Caesar, in his consulship in 59 B.C., advised the Senate to conclude a formal friendship with him. This merely committed Rome to recognizing, for the time being, Ariovistus' conquests in Gaul. Transalpine Gaul had not then been assigned to Caesar as one of his provinces, and if he was likely to be occupied with fighting elsewhere he may have thought it prudent to secure the neutrality of Ariovistus. Probably he did not yet realize how dangerous Ariovistus' presence in Gaul might be.

§ 4

THE ROMAN ARMY

APART from an unknown number of auxiliary troops (Gallic and Numidian light infantry, Cretan archers, and slingers from the Balearic Isles), the forces which Caesar commanded in Gaul consisted of a number of legions varying between six and eleven, and a cavalry force composed entirely of foreigners. The bulk of the cavalry, which at one time numbered at least four thousand, were Gauls requisitioned from friendly or conquered tribes. On the conclusion of a campaign most of them were sent home, and a new force raised the next year. In the campaign of 52 B.C. Caesar had some squadrons of German cavalry, with light infantry trained to fight among its ranks.

The legions were supposed to consist entirely of men possessing Roman citizenship; but when troops were urgently needed no doubt many exceptions were made, and towards the end of the war Caesar enrolled a whole legion in the province of Transalpine Gaul. The rest of the legions which he raised in the Gallic war were recruited in northern Italy. The legionaries were volunteers serving for pay and signed on for a definite term of service. In Caesar's time they were recruited mainly by the generals who required them, and were often paid out of booty or funds raised by him. This bad system, which made the men dependent on their commander rather than on the state, was largely responsible for the excessive power of military chiefs in this period.

The nominal strength of a legion was six thousand, divided into ten cohorts of six hundred each – the most important tactical units. Each cohort contained three maniples of two hundred each, and each maniple two centuries of one hundred each. But legions were often considerably under their nominal strength. The legion had at this date no permanent commander. The generals serving under Caesar were men of Senatorial rank (i.e. ex-magistrates) appointed by the Senate on his recommendation. He had five at the start of the war, and eventually ten. Their duties were assigned to them from time to time entirely at Caesar's discretion, and included taking command of legions in battle or on the march or in winter quarters, procuring supplies, superintending shipbuilding, raising fresh levies, and so on. Some of them may have been men without much military experience. Each legion had six military tribunes (nominated, and perhaps actually appointed, by the commander-in-chief), who were often young aspirants to public office and were sometimes chosen merely on personal or political grounds. They manoeuvred their legions in action under the direction of a general (pp. 87, 207), and sometimes acted on their own initiative (p. 216). No doubt they also discharged routine administrative duties. Perhaps more important than the military tribunes on the actual battlefield – certainly mentioned and praised much more often by Caesar – were the centurions, ex-rankers promoted for bravery and powers of leadership to the command of centuries. Of the sixty centurions in a legion, the six belonging to the first cohort (referred to in this translation as 'first grade centurions') held posts of special responsibility and were summoned with the generals and military tribunes to councils of war. Their duties on occasion must have been at least as important as those of a company commander in a modern army. The most responsible post of all was held by the chief centurion of the legion – i.e. the centurion of the first century of the first cohort.

The legionaries wore a woollen tunic, a leather coat protected by metal bands, long puttees, and a cloak or blanket for protection from cold or rain. Their armour consisted of a helmet (slung over the chest when they were on the march), a large rectangular shield of wood covered with leather, greaves, and probably a leather cuirass. Their weapons were pointed two-edged swords and heavy throwing-spears. The latter were sometimes nearly seven feet long; between the tempered point and the handle was a shank made of soft iron, which bent when the spear pierced an enemy's shield, so that it could not easily be pulled out and was useless for throwing back (p. 53).

The kit that the soldiers had to carry on the march included, besides their rations, cooking-vessels, and so on, the tools required for the constructional work on which they were constantly engaged – a spade, hatchet, and saw. The heavy baggage contained the military stores – including pieces of artillery,[1] material for making mantlets,[1] and other apparatus – as well as personal property belonging not only to the officers but apparently to the common soldiers also (p. 147). For carrying it a large number of horses or mules was needed, and no doubt wagons, though these are not mentioned in the *Gallic War*. The non-combatants included the animal drivers, officers' servants, sutlers, and dealers who sold goods to the sutlers and bought booty from the soldiers.

1. See the Glossary.

§ 5

THE COURSE OF THE WAR

IT is not likely that when Caesar went to his Transalpine province in March, 58 B.C., he intended to embark on a vast scheme of conquest in Gaul. If he had already formed such a design he would hardly have left three out of his four legions in northern Italy. But by the end of the year, after turning back the Helvetian migration and expelling Ariovistus from Gaul, he had clearly determined upon the conquest of the whole country. He already had two important tribes on his side – the Aedui in central Gaul and the Remi in the north. In 57 B.C. he overcame almost all the Belgic tribes – the fiercest resistance being offered by the Nervii – and the maritime tribes of Normandy and Brittany submitted for the moment without a fight. Thus by the end of that year the whole of Gaul between the Rhine and the Garonne, with the exception of the Morini and Menapii in the extreme north, was for the time being under Roman control.

The remaining six years of the war were occupied (apart from Caesar's invasions of Germany and Britain, which had little real connexion with the conquest of Gaul) in crushing a series of four rebellions by various combinations of tribes. The first to rebel were the Veneti and the other tribes on or near the Atlantic coast (56 B.C.). In 54–53 there were widespread revolts in the north by the Eburones, Atuatuci, Nervii, and Treveri, and less serious risings in central Gaul. Most serious of all was the rebellion of the central tribes in 52; for the Gauls produced at last an outstanding leader in the youthful Vercingetorix. By his defeat the conquest was virtually completed. The risings of 51 were only a fruitless prolongation of a struggle whose issue was already decided.

Although no accurate estimate can be made of the strength of the Gallic armies, and some of the figures which Caesar gives are probably exaggerated, it is obvious that the Gauls had an enormous numerical advantage.[1] It is also clear that many of them were

1. It is said that in all a million Gauls were killed and another million captured.

very brave fighters. The almost unbroken series of Roman victories is to be accounted for by the superiority of Caesar's armies in everything except numbers and physical courage. They were formed of better material, better trained, better disciplined, better equipped, and better led.

Caesar's own contribution was that of a superb tactician and a superb leader of men. No man ever knew better how to surprise and baffle his opponents by speed of movement, or how to snatch victory out of a battle that was very nearly a defeat by throwing in reserves at just the right place and the right time. No man ever won greater respect or more affectionate loyalty from his troops. For eight years of hard fighting, hard digging, and hard living, they gave him everything he asked of them. There was never a sign of mutiny. At the start of the civil war, when he was without means to pay them, they did not hesitate to serve him without present payment; and many who were captured by the Pompeians preferred to die rather than take the chance of life that was offered them on condition of fighting against their old commander. He secured this hold upon them partly by his personal courage and soldierly qualities – he was an excellent rider, swimmer, and man-at-arms, as patient of fatigue as any man in the ranks, and capable of rallying frightened troops single-handed, throwing himself in the path of runaways and stopping them with his own hands – partly, too, by his combination of an iron discipline in face of the enemy with an easy-going indulgence off duty.

The legionaries had a splendid military tradition and an efficient organization behind them, and were excellently equipped for their task by temperament and training. They knew what to do and how to do it, they had the tools for the job, they had the patience and determination to carry on till it was finished, and above all they were all of one mind about it. The Gauls had none of these things. They were distracted by jealousies and quarrels and hopelessly outclassed in the technical side of warfare; and though they had plenty of dash and gallantry they lacked staying-power and tenacity of purpose. If they had pulled together and all continued to resist simultaneously, they should have been able to wear down the Romans. But until 52 B.C. the Belgae and the maritime tribes were left to bear the brunt of the fight; many of the central tribes submitted without much effort to defend themselves. Then, when Vercingetorix roused the central tribes to a heroic struggle, the Belgae – perhaps because they were nearly exhausted – held aloof till it was too late.

In most of the tribes the cavalry, composed of noblemen and their retainers, was the only efficient and disciplined arm. Only the Helvetii and the Nervii had infantry forces formidable enough to meet the legions in a pitched battle with any hope of success. The infantry contingents supplied by some of the other tribes were unwieldy and unwarlike mobs. Most of the Gallic leaders' strategy was crude and they had little idea of organizing a commissariat. Only Vercingetorix showed ability of a high order, and his sub-ordinates failed to help him much. Caesar, on the other hand, was excellently served by some of his officers – notably by Labienus, who more than once saved an almost desperate situation – and by his Gallic allies. The Remi stood by him throughout the war, the Aedui till near the end; and in the great rebellion of 52 B.C. in-valuable aid was rendered both by the inhabitants of the Pro-vince and by Caesar's German auxiliaries. In these circumstances there could be only one end. Discipline and organization were bound to triumph over inefficiency, disunion, and disorder.

§ 6

CAESAR AS AUTHOR

OUR POSSESSION of Caesar's *Gallic War* is a unique piece of good fortune. No other great general of antiquity has left us his own account of his campaigns; and it is doubtful if any other great general, of any age or country, has possessed Caesar's literary talent.

In the original, the work is divided into eight books, but only the first seven, which take the narrative down to the autumn of 52 B.C., were written by Caesar. The eighth book was written, shortly after Caesar's death on the 15th of March, 44 B.C., by his friend Aulus Hirtius, who was with him on most of his campaigns and may have served as his secretary. Hirtius was consul in 43 B.C., and was killed in a battle fought against Mark Antony at Modena in April of that year. We cannot tell for certain why Caesar did not add a final book himself after the conclusion of the campaigns of 51 B.C. Probably he had more urgent matters to attend to, and – since the last year's campaigns were of only minor importance – considered that he had already written enough to serve his purpose.

Many scholars think that each of the first seven books was written and published separately at the close of each summer's campaign. But on the whole it is more probable that they were written all together in the autumn of 52 B.C., after the defeat of Vercingetorix, and finished by the end of the year, when Caesar began a fresh campaign against the Bituriges.[1] In his preface to the last book Hirtius remarks on the ease and speed with which Caesar wrote. Apart from his personal recollection, Caesar would doubtless have before him copies of the dispatches which he sent to the Senate after each campaign and of the reports submitted to him by his generals, and memoranda compiled by himself during the course of the war. The work is generally known as *The Gallic War*, but the original title seems to have been *Gaius Julius Caesar's Notes on his Achievements*. Both Hirtius and Cicero say that Caesar regarded his book not as a finished history but as a collection of material for the use of future historians. They add, however, that he wrote it so well that no sane man would ever think of trying to rewrite it.

It is clear that Caesar wrote not only for the information of posterity. The book was also a piece of personal propaganda intended to impress his contemporaries. He knew that, as well as many admirers, he had powerful enemies and detractors, and before standing for a second consulship it was natural that he should wish to justify himself before public opinion by publishing an account of the wars by which he had carried Roman arms in triumph to the Atlantic and the North Sea and added a huge territory to the empire.

The reliability of Caesar's narrative has been impugned by cer-

1. The only possible alternative is 50 B.C., between the end of the Gallic war and the start of the civil war. But in that case Caesar would surely have included an account of the campaigns of 51 B.C.

tain critics ancient and modern, some of whom have not scrupled to charge him with deliberate and repeated lying. Practically all good judges are agreed that these accusations are groundless. Such independent evidence as other ancient writers provide generally confirms the accuracy of Caesar's statements, and the few small inconsistencies that are found between different passages of the *Gallic War* are mere mistakes or lapses of memory. Caesar must have had before him a mass of documents written at different times by himself and by others, and evidently he was in too great a hurry to notice some points of detail in which they disagreed – or if he noticed them he did not always think it worth while to reconcile the discrepancies.

At the same time it would be absurd to suppose that he has told us everything there was to tell. Few men care to publish to the world their true motives for all they do, and few have written a narrative of events in which they were the chief actors without colouring it to some extent, if only by omitting or passing lightly over what they did not wish to emphasize. As a modern editor of the *Gallic War* puts it, 'Des *Mémoires* ne sont pas des *Confessions.*' Caesar could be very discreet when he chose. He says nothing of the personal ambition which clearly was a motive at least as strong as any other for his embarking on the war, and nothing of the huge fortunes which he and some of his friends made by pillaging and exploiting the Gauls. A casual reader would hardly gather from the narrative that the expeditions into Germany and Britain were failures in the sense that they achieved no lasting result. But such reticence is a very different thing from deliberate falsification of facts, of which no one has been able to convict Caesar.

The *Gallic War* is written in Latin of the utmost lucidity and elegance and in a simple and sober style, without any obvious attempt at fine writing or dramatic effect – though its very restraint often makes it highly effective. There is much detailed and vivid description of the places where events happened, but the events themselves are recorded with a minimum of comment and with scarcely a hint of the writer's own feelings about them. The only striking exception is the passage where he describes his joy at the escape of his friend Valerius Procillus (p. 72). Generally speaking, the tone is as objective and impersonal as that of an official communiqué.

The digressions which appear at certain points of the narrative – on geography, natural history, and national customs – may not all be of Caesar's own composition, but it is fairly clear that he himself inserted them for his readers' edification. Much of the information contained in them – some of it, as explained in the notes, erroneous – was derived from books, maps, or hearsay, and not from Caesar's personal observation.

§ 7

TRANSLATOR'S PREFACE

THE FOLLOWING BOOKS are particularly valuable for the study of the *Gallic War*:

T. Rice Holmes: *Caesar's Conquest of Gaul* (second edition).[1]

T. Rice Holmes: *Ancient Britain and the Invasions of Julius Caesar* (second edition).[1]

L. A. Constans: *César, Guerre des Gaules* (second edition – Latin text and French translation).

C. Hignett: *Cambridge Ancient History*, Vol. IX, Chap. xiii.

The present translation owes much to these books and also to Rice Holmes's English version (now out of print), which has suggested several happy turns of phrase.

The footnotes appended to the translation, including the cross references, are to be regarded as an integral part of it. They contain matter which stands in Caesar's Latin text, but which he might perhaps have put in the form of footnotes if footnotes had then been in use. The chapter and section headings, and the dates inserted in the text in brackets, have of course been added by the translator. In order to save the reader unnecessary trouble, meas-

1. Much of the information contained in these books is given in a condensed form in Rice Holmes's annotated edition of the Latin text (*Caesar, De Bello Gallico*).

ures of length and times of day and night have been expressed in English terms.

The eight chapters into which the translation is divided do not correspond with the eight books of the original. The following table shows the relation between them (the references are to chapters and sections of the translation, and to books and sections of the Latin text):

Trans-lation	Text	Trans-lation	Text	Trans-lation	Text
I 1	I 1; VI 11–20	III 3	III 28–29	VI 4	VI 9–10, 29
I 2	VI 21–28	IV 1	IV 1–15	VI 5	VI 29–44
II 1	I 1–29	IV 2	IV 16–19	VII 1	VII 1–13
II 2	I 30–54	V 1	IV 20–38	VII 2	VII 14–31
II 3	II 1–11	V 2	V 1–23	VII 3	VII 32–53
II 4	II 12–35	VI 1	V 24–37	VII 4	VII 54–67
II 5	III 1–6	VI 2	V 38–52	VII 5	VII 68–90
III 1	III 7–19	VI 3	{ V 53–58; VI 1–8	VIII 1	VIII 1–23
III 2	III 20–27			VIII 2	VIII 24–49

The following passages of Book VIII are not included in this translation: Hirtius' Preface, part of § 48, and the whole of §§ 50–55. These final sections have little connexion with the conquest of Gaul; they were written to provide a link between the *Gallic War* and Caesar's account of the civil war.

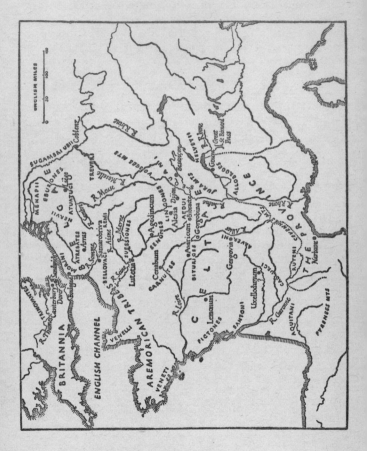

ENGLISH MILES

50   100   150

R. Rhine

SUGAMBRI UBII Cologne
MENAPII
EBURONES
NERVII ATUATUCI TREVERI
R. Scheldt R. Meuse R. Moselle VOSGES MTS.
MORINI Arras R. Sambre
St. Omer Arras
Boulogne Samarobriva R. Aisne REMI
Dover Amiens BELLOVACI SUESSIONES Agedincum
Canterbury Sandwich LINGONES Besançon
R. Thames R. Seine Lutetia SENONES Alesia Dijon JURA MTS. HELVETII
Great St. Bernard Pass
BRITANNIA Geneva ALLOBROGES Goutto
CARNUTES AEDUI THE
AREMORICAN TRIBES C E L T Avaricum Bibracte
R. Loire Gergovia ARVERNI CEVENNES MTS. PROVINCE
VENELLI Limonum Uxellodunum RUTENI Narbonne
VENETI PICTONES SANTONI CADURCI
AQUITANI R. Garonne
PYRENEES MTS.

ENGLISH CHANNEL

THE CONQUEST OF GAUL

CHAPTER I

CUSTOMS AND INSTITUTIONS OF THE GAULS AND GERMANS

§ I THE GAULS

GAUL comprises three areas, inhabited respectively by the Belgae, the Aquitani, and a people who call themselves Celts, though we call them Gauls. All of these have different languages, customs, and laws. The Celts are separated from the Aquitani by the river Garonne, from the Belgae by the Marne and Seine. The Belgae are the bravest of the three peoples, being farthest removed from the highly developed civilization of the Roman Province, least often visited by merchants with enervating luxuries for sale, and nearest to the Germans across the Rhine, with whom they are continually at war. For the same reason the Helvetii are braver than the rest of the Celts; they are in almost daily conflict with the Germans, either trying to keep them out of Switzerland or themselves invading Germany. The region occupied by the Celts, which has one frontier facing north, is bounded by the Rhone, the Garonne, the Atlantic Ocean, and the country of the Belgae; the part of it inhabited by the Sequani and the Helvetii also touches the Rhine. The Belgic territory, facing north and east, runs from the northern frontier of the Celts to the lower Rhine. Aquitania is bounded by the Garonne, the Pyrenees, and the part of the Atlantic coast nearest Spain; it faces north-west.

In Gaul, not only every tribe, canton, and subdivision of a canton, but almost every family, is divided into rival factions. At the head of these factions are men who are regarded by their followers as having particularly great prestige, and these have the final say on all questions that come up for judgement and in all discussions of policy. The object of this ancient custom seems to have been to ensure that all the common people should have protection against the strong; for each leader sees that no one gets the better of his supporters by force or by cunning – or, if he fails to do so, is utterly discredited.

The same principle holds good in inter-tribal politics: all the tribes are grouped in two factions, which, at the time of Caesar's arrival, were headed respectively by the Aedui and the Sequani. As the Aedui had long enjoyed very great prestige and had many satellite tribes, the Sequani were the weaker of the two, while they depended on their own resources. They therefore secured the alliance of Ariovistus and his Germans, at the cost of heavy sacrifices and the promise of still further concessions [70–65 B.C.]. Then, as a result of several victories in which all the Aeduans of rank were killed, the Sequani became so much stronger than their rivals that they were able to bring over to their side a considerable part of the Aeduan dependencies, and to make the Aeduans surrender the sons of their chiefs as hostages and swear to form no hostile designs against the Sequani. They had also seized and retained a part of the Aeduan territory that lay near their own frontier, and had in fact established a hegemony over the whole of Gaul. Reduced to this extremity, Diviciacus the Aeduan went to Rome to solicit aid from the Senate, but returned without success [61 B.C.]. Caesar's arrival changed the situation: the Aedui had their hostages restored to them, and not only regained their former dependencies but acquired new ones with Caesar's help, because those who became their allies found that they were better off and more equitably governed than before. In other respects, too, their influence and standing were enhanced, and the Sequani lost their supremacy. Their place was taken by the Remi; and as it was known that they stood as high in Caesar's favour as the Aedui, tribes which on account of old feuds could not be induced to join the Aedui were placing themselves under the protection of the Remi, who by taking good care of them were able to maintain the unaccustomed power that they had suddenly acquired. At this time, therefore, the position was that, while the Aedui were acknowledged to be easily ahead of all the other tribes, the Remi came next in importance.

Everywhere in Gaul there are only two classes of men who are of any account or consideration. The common people are treated almost as slaves, never venture to act on their own initiative, and are not consulted on any subject. Most of them, crushed by debt or heavy taxation or the oppression of more powerful persons, bind themselves to serve men of rank, who exercise over them all the rights that masters have over slaves. The two privileged classes are the Druids and the Knights. The Druids officiate at the worship of the gods, regulate public and private sacrifices, and give rulings on all religious questions. Large numbers of young men flock to them for instruction, and they are held in great honour by the people. They act as judges in practically all disputes, whether between tribes or between individuals; when any crime is committed, or a murder takes place, or a dispute arises about an inheritance or a boundary, it is they who adjudicate the matter and appoint the compensation to be paid and received by the parties concerned. Any individual or tribe failing to accept their award is banned from taking part in sacrifice – the heaviest punishment that can be inflicted upon a Gaul. Those who are laid under such a ban are regarded as impious criminals. Everyone shuns them and avoids going near or speaking to them, for fear

31

of taking some harm by contact with what is unclean; if they appear as plaintiffs, justice is denied them, and they are excluded from a share in any honour. All the Druids are under one head, whom they hold in the highest respect. On his death, if any one of the rest is of outstanding merit, he succeeds to the vacant place; if several have equal claims, the Druids usually decide the election by voting, though sometimes they actually fight it out. On a fixed date in each year they hold a session in a consecrated spot in the country of the Carnutes, which is supposed to be the centre of Gaul. Those who are involved in disputes assemble here from all parts, and accept the Druids' judgements and awards. The Druidic doctrine is believed to have been found existing in Britain and thence imported into Gaul; even to-day those who want to make a profound study of it generally go to Britain for the purpose.

The Druids are exempt from military service and do not pay taxes like other citizens. These important privileges are naturally attractive: many present themselves of their own accord to become students of Druidism, and others are sent by their parents or relatives. It is said that these pupils have to memorize a great number of verses – so many, that some of them spend twenty years at their studies. The Druids believe that their religion forbids them to commit their teachings to writing, although for most other purposes, such as public and private accounts, the Gauls use the Greek alphabet. But I imagine that this rule was originally established for other reasons – because they did not want their doctrine to become public property, and in order to prevent their pupils from relying on the written word and neglecting to train their memories; for it is usually found that when people have the help of texts, they are less diligent in learning by heart, and let their memories rust. A lesson which they take particular pains to inculcate is that the soul does not perish, but after death passes from one body to another; they think that this is the best incentive to bravery, because it teaches men to disregard the terrors of death. They also hold long discussions about the heavenly bodies and their movements, the size of the universe and of the earth, the physical constitution of the world, and the power and properties of the gods; and they instruct the young men in all these subjects.

The second class is that of the Knights. When their services are required in some war that has broken out – and before Caesar's arrival in the country the Gallic states used to fight offensive or defensive wars almost every year – these all take the field, surrounded by their servants and retainers, of whom each Knight has a greater or smaller number according to his birth and fortune. The possession of such a following is the only criterion of position and power that they recognize.

As a nation the Gauls are extremely superstitious; and so persons suffering from serious diseases, as well as those who are exposed to the perils of battle, offer, or vow to offer, human sacrifices, for the performance of which they employ Druids. They believe that the only way of saving a man's life is to propitiate the god's wrath by rendering another life in its place, and they have regular state sacrifices of the same kind. Some tribes have colossal images made of wickerwork, the limbs of which they fill with living men; they are then set on fire, and the victims burnt to death. They think that the gods prefer the execution of men taken in the act of theft or brigandage, or guilty of some offence; but when they run short of criminals, they do not hesitate to make up with innocent men.

The god they reverence most is Mercury. They have very many images of him, and regard him as the inventor of all arts, the god who directs men upon their journeys, and their most powerful helper in trading and getting money. Next to him they reverence Apollo, Mars, Jupiter, and Minerva, about whom they have much the same ideas as other nations – that Apollo averts illness, and Minerva teaches the principles of industries and handicrafts; that Jupiter is king of the gods, and Mars the lord of war. When they have decided to fight a battle they generally vow to Mars the booty that they hope to take, and after a victory they sacrifice the captured animals and collect the rest of the spoil in one spot. Among many of the tribes, high piles of it can be seen on consecrated ground; and it is an almost unknown thing for anyone to dare, in defiance of religious law, to conceal his booty at home or to remove anything placed on the piles. Such a crime is punishable by a terrible death under torture.

The Gauls claim all to be descended from Father Dis, declaring that this is the tradition preserved by the Druids. For this reason they measure periods of time not by days but by nights; and in celebrating birthdays, the first of the month, and new year's day, they go on the principle that the day begins at night. As regards the other usages of daily life, the chief difference between them and other peoples is that their children are not allowed to go up to their fathers in public until they are old enough for military service; they regard it as unbecoming for a son who is still a boy to stand in his father's sight in a public place.

When a Gaul marries, he adds to the dowry that his wife brings with her a portion of his own property estimated to be of equal value. A joint account is kept of the whole amount, and the profits which it earns are put aside; and when either dies, the survivor receives both shares together with the accumulated profits. Husbands have power of life and death over their wives as well as their children. When a high-born head of a family dies, his relatives assemble, and if the circumstances of his death are suspicious, they examine his widow under torture, as we examine slaves; if her guilt is established, she is consigned to the flames and put to death with the most cruel torments. Gallic funerals are splendid and costly, for a comparatively poor country. Everything that the dead man is supposed to have been fond of, including even animals, is placed upon his pyre; and not long ago there were people still alive who could remember the time when slaves and retainers known to have been beloved by their masters were burnt with them at the conclusion of the funeral rites.

The tribes which are considered to manage their affairs best have a law that if anyone hears from a neighbouring country any rumour or news that concerns the state, he is to communicate it to a magistrate without speaking of it to anyone else. For experience has shown that impulsive and ignorant persons are often frightened by false reports into subversive action, and meddle with important affairs of state. The magistrates suppress what they think it advisable to keep secret, and publish only what they deem it expedient for the people to know. The discussion of politics is forbidden except in a public assembly.

§ 2 THE GERMANS

THE customs of the Germans are entirely different. They have no Druids to control religious observances, and are not much given to sacrifices. The only beings they recognize as gods are things that they can see, and by which they are obviously benefited, such as Sun, Moon, and Fire; the other gods they have never even heard of. They spend all their lives in hunting and warlike pursuits, and inure themselves from childhood to toil and hardship. Those who preserve their chastity longest are most highly commended by their friends; for they think that continence makes young men taller, stronger, and more muscular. To have had intercourse with a woman before the age of twenty is considered perfectly scandalous. They attempt no concealment, however, of the facts of sex : men and women bathe together in the rivers, and they wear nothing but hides or short garments of hairy skin, which leave most of the body bare.

The Germans are not agriculturalists, and live principally on milk, cheese, and meat. No one possesses any definite amount of land as private property; the magistrates and tribal chiefs annually assign a holding to clans and groups of kinsmen or others living together, fixing its size and position at their discretion, and the following year make them move on somewhere else. They give many reasons for this custom: for example, that their men may not get accustomed to living in one place, lose their warlike enthusiasm, and take up agriculture instead; that they may not be anxious to acquire large estates, and the strong be tempted to dispossess the weak; to prevent their paying too much attention to building houses that will protect them from cold and heat, or becoming too fond of money – a frequent cause of division and strife; and to keep the common people contented and quiet by letting every man see that even the most powerful are no better off than himself.

The various tribes regard it as their greatest glory to lay waste as much as possible of the land around them and to keep it uninhabited. They hold it a proof of a people's valour to drive their neighbours from their homes, so that no one dare settle near them, and also think that it gives them greater security by removing any fear of sudden invasion. When a tribe is attacked or intends to attack another, officers are chosen to conduct the campaign and invested with powers of life and death. In peace-time there is no central magistracy; the chiefs of the various districts and cantons administer justice and settle disputes among their own people. No discredit attaches to plundering-raids outside the tribal frontiers; the Germans say that they serve to keep the young men in training and prevent them from getting lazy. When a chief announces in an assembly his intention of leading a raid and calls for volunteers, those who like the proposal, and approve of the man who makes it, stand up and promise their assistance amid the applause of the whole gathering; anyone who backs out afterwards is looked on as a deserter and a traitor, and no one will ever trust him again. To wrong a guest is impious in their eyes. They shield from injury all who come to their houses for any purpose whatever, and treat their persons as sacred; guests are welcomed to every man's home and table.

There was a time when the Gauls were more warlike than the Germans, when they actually invaded German territory, and sent colonists across the Rhine because their own country was too small to support its large population. It was in this way that the most fertile district of Germany, in the neighbourhood of the Hercynian forest,[1] was seized and

1. I see that this forest was known to Eratosthenes and other Greeks, who call it Orcynia. It is so wide that it takes a lightly-equipped traveller nine days to cross it; this is the only way the Germans have of estimating its size, as they know nothing of measures of length. Starting from the frontiers of the Helvetii, Nemetes, and Rauraci, it runs straight along the Danube to the country of the Dacians and the Anartes. At this point it turns north-east away from the river, and in its huge length extends through the territories of many different peoples. No western German claims to have reached its eastern extremity, even after travelling for two months, or to have heard where it ends. The forest is known to contain many kinds of animals not seen elsewhere, some of which seem worthy of mention because they differ greatly from those found in other countries. There is an ox shaped like a deer, with a single horn in the middle of its forehead between the ears, which sticks up higher and straighter than those of the animals we know, and at the top branches out widely like a man's hand or a tree. The male and female are alike, and their horns are of the same shape and size. There are also animals called elks, which resemble goats in shape and in their piebald colouring, but are somewhat larger, and have stunted horns and legs without joints or knuckles. They do not lie down to rest, and if they fall by accident, cannot get up or raise themselves from the ground. Trees serve them as resting-places; they support themselves against the trunks, and rest in that way, leaning over only slightly. When the hunters have found out their usual retreats by following their tracks, they

occupied by the Volcae Tectosages, who remain there to this day and have a high reputation for fair dealing and gallantry. Nowadays, while the Germans still endure the same life of poverty and privation as before, without any change in their diet or clothing, the Gauls, through living near the Roman Province and becoming acquainted with sea-borne products, are abundantly supplied with various commodities. Gradually accustomed to inferiority and defeated in many battles, they do not even pretend to compete with the Germans in bravery.

---

either sever the roots of all the surrounding trees or cut nearly through the trunks, so that they only *look* as if they were still standing firm. When the elks lean against them as usual, they push over the insecure trunks with their weight, and fall down with them. A third species is the aurochs, an animal somewhat smaller than the elephant, with the appearance, colour, and shape of a bull. They are very strong and agile, and attack every man and beast they catch sight of. The natives take great pains to trap them in pits, and then kill them. This arduous sport toughens the young men and keeps them in training; and those who kill the largest number exhibit the horns in public to show what they have done, and earn high praise. It is impossible to domesticate or tame the aurochs, even if it is caught young. The horns are much larger than those of our oxen, and of quite different shape and appearance. The Germans prize them greatly; they mount the rims with silver and use them as drinking-cups at their grandest banquets.

CHAPTER II

THE MILITARY OCCUPATION
OF GAUL

(58–57 B.C.)

THE foremost man among the Helvetii, in rank and wealth, was Orgetorix. In the consulship of Marcus Messala and Marcus Piso [61 B.C.] he was induced by the hope of obtaining royal power to organize a conspiracy of noblemen, and persuaded his countrymen to emigrate *en masse*, telling them that they were the best fighters in Gaul and could very easily conquer the whole country. They listened the more readily to his proposal because their territory is completely hemmed in by natural barriers – on one side by the Rhine, a very broad and deep river, which is the frontier between them and the Germans; on another side by the high mountain range of the Jura, between them and the Sequani; on a third, by the Lake of Geneva and the Rhone, which form the boundary between the Helvetii and the Roman Province. These obstacles restricted their movement and made it more difficult to attack their neighbours; and as they are a warlike people they greatly resented this restraint. Considering their large population, military prestige, and reputation for bravery, they felt that their territory – only two hundred and twenty miles long, one hundred and sixty-five wide – was unduly small.

Impelled by this feeling and by the influence of Orgetorix, they determined to prepare for emigration by buying up all the draught cattle and wagons they could, sowing as much land as possible in order to secure an adequate supply of corn for the journey, and establishing peaceful and friendly relations with their neighbours. They thought that two years would suffice for completing these preparations, and passed a formal resolution fixing their departure for the third year. Orgetorix was put in charge of the arrangements and undertook a mission to the neighbouring peoples, in the course of which he persuaded a Sequanian named Casticus, whose father Catamantaloedis had been king of his tribe for many years and had been honoured by the Senate with the title of 'Friend of the Roman People', to seize the royal power which his father had held before him. He also induced the Aeduan Dumnorix, Diviciacus' brother, who at that time held the chief magistracy of his tribe and enjoyed great popularity, to make a similar attempt, and gave him his daughter in marriage. Orgetorix convinced them that these schemes were quite easy of achievement by telling them that he intended to usurp the sovereignty of his own state, which he said was beyond question the most powerful in Gaul, and that he would use his wealth and military strength to secure them the possession of their thrones. His arguments proved effective. The three men swore an oath of mutual loyalty, hoping that once they had made themselves kings the great power of the warlike peoples they ruled would enable them to get control of all Gaul.

The intrigue was revealed to the Helvetii by informers, and in accordance with the national custom Orgetorix was summoned to stand his trial in chains. Since condemnation would mean death at the stake, he collected all his slaves, numbering some ten thousand, from his various estates, and brought them to the place of trial on the day appointed for the hearing, together with all his numerous retainers and debtor-bondsmen. By means of their protection he escaped trial. His countrymen were angered by this behaviour and attempted to assert their rights by armed force. But while the magistrates were calling up a large body of men from the countryside, Orgetorix died – perhaps, as the Helvetii believe, by his own hand.

The Helvetii however did not relax their efforts to carry out their intended migration. As soon as they considered themselves ready, they burnt all their twelve towns and four hundred villages, as well as the isolated buildings belonging to private individuals, and also the whole of their grain, except what they intended to carry with them. For they thought that, if there was no possibility of returning home, they would be more willing to face all the perils that awaited them. Every man was directed to take with him from home three months' supply of flour for his own use. They persuaded their neighbours the Rauraci, Tulingi, and Latovici to follow their example – to burn their towns and villages and go with them – and were joined also by the Boii, who formerly lived on the other side of the Rhine, but had recently migrated into Austria and attacked the town of Noreia.

There were only two routes by which the Helvetii could leave their country. One led between the Jura mountains and the Rhone through the land of the Sequani, and was so narrow and difficult that wagons could scarcely pass along it in single file; and a high mountain overhung it, so that a mere handful of men could easily make it impassable. The other route, leading through the Roman Province, was much easier and more convenient; for the Rhone, which forms the frontier between the Helvetii and the Allobroges,[1] is fordable at several places. The frontier town of the Allobroges, nearest to Switzerland and connected with it by a bridge, is Geneva. The Helvetii thought that they could either induce the Allobroges to let them pass through, as they were believed to be still unfriendly towards the Romans, or compel them by force to do so. When everything was ready for their departure, they fixed

1. Recently subdued by Rome [61 B.C.].

a day for a general muster on the bank of the Rhone – the 28th of March in the consulship of Lucius Piso and Aulus Gabinius [58 B.C.].

When Caesar was informed that they were attempting to pass through the Province, he left Rome at once and travelled post-haste to the neighbourhood of Geneva. As there was only one legion stationed in Gaul, he ordered as many fresh troops as possible to be raised throughout the Province, and had the bridge at Geneva destroyed. On hearing of his arrival the Helvetii sent an embassy, composed of their most illustrious citizens and headed by Nammeius and Verucloetius, to say that they intended to march through the Province because there was no other route open to them. They promised to do no harm and asked for his consent. As Caesar remembered that the consul Lucius Cassius had been killed by the Helvetii, and his army routed and sent under the yoke [107 B.C.], he was not disposed to grant their request. If people so hostile to Rome were permitted to go through the Province, he did not think they were likely to refrain from damage to persons and property. However, to gain time for the assembly of the troops he had ordered to be levied, he told the envoys that he would consider the matter at leisure: if they wished to present their request again, they were to return on the 13th of April. In the meantime he employed the legion he had with him, and the troops that had been raised in the Province, to fortify the bank of the Rhone for a distance of eighteen miles between the Lake of Geneva and the Jura, the frontier between the Helvetii and the Sequani. This was effected by means of a rampart sixteen feet high with a trench running parallel. He then placed redoubts at intervals along the forfication and garrisoned them with pickets, so that he could stop the Helvetii more easily, should they attempt to force a passage. When on the appointed day the envoys returned, he told them that it would be contrary to precedent and the traditions of the Roman state to allow anyone to march through the Province, and that if they tried to use force he would stop them. Disappointed of this hope, some of the Helvetii endeavoured – generally, though not always, by night – to get across by lashing boats together and making a number of rafts, others by wading through the shallowest places. But the Roman troops always hastened up to the danger-points, and aided by the fortifications drove them back with volleys of missiles and forced them to abandon their attempts.

There remained only the route through the land of the Sequani, which was so narrow that it could not be used without their consent. Being unable to obtain permission by their own efforts, the Helvetii sent an embassy to Dumnorix the Aeduan, hoping by his intercession to gain what they desired. Dumnorix's popularity and open-handedness had won him great influence among the Sequani, and he was well-disposed towards the Helvetii because he had married a woman of their country, a daughter of Orgetorix. His ambition for kingly power made him favour political change, and he wanted to lay as many tribes as possible under obligations to himself. Accordingly he undertook the commission, induced the Sequani to let the Helvetii go through, and arranged an exchange of hostages between them. The Helvetii undertook to pass through without harming anyone or doing any damage; the Sequani, to let them travel without interference.

Caesar was informed that the Helvetii intended to cross the territories of the Sequani and the Aedui and to enter the country of the Santoni, which is not far from that of the Tolosates, a tribe living in the Roman Province. He saw that it would be very dangerous to the Province to have a war-like people, hostile to Rome, established close to its rich cornlands, which were without any natural defences. Accordingly, leaving Titus Labienus, one of his generals, in charge of the fortifications he had constructed, he marched at top speed into northern Italy, enrolled two new legions there, sent for the three which were in winter quarters near Aquileia, and hastened back with all five by the shortest route over the Alps into Gaul. An attempt was made to hinder his march by the Ceutrones, Graioceli, and Caturiges, who seized some commanding heights. Beating them off in several engagements, Caesar marched in six days from Ocelum, the westernmost town in the Alpine district of Italy, into the territory of the Vocontii in the Province, and then continued through the country of the Allobroges into that of the Segusiavi, the first people on the west bank of the Rhone who live beyond the Provincial frontier.

By this time the Helvetii had marched through the pass and across the country of the Sequani, and had reached that of the Aedui, whose land they were pillaging. Unable to protect themselves or their property, the Aedui sent to ask Caesar for help, pleading that they had always been loyal to Rome, and that it was not right to allow their land to be ravaged almost under the eyes of his army, their children carried off into slavery, and their towns taken by storm. At the same time the Ambarri, who had ties of friendship and kindred with the Aedui, informed Caesar that their fields too had been pillaged, and that it was almost more than they could do to repel the Helvetii's assaults upon their towns. The Allobroges also, who had villages and estates beyond the Rhone, came fleeing for refuge and said that they had been robbed of everything but the bare soil of their country. These complaints convinced Caesar that he must act immediately: if he delayed, his allies would have all their property destroyed and the Helvetii get clear away to the country of the Santoni.

There is a river called the Saône, which flows through the territories of the Aedui and the Sequani into the Rhone with an extremely sluggish current, so that the eye cannot tell in which direction it is going. The Helvetii were crossing this river on rafts and small boats tied together. On learning from his patrols that they had got three-quarters of their forces across, but that the remaining quarter was still on the east bank, Caesar left camp with three legions some time after midnight and came into contact with the division that had not yet crossed. Attacking them unexpectedly when they were hampered by baggage, he destroyed a large number, and the rest took to flight and hid in the neighbouring woods. The troops in this division formed one of the four clans into which the Helvetian people was divided, known as the Tigurini. Fifty years earlier, the men of this clan had left home independently of the others, and after the battle in which the consul Cassius was killed had sent his army under the yoke. Thus, whether by accident or by divine providence, the section of the Helvetii that had inflicted a signal defeat upon Rome was the first to suffer for it. In thus punishing the Tigurini Caesar avenged a private injury as well as that done to his country; for a general named Lucius Piso, grandfather of the Lucius Piso who was Caesar's father-in-law, had been killed in the same battle as Cassius.

After this success Caesar wanted to pursue the remaining forces of the Helvetii. He therefore built a bridge over the Saône and led his army across. Alarmed by his unexpected arrival, and seeing that he had effected in one day the crossing which they had the greatest difficulty in accomplishing in twenty days, they sent an embassy to him headed by Divico, who had been their commander in the campaign against Cassius. He told Caesar that if Rome made peace with the Helvetii they would go and remain wherever Caesar chose to settle them. If, however, he persisted in making war upon them, he would do well to remember the Romans' previous reverse and the traditional bravery of the Helvetii. He had made a surprise attack on one clan at a moment when their comrades who had crossed the river could not come to their help; but he should not on that account exaggerate his own prowess or despise them. They had learned from their fathers and ancestors to fight like brave men, and not to rely on trickery or stratagem. So let him beware; or it might be that the place where they stood would become famous in future ages as the scene of a Roman disaster and the destruction of a Roman army. Caesar replied that he had no hesitation about the action he should take, especially as he had not forgotten the Roman reverse to which the envoys referred, a misfortune that he resented all the more because it was undeserved. If the Romans at that time had been conscious of any act of oppression, it would have been easy to take precautions; they were caught off their guard because they knew they had done nothing to justify apprehension and thought it undignified to fear without cause. Even if he were willing to forget this old affront, could he banish the recollection of their fresh insults – their attempt to force a passage through the Province in defiance of his prohibition, and their attacks upon the Aedui, the Ambarri, and the Allobroges? 'The victory of which you boast so arrogantly,' he said, 'and the surprisingly long time during which you have escaped punishment, are both due to the same cause. When the gods intend to make a man pay for his crimes, they generally allow him to enjoy moments of success and a long period of impunity, so that he may feel his reverse of fortune, when it eventually comes, all the more keenly. However, if you will give hostages as a guarantee that you mean to carry out your undertakings, and will recompense the Aedui and the Allobroges for the injury you have done to them and their allies, I am willing to make peace with you.' Divico replied that it was the traditional custom of the Helvetii to demand hostages of others, but never to give them – as the Romans had good cause to know. With this rejoinder he departed.

The next day the Helvetii quitted their encampment.

Caesar did the same, sending ahead, to discover in what direction they were marching, his entire force of four thousand cavalry, raised from various parts of the Province and from the Aedui and their allies. These pursued the Helvetian rearguard too eagerly, and engaging their cavalry on unfavourable ground suffered a few casualties. The Helvetii were elated at repulsing such a large force with only five hundred horsemen, and with increased boldness halted several times and challenged the Romans with their rearguard. Caesar would not allow his men to fight them, and contented himself for the moment with preventing them from foraging, looting, and ravaging the country. So the two armies marched for about a fortnight, the enemy's rear and the Roman vanguard being never more than five or six miles apart.

Meanwhile Caesar was daily demanding from the Aedui the grain which, as he reminded them, their government had promised. For on account of the cold climate the standing corn was still unripe, and there was not even a sufficient supply of hay. Some grain that Caesar had brought up the Saône was of little use at the moment because the Helvetii had diverged from the river, and he did not want to lose contact with them. The Aedui kept putting him off from day to day, saying that the grain was being collected, was in transit, was on the point of arriving, and so forth. When he saw that there was going to be no end to this procrastination, and the day on which the soldiers' rations were due was approaching, he summoned the numerous Aeduan chiefs who were in the camp, including Diviciacus and Liscus, their chief magistrate.[1] Caesar reprimanded them severely for failing to help him at such a critical moment, when the enemy was at hand and it was impossible either to buy corn or to get it from the

1. The Vergobret, as the Aedui call him – an annually elected officer holding power of life and death over his countrymen.

fields. He pointed out that it was largely in response to their entreaties that he had undertaken the campaign, and in still stronger terms than he had yet used accused them of betraying him by this neglect.

His remarks at last induced Liscus to drop concealment and speak out. 'There are a number of private individuals in our state,' he said, 'who have great influence over the masses, and are more powerful than the magistrates themselves. It is these who, by criminal and seditious talk, work on the fears of the people to prevent them from bringing in the grain that is due. They argue that if the Aedui are no longer able to maintain their supremacy in Gaul, it is better to have Gauls as masters than Romans, and say they are certain that, if you defeat the Helvetii, you mean to rob the Aedui of their liberty, along with all the rest of the Gauls. These men also keep the enemy informed of your plans and of all that goes on in the camp, and I have no power to control them. Indeed – in case you wonder why I have waited to be compelled before revealing these facts – I realize I am running a very grave risk in doing so. That is why I held my tongue as long as I could.'

Caesar perceived that Liscus' remarks alluded to Diviciacus' brother Dumnorix, and as he did not want the matter discussed with a number of others present, he promptly dismissed the assembly, telling Liscus to stay behind. When they were alone he questioned him about what he had said in the meeting, and Liscus now spoke with greater freedom and confidence. On putting the same questions to others in private, Caesar found that his report was true. It was indeed Dumnorix that he had referred to, a man of boundless daring, extremely popular with the masses on account of his liberality, and an ardent revolutionary. For many years he had bought at a cheap price the right of collecting the river-tolls and other taxes of the Aedui, because when he made a bid at the auction not a soul dared bid against him. In this way he had made a fortune and amassed large resources to expend in bribery. He maintained at his own expense a considerable force of cavalry, which he kept in attendance upon him, and his power was not confined to his own country, but extended over the neighbouring tribes. To increase it he had arranged a marriage for his mother with a nobleman of very great influence among the Bituriges; his own wife was a Helvetian, and he had married his half-sister and other female relations to members of other tribes. On account of his matrimonial connection he was a keen partisan of the Helvetii, and he had his own reasons for hating Caesar and the Romans, because their arrival in Gaul had decreased his power and restored his brother Diviciacus to his former position of honour and influence. If disaster should befall the Romans, he felt sure that with the aid of the Helvetii the throne was within his grasp, whereas a Roman conquest of Gaul would mean that he could not hope even to retain his present standing, much less make himself king. Caesar also learnt in the course of his inquiries that, in the cavalry reverse a few days before, it was Dumnorix and the Aeduan horsemen under his command – sent to Caesar's aid by the tribal authorities – who had been the first to turn tail, and so made the rest of the cavalry lose their nerve.

The suspicions aroused by these revelations were confirmed by certain indubitable facts. Dumnorix had secured a passage for the Helvetii through the territory of the Sequani, and arranged an exchange of hostages between them. He had done this not merely without the authority of Caesar or the Aeduan government, but actually without their knowledge; and he was denounced by the chief magistrate of his tribe. Caesar therefore decided that he had good grounds for either punishing him himself or calling on his fellow-tribesmen to do so. The one objection to this course was that he knew Dumnorix's brother Diviciacus to be an enthusiastic supporter of Roman interests, a very good friend

49

to him personally, and a man of exceptional loyalty, fair-
mindedness, and moderation; and there was reason to fear
that he would be much displeased if his brother were executed. Accordingly, before taking any action he sent for
Diviciacus, and dismissing the ordinary interpreters talked
to him with the assistance of Gaius Valerius Troucillus, a
prominent man in the Province of Gaul and an intimate
friend of his own, in whom he had entire confidence. He
reminded Diviciacus of what he himself had heard said
about Dumnorix in the meeting, informed him of what had
been stated in his private interviews with various persons,
and earnestly begged him not to take offence, but to consent to his either hearing the case himself and passing judgement on Dumnorix, or else instructing the Aeduan state
to do so. Bursting into tears, Diviciacus embraced Caesar
and besought him not to deal too severely with his brother.
'I know,' he said, 'that the allegations against him are true,
and no one regrets it more than I do. For when I had great
power at home and in the rest of Gaul, while he was too
young to have much influence, it was I that raised him to
greatness; and the resources and strength that he thus acquired he is now using, not only to weaken my position,
but to bring me near to ruin. Nevertheless, he is my brother;
and apart from my own feelings, I cannot afford to be indifferent to public opinion. If you take severe measures
against him, everyone will think – in view of my friendly
relations with you – that I desired it, and I shall become very
unpopular throughout Gaul.' He was continuing to plead at
some length, with tears in his eyes, when Caesar grasped his
hand, reassured him, and bade him say no more. 'So high is
my regard for you,' he said, 'that, since you wish it and beg
me so earnestly, I will both overlook the injury to Roman
interests and swallow my own indignation.' He then summoned Dumnorix and in his brother's presence stated his
reasons for complaint about his conduct, mentioning the

information he had received and the charges made against him by his own government. He warned him to avoid henceforth giving any cause for suspicion; what was past, he would overlook for his brother's sake. However, he placed Dumnorix under surveillance in order to ascertain what he was doing and whom he talked with.

That same day the patrols brought word that the Helvetii had stopped at the foot of a hill eight miles from Caesar's camp, whereupon he sent a party to reconnoitre the hill and find out what the ascent was like on the farther side. They reported that it was quite easy. Shortly after midnight he explained his plans to Labienus, his second-in-command, and detailed him to climb to the summit with two legions, taking as guides the men who had reconnoitred the ground. In the early hours of the morning Caesar himself marched towards the enemy, following the route by which they had proceeded, and sending all the cavalry in front. They were preceded by a patrol under command of Publius Considius, who was reputed a first-class soldier, and had served under Sulla and later under Crassus. At daybreak Labienus was actually in possession of the summit, while Caesar was not more than a mile and a half from the enemy's camp; and he learned afterwards from prisoners that neither his own approach nor that of Labienus had been observed. But suddenly Considius galloped up and said that the hill Labienus had been sent to occupy was held by the enemy; he knew this, he said, because he had recognized their Gallic arms and the crests of their helmets. Accordingly Caesar withdrew to a hill close by and formed line of battle. Labienus had been instructed not to engage until Caesar's force was seen close to the enemy's camp, so that they might be attacked on all sides at once. After occupying the hill, therefore, he was waiting for Caesar to appear, without offering battle. It was only quite late in the day that Caesar learned the truth from his patrols – that it was the Romans who were in possession of the hill, that the Helvetii had moved camp, and that Considius had lost his head and reported that he had seen what was not there to be seen. During that day Caesar followed the enemy at the usual interval and pitched his camp three miles from theirs.

Next day, as the distribution of rations was due in two days' time and he was only seventeen miles from Bibracte, far the largest and richest town of the Aedui, he thought it advisable to secure his food-supply, and therefore diverged from the route that the Helvetii were following and marched towards the town. His movements were reported to the enemy by some runaway slaves of Lucius Aemilius, the commander of Caesar's Gallic cavalry. The Helvetii perhaps thought that we were breaking contact with them out of fear, especially as we had declined an engagement the day before, although we had the advantage of position; or it may be they were confident of being able to cut us off from access to supplies. In any case they changed their plan, altered the direction of their march, and began to hang upon our rear and harass it. Observing this, Caesar withdrew to a hill close at hand and sent out his cavalry to meet the enemy's attack. In the meantime he formed up his four veteran legions in three lines half-way up the hill, and posted the two recently levied in Italy on the summit with all the auxiliaries, so that the whole of the hillside above him was occupied with troops. The baggage and packs he ordered to be collected in one place, and defence works to be dug round them by the veterans posted in the top line. The Helvetii, who were following us with the whole of their transport, now parked it all together, and, after repulsing our cavalry with a battle-line drawn up in very close order, formed a phalanx and climbed towards our first line.

Caesar had all the horses – starting with his own – sent away out of sight, so that everyone might stand in equal danger and no one have any chance of flight. Then he

addressed the men and joined battle. By throwing down
spears from their commanding position the troops easily
broke the enemy's phalanx, and then drew their swords and
charged. The Gauls were much hampered in action because
a single spear often pierced more than one of their overlapping shields and pinned them together; and, as the iron
bent, they could not pull them out. With their left arms thus
encumbered it was impossible for them to fight properly,
and many, after repeated attempts to jerk their arms free,
preferred to drop the shields and fight unprotected. At
length, exhausted by wounds, they began to fall back towards a hill about a mile away. They had gained the hill,
and our men were approaching to dislodge them, when the
fifteen thousand Boii and Tulingi who protected the rear of
their column suddenly marched up, attacked us on the right
flank, and surrounded us. Thereupon the Helvetii who had
retreated to the hill began to press forward again and renew
the battle. We changed front and advanced in two divisions
– the first and second lines to oppose the Helvetii whom
we had already once defeated and driven back, the third to
withstand the newly-arrived troops.

This double battle was long and fiercely fought. When
they could no longer sustain the Roman charges, the Helvetii resumed their retreat up the hill, while the Boii and
Tulingi retired to the laager where the baggage was stacked,
to continue the struggle – for throughout this battle, which
lasted from midday till evening, not a single man of them
was seen in flight. At the laager fighting actually continued
until late at night. For the enemy had made a barricade of the
wagons, and rained down missiles on all who approached;
some also wounded our men with spears and javelins discharged low down between the wagons and between the
wheels. After a long struggle we captured the laager and the
baggage it contained, and also Orgetorix's daughter and
one of his sons. About a hundred and thirty thousand

Helvetii who survived the battle marched without halting all that night, and arrived after three days in the country of the Lingones. We had not been able to pursue immediately because we spent these days in attending to the wounded and burying the dead. But Caesar sent a letter and a message to the Lingones warning them not to supply the Helvetii with grain or aid them in any way, on pain of being treated as enemies, and three days later he started in pursuit with the whole army.

The Helvetii were compelled by want of all kinds of supplies to send envoys offering surrender. These met Caesar on the march, prostrated themselves before him, and with tears of supplication besought him to grant them peace. Caesar commanded that the Helvetii should stay where they were until he arrived. They obeyed, and on reaching the place he required them to give hostages and to surrender their arms and the slaves who had deserted to them. While these were being searched for and collected, six thousand men of the clan known as the Verbigeni quitted the encampment in the early hours of the night and set out for the German frontier on the Rhine. Either they were afraid that they would be massacred when once they had given up their arms, or they hoped to escape punishment altogether, thinking that they could get away unobserved in such a large crowd of prisoners, and that the Romans might never learn of their departure. But Caesar heard of it, and sent word to the tribes through whose territory the fugitives were passing that they were to hunt them down and bring them back, or he would hold them responsible. When they were brought back he put them to death; but all the rest were allowed to surrender after handing over the hostages, deserters, and arms. The Helvetii, together with the Tulingi, Latovici, and Rauraci, were bidden to return to their own country; and as all their produce was gone, so that they had nothing at home to live on, Caesar directed the Allobroges

to supply them with grain, and ordered the Helvetii themselves to rebuild the towns and villages they had burnt. His
chief reason for doing this was that he did not want the
country they had abandoned to remain uninhabited, lest the
Germans across the Rhine might be induced by its fertility
to migrate into Switzerland, and so become near neighbours of the Roman Province, and especially of the Allobroges. The Boii were given a home in the country of the
Aedui, who asked Caesar to consent to this arrangement because the Boii were known as a people of exceptional bravery. The Aedui assigned them land, and later admitted
them to equality of rights and liberties with themselves.

Some documents found in the Helvetian camp were
brought to Caesar. They were written in Greek characters,
and contained a register of the names of all the emigrants
capable of bearing arms, and also, under separate heads, the
numbers of old men, women, and children. The grand total
was 368,000, comprising 263,000 Helvetii, 36,000 Tulingi,
14,000 Latovici, 23,000 Rauraci, and 32,000 Boii; and the
list of men fit for military service contained 92,000 names.
By Caesar's orders a census was taken of those who returned
home, and the number was found to be 110,000.

§ 2 EXPULSION OF ARIOVISTUS FROM GAUL (58 B.C.)

ON the conclusion of the Helvetian campaign the leading
men of tribes in almost every part of Gaul came to offer
Caesar congratulations. They realized, they said, that although his motive in fighting the Helvetii was to punish
them for their past injuries to Rome, what had happened
was just as much to the advantage of Gaul as of the Romans.
For the intention of the Helvetii, in abandoning their home at
a time when they enjoyed great prosperity, was to make war

on all Gaul and become masters of it, and so to have the whole country from which to select the district they thought most fertile and convenient for settlement, and to compel the other tribes to pay tribute. The deputies asked Caesar to let them fix a day for convening a pan-Gallic assembly, saying that there were certain requests they would like to submit to him when they were all agreed about them. With Caesar's consent they appointed a date for this assembly, and swore to one another not to disclose its proceedings without its express authority.

When the assembly had met and concluded its business, the same chieftains who had been with Caesar before returned and asked leave to interview him privately in a place secluded from observation, in order to discuss a matter that concerned not only their own interest, but that of the whole country. When the interview was granted they all prostrated themselves before him with tears in their eyes. They explained that they were very anxious to prevent what they said from being disclosed; this was just as important to them as obtaining the request that they had come to make, because its disclosure would bring the most cruel punishment upon them. Their spokesman was the Aeduan Diviciacus. The Gauls, he said, were divided into two parties, one dominated by the Aedui, the other by the Arverni. After a fierce struggle for supremacy, lasting many years, the Arverni and Sequani hired some German mercenaries to help them [70–65 B.C.]. A first contingent of about fifteen thousand had crossed the Rhine; but when the uncivilized Barbarians had acquired a taste for residence in Gaul, with its good land and high standard of life, more were brought over, and there were at present about a hundred and twenty thousand of them in the country. The Aedui and their satellite tribes had fought the Germans more than once, and had suffered disastrous defeats, by which they lost all their noblest citizens, councillors, and knighthood. These calamities had broken the supremacy which they formerly maintained in Gaul by their own prowess and by the ties of hospitality and friendship that united them with the Romans; and they had been forced to surrender their most distinguished citizens as hostages to the Sequani, and to bind themselves by oath not to attempt to recover them and not to solicit the aid of Rome, but to submit for ever without demur to the sovereign power of their conquerors. 'I myself,' he said, 'am the only man of the whole Aeduan nation who could not be prevailed upon to swear this oath or to give my children as hostages. That was why I fled from my country and went to Rome to claim assistance from the Senate – because I alone was not restrained either by an oath or by the surrender of hostages.' But a worse fate, he went on to say, had befallen the victorious Sequani than the conquered Aedui. For the German king Ariovistus had settled in their territory and seized a third of their land – the best in all Gaul. And now he was bidding them evacuate another third, because a few months previously he had been joined by twenty-four thousand men of the Harudes, and must find them a home to settle in. In a few years' time the whole population of Gaul would be expatriated and all the Germans would migrate across the Rhine; for there was no comparison between the soil of Germany and that of Gaul, or between their respective standards of living. After a single victory over the united Gallic forces at Admagetobriga [61 B.C.], Ariovistus had shown himself an arrogant and cruel tyrant, demanding the children of every man of rank as hostages, and making an example of them by the infliction of all manner of torture, if the least indication of his will and pleasure was not instantly complied with. The man was an ill-tempered, headstrong savage, and it was impossible to endure his tyranny any longer. Unless Caesar and the Romans would help them, the Gauls must all do as the Helvetii had done – leave their homes, seek other dwelling-places out of reach of the Germans, and take their chance of whatever fortune might befall them. 'If my words come to the ears of Ariovistus,' he concluded, 'I do not doubt that he will inflict the most inhuman punishment on all the hostages he has in his power. But your great prestige, the recent victory of your army, and the terror of the Roman name, could deter him from bringing fresh German hordes across and protect all Gaul from his depredations.'

When Diviciacus had finished his speech, the whole deputation began with many tears to implore Caesar's aid. He noticed however that the Sequanian representatives did not follow the example of all the rest, but hung their heads in dejection with their eyes fixed on the ground. In astonishment he asked them the reason for this behaviour, but without making any reply they maintained their attitude of silent dejection. After he had questioned them repeatedly without being able to get a word out of them, Diviciacus spoke again. The lot of the Sequani, he explained, was even more grievous and miserable than that of the rest, because they alone dared not, even in secret, complain or beg for relief. They stood in terror of Ariovistus' cruelty, even when he was far away, just as much as if they were in his presence. For while the others could at any rate flee away out of his reach, the Sequani, having admitted him into their midst and allowed all their towns to fall into his power, must submit to any atrocities he chose to commit against them.

On receiving this information Caesar reassured the Gauls and promised to attend to the matter, adding that he had great hopes that the privilege he had secured for Ariovistus, as well as the weight of his authority, would induce him to cease his oppression. He then dismissed the meeting. In addition to what he had been told, many other considerations convinced him that this problem must be faced and some action taken. The most important was the fact that the Aedui, who had frequently been styled by the Senate

'Brothers and Kinsmen of the Roman People', were en-slaved and held subject by the Germans, and that Aeduan hostages were in the hands of Ariovistus and the Sequani, which, considering the mighty power of Rome, Caesar re-garded as a disgrace to himself and his country. Further-more, if the Germans gradually formed a habit of crossing the Rhine and entering Gaul in large numbers, he saw how dangerous it would be for the Romans. If these fierce Bar-barians occupied the whole of Gaul, the temptation would be too strong for them: they would cross the frontier into the Province, as the Cimbri and Teutoni had done before them [109–101 B.C.], and march on Italy. For the Roman Province lay just across the Rhone from the territory of the Sequani. This danger, he considered, must be provided against immediately. Moreover, Ariovistus personally had behaved with quite intolerable arrogance and pride.

Accordingly Caesar decided to send envoys requiring him to select for a conference some place lying between their present positions, as he wished to discuss business of state of the highest importance to them both. To this delegation Ariovistus replied: 'If I wanted anything from Caesar, I should go to him; so if he wants anything of me, he must come to me.' He added that he dared not come without the protection of his army into the part of Gaul occupied by Caesar, and that to concentrate his forces would mean making elaborate and troublesome arrangements for pro-visioning them. He could not imagine what business Caesar, or the Romans at all for that matter, had in the part of Gaul which was his by right of conquest.

At this Caesar sent a second embassy to remind Ariovis-tus of the important privilege conferred upon him by him-self and the Roman government, when during Caesar's consulship [59 B.C.] he received from the Senate the titles of 'King' and 'Friend'. Since his way of showing his grati-tude was to refuse an invitation to a conference for the discussion of matters affecting their common interest, the envoys were instructed to deliver him an ultimatum: first, he was not to bring any more large bodies of men across the Rhine into Gaul; secondly, he was to restore the Aeduan hostages he held, and to authorize the Sequani to restore those whom they held; finally, he was not to oppress the Aedui or to make war on them or their allies. On these conditions Caesar and the Roman government would maintain cordial and friendly relations with him. If these demands were refused, then, in accordance with a decree of the Senate passed in the consulship of Marcus Messala and Marcus Piso [61 B.C.], directing all governors of the Province of Gaul to do everything consistent with the public interest to protect the Aedui and other Roman allies, Caesar would not fail to punish his ill-treatment of them.

In reply Ariovistus said that it was the recognized custom of war for victors to rule the vanquished in any way they pleased, and that the Romans acted on this principle by governing their conquered subjects, not according to the dictates of any third party, but at their own discretion. Since he did not dictate to them how they were to exercise their rights, he ought not to be interfered with in the exercise of his. It was because the Aedui had tried the fortune of war, and were the losers in the fight, that they had to pay him tribute; and Caesar was doing him a serious wrong in coming to Gaul and causing him a loss of revenue. He would not return the hostages to the Aedui, but would refrain from making any wanton attack upon them or their allies, if they kept their agreement and paid the tribute regularly every year; if they did not, the title of 'Brothers of the Roman People' would not save them from the consequences. 'I am not impressed,' he concluded, 'by Caesar's threat to punish my "oppression" of these people. No one has ever fought me without bringing destruction upon himself. Let him attack whenever he pleases. He will discover what German valour is capable of. We have never known defeat, we have had a superb training in arms, and for fourteen years have never sheltered beneath a roof.'

At the very moment when this message was being reported to Caesar, delegations arrived from the Aedui and the Treveri. The Aedui came to complain that the Harudes, who had lately crossed into Gaul, were ravaging their territory, and that even the surrender of hostages had failed to induce Ariovistus to leave them in peace. The Treveri stated that a hundred clans of the Suebi had encamped on the bank of the Rhine and were trying to cross under the command of Nasua and his brother Cimberius. Caesar was much perturbed by this news, and decided that he must act immediately, lest, if this fresh horde of Suebi joined forces with Ariovistus' veteran troops, it might become more difficult to resist them. Accordingly, he arranged for a supply of grain as quickly as he could, and advanced at top speed towards Ariovistus. After three days' march it was reported that the German was hastening with all his forces to occupy Besançon, the largest town of the Sequani, and had already advanced three days' journey beyond his own frontier. Caesar felt that he must take energetic measures to prevent the fall of this town. For it contained an abundance of military stores of every kind, and its natural defences were so strong that it offered every facility for protracting hostilities. The river Doubs forms an almost complete and perfect circle round it; the gap left unprotected is little more than five hundred yards wide, and is blocked by a high hill so completely that the spurs at its base run right down to the river bank on either side. This hill was girt by a wall which gave it the strength of a citadel and joined it with the town. Caesar hastened there by forced marches continued day and night, occupied the town, and placed a garrison in it.

During the few days that they spent near Besançon to lay in a stock of corn and other provisions, the soldiers began to question the Gauls and merchants there, who talked about the enormous stature, incredible courage, and splendid military training of the Germans. Some affirmed that on many occasions when they had met them in battle, the very expression on their faces and the fierce glance of their eyes were more than they could endure. This gossip threw all ranks into a sudden panic that completely unnerved them. It began with the military tribunes, the prefects of the auxiliary troops, and the men with little experience of war who had followed Caesar from Rome in order to cultivate his friendship. Most of these alleged some urgent reason or other for leaving camp, and asked Caesar's permission to go. Some stayed out of shame and a desire to avoid the suspicion of cowardice. But they were unable to hide their feelings, and at times could not help shedding tears; skulking in their tents, they bemoaned their fate or joined their friends in lamenting the peril that threatened them all alike. All over the camp men were signing and sealing their wills. The talk of these frightened people gradually affected even seasoned campaigners, including some centurions and cavalry officers. Those who wished to be thought less timid than the rest said that it was not the enemy they feared, but the narrow defiles through which they had to pass and the great forests that lay between them and Ariovistus, or pretended to be afraid that it would prove impossible to maintain an adequate supply of corn. Some even went so far as to tell Caesar that when he gave the command to strike camp and advance, the soldiers would be too panic-stricken to obey.

Observing this state of affairs, Caesar summoned the centurions of every grade to a council, and began by severely reprimanding them for presuming to inquire or conjecture where he was leading them, or with what object. At the time of his consulship, he said, Ariovistus had sought the friendship of Rome with great eagerness; and what reason was there for thinking that he would so light-heartedly refuse to carry out his obligations? For his own part, he was convinced that when the king was acquainted with his demands and saw the fairness of the terms proposed, he would not reject the friendship offered by the Roman government and by himself. If, however, a mad impulse should lead him to make war, what reason had they after all for being afraid? Both their own courage and his careful attention to his duties gave good grounds for confidence. 'Our countrymen faced this enemy,' he continued, 'in our fathers' time, when Gaius Marius won a victory over the Cimbri and Teutoni by which, as all agreed, the whole army earned as much glory as its commander. They faced them again more recently in Italy, when they defeated the rebellious slaves, aided though these were to some extent by the military training and discipline that they had acquired from their Roman masters. This shows what a great advantage resolute courage is: for a long time the Romans had an unreasoning fear of the slaves while they were still unarmed, yet afterwards defeated them when they were not only armed but flushed with victory. Moreover these Germans are the same men whom the Helvetii have often met in battle, not only in Switzerland but also in Germany, and have generally beaten; yet the Helvetii were not a match for our army. If anyone is alarmed by the fact that the Germans have defeated the Gauls and put them to flight, he should inquire into the circumstances of that defeat. He will find that it happened at a time when the Gauls were exhausted by a long war. Ariovistus had remained for many months under cover of his camp and the surrounding marshes, so that they had no chance of fighting him, and then he attacked suddenly, when in despair of bringing him to battle they had broken up into scattered groups. Thus his victory resulted from his cunning strategy rather than the bravery of his troops. The employment of such strategy was possible against inexperienced natives, but even Ariovistus can have no hope of being able to trick our armies by such means.' He went on to say that those who tried to disguise their cowardice by pretending to be anxious about the corn-supply or the difficulties of the route were acting presumptuously: it was plain that they either lacked confidence in their general's sense of duty or else meant to dictate to him. He was attending to these matters. Corn was being supplied by the Sequani, Leuci, and Lingones, and the harvest was already ripe in the fields; and as to the route, they would soon be in a position to judge for themselves. The suggestion that the men would not obey orders to advance did not trouble him at all; for he knew that in all cases in which an army had refused obedience, it was either because their generals had been unsuccessful and were regarded as unlucky, or because they were proved dishonest by the discovery of some misconduct. His own integrity was attested by his whole life; his power of commanding success, by the campaign against the Helvetii. Therefore he was going to do that very night what he had at first intended to defer till later: he would move camp in the early hours of the morning, so as to find out with the least possible delay whether their sense of honour and duty or their fear was the stronger. If no one else would follow him, he would go all the same, accompanied only by the 10th legion; [1] of its loyalty he had no doubt, and it should serve as his bodyguard.

This address had a dramatic effect on all ranks, and inspired them with the utmost enthusiasm and eagerness for action. First of all, the men of the 10th commissioned their military tribunes to thank Caesar for his high opinion of them, and to assure him that they were ready to take the field at any moment. Then the other legions prevailed on their tribunes and first grade centurions to make their peace

1. Caesar placed the highest confidence in this legion for its bravery and had shown it particular favour.

with him, professing that they had never entertained doubts or fears, and had never imagined that it was for them to direct the campaign, which they realized was their commander's business. Accepting their excuses, Caesar told Diviciacus to study the available routes, because he trusted him more than any of the other Gauls, and was advised by him to make a detour of some fifty miles, which would enable them to march through open country. Starting in the small hours, as he had said he would, he marched without interruption for six days, and was then informed by his patrols that Ariovistus' forces were twenty-three miles away.

Hearing that Caesar had moved nearer, Ariovistus sent a message saying that he had no objection to arranging the interview previously requested, as he thought he could now do so without risk. Caesar did not reject his offer, thinking that Ariovistus was now coming to his senses again, since he undertook of his own accord to do what he had refused before when asked. He hoped too that the recollection of the great favours the king had received from himself and the Roman government would make him abandon his stubborn attitude, when he heard what was required of him. The interview was arranged for the fifth day following, and in the meantime messengers kept going to and fro between them. Ariovistus insisted that Caesar should not bring any infantry to the conference; he was afraid, he said, of being caught in a trap. Each of them must come with a mounted escort only; otherwise he would not come at all. As Caesar did not want to give him an excuse for cancelling the meeting, yet dared not entrust his safety to the Gallic cavalry, he decided that his best course would be to take away all their horses and mount upon them the infantrymen of the 10th legion, in whom he had such complete confidence, and thus have an escort on whose devotion he could rely absolutely in case of need. While this was being done

one of the legionaries made quite a witty remark: 'Caesar's being better than his word,' he said. 'He promised to make the 10th his bodyguard, and now he's knighting us.'

In an extensive plain there stood a fairly high mound of earth, about equidistant from the camps of Caesar and Ariovistus. Here they came, as agreed, to hold their conference. The mounted legion that Caesar had brought was posted some three hundred yards away from the mound, and Ariovistus' horsemen took up their position at an equal distance. The king stipulated that they should confer on horseback, each accompanied by ten men. On reaching the place Caesar began by recalling the favours that he himself and the Senate had conferred on Ariovistus – how he had been honoured with the titles of 'King' and 'Friend', and had received handsome presents – pointing out that very few princes had been granted such distinctions, which were usually reserved for those who had rendered important services to Rome. 'You would have had no right,' he said, 'to apply to the Senate for any such favours; you owe them entirely to my kindness and generosity and that of the Senate. The friendship between my country and the Aedui is of long standing and founded on solid grounds. Resolutions of the Senate, expressed in most complimentary terms, have repeatedly been passed in their honour. They held a position of supremacy in Gaul all along, even before they sought our friendship; and since it has always been our policy to see that our allies and friends, far from losing anything they had already, should have their credit, honour, and importance increased, how can we allow them to be robbed of what they already had when they became our friends?' He then repeated the demands which he had instructed his envoys to present – that Ariovistus should not make war on the Aedui or their allies; that he should restore their hostages; and that even if he could not send any of the Germans back home, he should at least not let any more cross the Rhine.

Ariovistus had little to say in reply to these demands, but spoke at length about his own merits. He had crossed the Rhine, he said, not of his own accord but in response to the invitation of the Gauls, and it had needed the prospect of a rich reward to induce him to leave his home and his relatives. The possessions he had in Gaul had been ceded to him by the Gauls themselves, and the hostages had been given voluntarily. As for the tribute he exacted, this was customarily regarded as the right of a victorious belligerent. He had not been the aggressor: the Gauls had attacked him, all their tribes having marched out and taken the field against him. He had completely routed their entire force in a single battle. If they wanted to try their luck again, he was quite ready for another fight; if they wanted peace, it was unfair for them to object to the tribute that they had hitherto paid without demur. The friendship of the Roman People ought to be a distinction and a protection to him, not an occasion of loss, and it was with this expectation that he had sought it. If through Roman interference his subjects were absolved from payment and withdrawn from his control, he would be just as ready to discard that friendship as he had been to seek it. The large numbers of Germans he was bringing into Gaul were brought to secure his safety, not for aggression; the proof of that was that he had not come till he was asked, and had fought only in self-defence. However, he had come there before the Romans, whose armies had never before marched beyond the frontier of the Province. What did Caesar mean by invading his dominions? 'This part of the country,' he said, 'is my province, just as the other part is yours. I could not expect you to let me make raids into your territory with impunity, and it is a gross injustice for you to interfere with me in the exercise of my lawful rights. You say that the Aedui have been called "Brothers" by the Roman Senate. Well, I may be a "Barbarian"; but I am not such a Barbarian, and not so ignorant, as not to know that in the recent revolt of the Allobroges [61 B.C.] you got no help from the Aedui, and that they had to do without the benefit of your assistance in the war they have just fought with me and the Sequani. I suspect that this talk of friendship is just so much pretence, and that your object in keeping an army in Gaul is to crush me. Unless you take yourself off from this country, and your army with you, it won't be as a "Friend" that I shall treat you. In fact, if I killed you, there are plenty of nobles and politicians in Rome who would thank me for it; I know this, because they themselves commissioned their agents to tell me so. I could make them all my grateful friends by putting an end to you. But if you will go away and leave me in undisturbed possession of Gaul, I will reward you handsomely, and whenever you want a war fought, I will see the job through for you, without your lifting a finger or running any risk.'

Caesar explained at some length why he could not think of abandoning his intention. It was contrary to his principles and to those of the Roman government to desert a loyal ally; and he could not admit that Gaul belonged to Ariovistus any more than to Rome. The Arverni and the Ruteni had been conquered by Quintus Fabius Maximus [121 B.C.], although the Roman People afterwards pardoned their hostility and refrained from annexing their land or exacting tribute from them. If priority of arrival was to be the criterion, the Romans' title to rule Gaul was unimpeachable. If they were to abide by the decision of the Senate, Gaul ought to be independent, since the Senate had determined that, although conquered, it should be allowed self-government.

While these questions were being argued, word was brought to Caesar that Ariovistus' horsemen were approaching nearer the mound, riding towards our soldiers, and throwing stones and javelins at them. Caesar broke off the conversation, went to his men, and forbade them to throw a single missile in retaliation. For although he knew that a legion of picked troops could engage cavalry without the slightest risk, he did not choose to give anyone the chance of saying, if the enemy were driven off, that he had broken his word by treacherously attacking them during a parley. When the news spread through the ranks of the army that Ariovistus had arrogantly warned the Romans off the whole of Gaul, and that his cavalry had interrupted the conference by attacking our troops, the men's enthusiasm and eagerness for battle knew no bounds.

The next day Ariovistus sent envoys to Caesar to say that he wished to resume their interrupted discussion, and to ask him either to appoint a day for another personal interview, or, if he did not want to do that, to send an officer to represent him. Caesar did not see that anything was to be gained by a further interview, especially as on the previous day Ariovistus had been unable to restrain his men from attacking the Roman troops, and he thought it would be running a great risk to send a Roman officer and place him at the mercy of such savages. He decided that his best plan was to send Gaius Valerius Procillus, a young man of high character and liberal education, whose father Gaius Valerius Caburus had been granted Roman citizenship by Gaius Valerius Flaccus. Procillus was a man who could be trusted; his knowledge of the Gallic language would be useful, since by long practice Ariovistus had learnt to speak it fluently; and in his case the Germans would have no motive for foul play. With him he sent Marcus Metius, who was bound to Ariovistus by ties of hospitality, and their orders were to hear what the king had to say, and report to Caesar. But as soon as Ariovistus saw them at his camp headquarters, he shouted out in front of his whole army: 'What are you coming here for? To play the spy, I suppose?'; and when they attempted to speak, he stopped them and had them put in chains. On the same day he advanced and took up a position at the foot of a mountain six miles from Caesar's camp. The next day he marched his army past the camp and himself encamped two miles farther on, with the object of intercepting the convoys of grain and other supplies that were being sent up from the Sequani and the Aedui. On each of the five days following, Caesar led his troops out in front of his camp and kept them for some time in line of battle, so as to give Ariovistus the opportunity of fighting if he wanted to; but each day the king kept his main forces in camp, merely engaging in cavalry skirmishes.[1]

Caesar saw that the Germans were not going to come out of their camp, and since he could not afford to be cut off from supplies any longer, he chose a suitable site for a camp about a thousand yards beyond the enemy's position, and marched there in battle formation of three lines. The first and second lines were ordered to stand by under arms; the third, to make fortifications for the camp. The place being less than a mile away, Ariovistus sent some sixteen thousand light infantry and all his cavalry to overawe our soldiers and prevent them from continuing the work. Caesar, however, did not vary his original plan; the first two lines were told to drive off the enemy, while the third finished their task. When the entrenchments of the camp were completed, he left two legions and a detachment of auxiliaries to occupy it, and led the other four legions back to the large camp. The next day he followed his usual routine by bringing the troops out of both camps, deploying them for action a short

1. The Germans were trained in the use of a special battle technique. They had a force of six thousand cavalry, each of whom had selected from the whole army, for his personal protection, one infantryman of outstanding courage and speed of foot. These accompanied the cavalry in battle and acted as a support for them to fall back upon. In a critical situation they ran to the rescue and surrounded any cavalryman who had been unhorsed by a severe wound. They acquired such agility by practice, that in a long advance or a quick retreat they could hang on to the horses' manes and keep pace with them.

distance from the large camp, and offering battle. Finding that even then the enemy would not come out, he returned to camp about midday, whereupon Ariovistus at last sent a detachment to attack the small camp, and a hotly-contested battle was kept up until evening. At sunset, after severe casualties had been sustained by both sides, Ariovistus retired. On inquiring from prisoners why he would not fight a general engagement, Caesar was told that the German matrons, who used to draw lots and employ other methods of divination to decide whether it was advisable to join battle, had pronounced that the Germans were not destined to win if they fought before the new moon.

Next day, leaving adequate garrisons in the two camps, Caesar posted all his auxiliaries in front of the small camp, where they would be visible to the enemy and give an impression of strength – since his regular infantry was numerically weak in comparison with the Germans. He then drew up the legions for action in three lines and advanced right up to Ariovistus' camp. The enemy was now compelled to lead his forces out, and drew up the various tribal contingents at equal intervals – Harudes, Marcomani, Triboci, Vangiones, Nemetes, Eudusii, and Suebi. So that there might be no hope of escaping by flight, they formed a barrier of carriages and wagons along the rear of their whole line, and in them placed their women, who as the men marched to battle stretched out their hands and implored them with tears not to let them be enslaved by the Romans.

Caesar placed each of his five generals at the head of a legion and detailed his quaestor to command the remaining legion, so that every soldier might know that there was a high officer in a position to observe the courage with which he conducted himself, and then led the right wing first into action, because he had noticed that the enemy's line was weakest on that side. Our troops attacked with such vigour when the signal was given, and the enemy also dashed forward so suddenly and swiftly, that there was no time to throw spears at them. So the men dropped their spears and fought hand to hand with their swords. By quickly adopting their usual phalanx-formation the Germans were able to withstand the sword-thrusts, but many of our soldiers actually threw themselves on the wall of shields confronting them, wrenched the shields out of the enemy's hands, and stabbed them from above. The Germans' left was thus routed, but their right began to press our troops hard by weight of numbers. Their perilous position attracted the attention of young Publius Crassus, who was in charge of the cavalry and better able to move about and see what was happening than those in the fighting line. He therefore sent up the third line to their relief. This move turned the battle once more in our favour, and the enemy's whole army broke and fled without stopping until they came to the Rhine, some fifteen miles away. A very few of the strongest tried to swim the river, and a few others saved themselves by finding boats – including Ariovistus, who had the luck to come across a small craft moored to the bank. All the rest were hunted down and killed by our cavalry. Ariovistus' two wives both perished in the flight – one a Suebic woman whom he had brought from Germany, the other a Norican whom her brother King Voccio sent to him while he was in Gaul; and of his two daughters, one was killed and the other captured. Valerius Procillus was being dragged along by his guards among the German fugitives, fettered with three chains, when Caesar himself, who was with the pursuing cavalry, came up with him. This fortunate chance pleased Caesar as much as the actual victory. For the man whom it rescued from the enemy's clutches and restored to him was the worthiest in the whole Province, besides being his own friend and host; and his death, which Providence thus averted, would have marred the pleasure and rejoicing that attended so splendid a triumph. Procillus recounted how, before his very eyes, the Germans had three times cast lots to decide whether he should be burnt to death at once or reserved for execution later, and how he owed his life to the way the lots had fallen. Metius also was found and brought back to Caesar. When the news of the battle reached the other side of the Rhine, the Suebi, who had advanced as far as the river bank, turned back homewards, and the Rhineland tribes, seeing what a panic they were in, pursued and killed a large number of them.

Caesar had completed two important campaigns in a single summer. He now took the army into winter quarters in the country of the Sequani somewhat earlier than the usual time of year, and leaving Labienus in command started for northern Italy to hold the assizes.

§ 3 COLLAPSE OF THE BELGIC COALITION (57 B.C.)

WHILE Caesar was in Italy, and the legions in their winter quarters, repeated rumours reached him, alleging what was confirmed by dispatches from Labienus – that all the Belgic tribes, whose territory comprises a third of Gaul,[1] were conspiring against the Romans and exchanging hostages. Their action was said to be due to two causes. In the first place, they were afraid that if all the rest of Gaul was subdued, our troops would advance against them. Secondly, they were instigated, from various motives, by a number of Celtic Gauls. Some of these were as much annoyed by the sight of a Roman army wintering in Gaul, and establishing itself there, as they had been by the continued presence of the Germans in the country; others, fickle and inconstant, merely hankered after a change of masters. There were also

1. See above, page 29.

some adventurers who saw that under Roman rule they would not find it so easy to usurp thrones, as was commonly done in Gaul by powerful men, and by those who could afford to hire mercenaries.

These alarming reports induced Caesar to raise two new legions in Italy, and to send them in the spring to Gaul under the command of Quintus Pedius, one of his generals. As soon as forage began to be plentiful he joined the army in person, and instructed the Senones and the other tribes whose territory bordered on that of the Belgae to find out what was going on among them and inform him. As their reports all agreed that troops were being levied and concentrated, he decided that he must take the offensive at once; and after arranging for a supply of grain he broke camp and in a fortnight was on the Belgic frontier.

On his arrival, which owing to the speed of his march was quite unexpected, the Remi, the nearest of the Belgae to Celtic Gaul, sent Iccius and Andecombogius, the leading men of their tribe, to tell him that they placed themselves and all they possessed under the protection and at the disposal of the Roman People. They explained that they had taken no part in the conspiracy which the rest of the Belgae had planned against the Romans, and that they were ready to give hostages, to obey his orders, to admit him into their strongholds, and to furnish corn and other supplies. The remainder of the Belgae, they said, were up in arms, and had been joined by the Germans living on the Gallic side of the Rhine; and all of them were possessed by such fury that even the Suessiones – their own near kinsmen, who enjoyed the protection of the same laws as themselves, and obeyed the same king and the same magistrate – had refused to listen when they tried to deter them from joining the movement.

On being asked for the names of the tribes that had taken up arms, and particulars of their numbers and military strength, the envoys stated that most of the Belgae were descended from tribes which long ago came across the Rhine from Germany and settled in that part of Gaul on account of its fertility, expelling the former inhabitants. The Belgae, they said, were the only people who half a century earlier, when all the rest of Gaul was overrun by the Teutoni and the Cimbri, prevented the invaders from entering their territory – the recollection of which made them assume an air of much importance and pride themselves on their military power. Regarding their numbers the Remi professed to have detailed information, explaining that they were united with the various tribes by ties of blood and marriage, and knew the strength of the contingent that each had promised in the general council of the Belgae. The most powerful of all, they said, were the Bellovaci, on account of their bravery, prestige, and large population; they could muster 100,000 troops, had promised 60,000 picked men, and claimed the direction of the whole campaign. The Suessiones, near neighbours of the Remi themselves, had an extensive and very fertile territory. They had been ruled within living memory by Diviciacus, the most powerful king in Gaul, who controlled not only a large part of the Belgic country, but Britain as well. Their present king was Galba, to whom, as a just and able man, the supreme direction of the war was being entrusted by common consent; he possessed twelve strongholds, and undertook to furnish 50,000 troops. An equal number was promised by the Nervii, who were considered by the Belgae themselves to be their fiercest fighters, and lived farthest to the north. The Atrebates were to provide 15,000 men, the Ambiani 10,000, the Morini 25,000, the Menapii 9,000, the Caleti 10,000, the Veliocasses and the Viromandui 10,000 between them, and the Atuatuci 19,000; the Condrusi, Eburones, Caerosi, and Paemani (who are all known as German tribes) thought they could raise an army about 40,000 strong.

Caesar addressed the Remi in gracious and reassuring terms, telling them to send their whole council to him and to place the children of their leading citizens in his hands as hostages. These orders were carefully and punctually obeyed. He impressed upon Diviciacus the Aeduan the importance, alike for Rome and for the general safety of Gaul, of preventing the junction of the various enemy contingents, in order to avoid the necessity of fighting such powerful forces all at once. He explained that the best way of effecting this was for the Aedui to invade the land of the Bellovaci and start devastating it, and dismissed Diviciacus with orders to do so. When, however, he learnt from his patrols, and from the Remi, that the Belgae had already completed their concentration and were approaching, he hastily crossed the river Aisne, just within the borders of the Remi, and encamped. This movement enabled him to protect one side of his camp by the river and to secure his rear, and assured the safety of the convoys that were to be sent up by the Remi and others. The river was spanned by a bridge, at the head of which he placed a strong guard, leaving one of his generals, Quintus Titurius Sabinus, on the left bank with six cohorts. He ordered the camp to be made with a rampart twelve feet high and a trench eighteen feet wide.

Eight miles away was a town of the Remi called Bibrax, which the Belgae, directly they reached it, assaulted so violently that the garrison had difficulty in holding out to the end of the day. The Belgae have the same method of attacking a fortress as the rest of the Gauls. They begin by surrounding the whole circuit of the wall with a large number of men and showering stones at it from all sides; when they have cleared it of defenders, they lock their shields over their heads, advance close up, and undermine it. These tactics were easy to employ on the present occasion; for with such a large force hurling stones and javelins, no one could possibly stay on the wall. When night stopped the assault, Iccius, the governor of the town – a Reman nobleman, who was very influential with his countrymen and had been one of the envoys deputed to ask Caesar for peace – sent word that unless relieved he could not hold out longer. Shortly after midnight, using as guides the men who had brought Iccius' message, Caesar sent some Numidians, Cretan archers, and Balearic slingers to help him. Their arrival restored the morale of the Remi and filled them with fresh ardour for the defence of the town, while the enemy gave up hope of capturing it. Accordingly, after staying there a short time longer, the Belgae proceeded to ravage the countryside and to burn all the villages and homesteads within reach, and then marched their whole army towards Caesar's camp and themselves encamped barely two miles away. The smoke and flame of their watchfires showed that their camp stretched for about eight miles.

As the Belgic forces were very strong and had a great reputation for bravery, Caesar determined at first not to fight a general action. But he engaged every day in cavalry skirmishes, in order to discover what the enemy could really do, and how his own men stood up to them; and he soon found that his troops were as good as theirs. The ground in front of his camp was ideal for deploying the army for action. The low hill on which the camp stood was of just the right width, on the side facing the enemy, for the legions to occupy in battle-formation; on each flank it descended steeply to the plain, while in front it formed a slight ridge and then sloped gently down. On either side of the hill Caesar had a trench dug, running for about six hundred and fifty yards at right angles to the line along which the troops would be drawn up, and placed redoubts and artillery at both ends of each trench, to prevent the enemy from using their numerical superiority to envelop his men from the flanks while they were fighting. He left the two newly enrolled legions in camp, to be used as reinforcements wherever they were needed, and drew up the other six in front in line of battle. The enemy also had marched out and deployed for action.

There was a small marsh between the two armies. The Belgae waited in the hope that our troops would try to cross it, and our men stood with weapons in their hands, ready to pounce upon them at a disadvantage if they attempted to cross first, while in the meantime a cavalry skirmish went on between the lines. Since neither side would make the first move, as soon as the cavalry fight ended in our favour Caesar led the infantry back into camp. The Belgae then marched straight from their battle-position to the Aisne, which I have explained was in the rear of our camp. They found a ford and tried to get a part of their forces across, intending to storm a redoubt commanded by Sabinus and break down the bridge, or, failing this, to deprive us of a very useful source of supplies for the campaign by devastating the land of the Remi, and to cut our communications. On being informed of this by Sabinus, Caesar crossed the bridge with all the cavalry, the light-armed Numidians, the slingers, and the archers, and advanced against them. A fierce battle ensued. He attacked them in the river, which impeded their movements, and killed a large number. Others made a very daring attempt to cross over their dead bodies, but were driven back by a shower of missiles, while some of the first comers who had succeeded in getting across were rounded up and destroyed by the cavalry. The Belgae now realized that their hope of crossing the river was as vain as their hope of capturing Bibrax had proved to be, and that the Romans would not advance into an unfavourable position to fight. Their own supply of grain, too, was running short. Summoning a council of war, therefore, they decided that the best course was for every man to return to his own home and wait to see whose territory the Romans invaded first; they would then rally from all parts to its defence, and would have the advantage of fighting in friendly country, where their home supplies of grain would be available. In addition to the other reasons, they were led to this decision by the knowledge that Diviciacus and his Aeduans were approaching the frontier of the Bellovaci, whose soldiers were so anxious to go to the help of their own people that they could not be induced to stay any longer where they were.

In pursuance of their resolve the Belgae left camp some time before midnight amid great uproar and confusion, without any proper order or discipline, since every man wanted to reach home quickly and tried to get the first place on the road. The result was that their departure resembled a rout. The movement was immediately reported to Caesar by his scouts, but he was afraid at first that an ambush was being laid, because the reason for their retreat was not yet apparent, and therefore kept all his forces in camp. At daybreak, however, the reports of his patrols satisfied him that the enemy really were retreating, whereupon he sent forward the generals Quintus Pedius and Lucius Aurunculeius Cotta, with all the cavalry, to delay the march of their rearguard, and ordered Labienus to follow in support with three legions. These troops attacked their column from behind and pursued it for many miles, killing a large number as they fled. For while the rearguard, with which our men were actually in contact, halted and put up a gallant resistance, all those in front, imagining that they were far enough off to be safe, and not being under the immediate necessity of defending themselves or under the control of anyone in authority, broke their ranks directly they heard the shouting of the combatants, and tried to escape. Thus our troops were able, without any risk, to kill as many of them as there was time to kill. When nightfall compelled them to stop, they returned to camp in accordance with their orders.

§ 4 PIECEMEAL CONQUEST OF THE BELGIC TRIBES
(57 B.C.)

THE next day, before the enemy could recover from their panic, Caesar advanced into the country of the Suessiones, which adjoined that of the Remi, and by a forced march reached the fortress of Noviodunum. Being informed that it was not garrisoned, he tried to storm it directly he arrived, but the width of the moat and the height of the wall enabled the few defenders to repel his assault. After constructing a camp, therefore, he formed a line of mantlets and set about the usual preparations for a siege. But the next night, before his arrangements were completed, the whole fugitive army of the Suessiones came crowding into the place. When they saw the mantlets rushed up to the wall, earth shovelled into the moat, and siege-towers erected, they were alarmed by the impressive size of this apparatus, which had never before been seen or heard of in Gaul, and by the speed with which the Romans worked. They therefore sent envoys asking to be allowed to surrender – a request which Caesar granted on the intercession of the Remi, who pleaded for the lives of their kinsmen. He took the leading men of the Suessiones as hostages, as well as two of King Galba's own sons, and accepted the surrender of the tribe after all the arms in the fortress had been handed over.

Caesar marched next against the Bellovaci, who retired with all their belongings into the fortress of Bratuspantium. When his army was about five miles off, all the older men came out, and signified by supplicatory gestures and cries that they placed themselves at his mercy and were not offering resistance. In the same way, when he marched close up to the fortress and began to make a camp, the women and children appeared on the wall with arms outstretched in their habitual manner of entreaty, and begged for peace.

Their plea was supported by Diviciacus, who after the re-treat of the Belgae had disbanded the Aeduan forces and returned to Caesar. He said that the Bellovaci had always lived under the friendly protection of the Aedui, until their leading men induced them to sever the connection and take up arms against Rome, by telling them that the Aedui were enslaved by Caesar and had to endure every kind of ill-usage and humiliation. 'The people responsible for the adoption of this policy,' he continued, 'have now realized what a calamity they have brought upon their country, and have fled to Britain. To the prayers of the Bellovaci we Aeduans add our own, begging you to treat them with your usual clemency and humanity. By so doing you will en-hance our prestige with all the Belgic tribes – a matter of importance to us, because we always rely on their troops and resources to see us through any war in which we are in-volved.' Caesar said that he would spare the Bellovaci and accept their submission out of respect for Diviciacus and the Aedui; but as the tribe was very influential among the Bel-gae, and had the largest population, he demanded six hun-dred hostages. When these had been handed over and all the arms in the fortress collected, he marched into the country of the Ambiani, who at once surrendered unconditionally.

The Ambiani were neighbours of the Nervii, about whose character and habits Caesar made inquiries. He learnt that they did not admit traders into their country and would not allow the importation of wine or other luxuries, because they thought such things made men soft and took the edge off their courage; that they were a fierce, warlike people, who bitterly reproached the other Belgae for throwing away their inheritance of bravery by submitting to the Romans, and vowed that they would never ask for peace or accept it on any terms. After three days' march through Nervian territory, Caesar learnt from prisoners that the river Sambre was not more than ten miles from the place where he was encamped, and that all the Nervian troops were posted on the farther side of it, awaiting the arrival of the Romans. Already with them in the field, he was told, were their neighbours the Atrebates and the Viromandui, whom they had persuaded to try the fortune of war along with them; and they were expecting to be joined by the forces of the Atuatuci, which were already on the way. They had hastily thrust their women, and all who were thought too young or too old to fight, into a place which marshes made inaccessible to an army.

On receiving this information Caesar sent forward a reconnoitring party, accompanied by some centurions, to choose a good site for a camp. A large number of Gauls, including some of the Belgae who had surrendered, had attached themselves to Caesar and were marching with the troops. Some of these, as was afterwards ascertained from prisoners, had observed the order in which our army marched during the previous days, and at night made their way to the Nervii and explained to them that each legion was separated from the following one by a long baggage-train, so that when the first reached camp the others would be far away; it would be quite easy to attack it while the men were still burdened with their packs, and when it was routed and its baggage plundered, the others would not dare to make a stand. There was one thing that favoured the execution of the plan suggested by these deserters. The Nervii, having virtually no cavalry,[1] long ago devised a method of hindering their neighbours' cavalry when it made plundering raids into their territory. They cut off the tops of saplings, bent them over, and let a thick growth of side branches shoot out; in between them they planted briers and thorns, and thus made hedges like walls, which gave such protection that no one could even see through them, much less

1. To this day they pay no attention to that arm, their whole strength consisting of infantry.

penetrate them. As these obstacles hindered the march of our column, the Nervii thought the proposed plan too good to leave untried.

At the place that the Romans had chosen for their camp a hill sloped down evenly from its summit to the Sambre. Opposite it, on the other side of the river, rose another hill with a similar gradient, on the lower slopes of which were some three hundred yards of open ground, while the upper part was covered by a wood which it was not easy to see into. In this wood the main part of the enemy's forces lay concealed, while on the open ground along the river bank a few pickets of cavalry were visible. The depth of the river was about three feet.

Caesar had sent his cavalry a little in advance and was following with the rest of his forces. But the column was formed up in a different manner from that which the Belgic deserters had described to the Nervii. In accordance with his usual practice when approaching an enemy, Caesar marched at the head of the column with six legions, unencumbered by heavy baggage; then came the transport of the entire army, protected by the two newly-enrolled legions, which brought up the rear. First of all, our cavalry crossed the river with the slingers and archers and engaged the enemy's horsemen. These kept on retiring into the wood where their comrades were and then reappearing to charge our troops, who dared not pursue them beyond the end of the open ground. Meanwhile the six legions that were the first to arrive measured out the ground and began to construct the camp. The Gauls concealed in the wood had already formed up in battle-order and were waiting full of confidence. As soon as they caught sight of the head of the baggage-train – the moment which they had agreed upon for starting the battle – they suddenly dashed out in full force and swooped down on our cavalry, which they easily routed. Then they ran down to the river at such an incredible speed that almost at the same instant they seemed to be at the edge of the wood, in the water, and already upon us. With equal rapidity they climbed the hill towards our camp to attack the men who were busy entrenching it.

Caesar had everything to do at once – hoist the flag which was the signal for running to arms, recall the men from their work on the camp, fetch back those who had gone far afield in search of material for the rampart, form the battle-line, address the men, and sound the trumpet-signal for going into action. Much of this could not be done in the short time left available by the enemy's swift onset. But the situation was saved by two things – first, the knowledge and experience of the soldiers, whose training in earlier battles enabled them to decide for themselves what needed doing, without waiting to be told; secondly, the order which Caesar had issued to all his generals, not to leave the work, but to stay each with his own legion until the camp fortifications were completed. As the enemy was so close and advancing so swiftly, the generals did not wait for further orders but on their own responsibility took the measures they thought proper.

After giving the minimum of essential orders, Caesar hastened down to the battlefield to address the troops and happened to come first upon the 10th legion, to which he made only a short speech, urging them to live up to their tradition of bravery, to keep their nerve, and to meet the enemy's attack boldly. Then, as the Nervii were within range, he gave the signal for battle. On going to the other side of the field to address the troops there, he found them already in action. The soldiers were so pushed for time by the enemy's eagerness to fight, that they could not even take the covers off their shields or put on helmets – not to speak of fixing on crests or decorations. Each man, on coming down from his work at the camp, went into action under the first standard he happened to see, so as not to waste time searching for his own unit. The battle-front was not formed according to the rules of military theory, but as necessitated by the emergency and the sloping ground of the hill-side. The legions were facing different ways and fighting separate actions, and the thick hedges obstructed their view. The result was that Caesar could not fix upon definite points for stationing reserves or foresee what would be needed in each part of the field, and unity of command was impossible. In such adverse circumstances there were naturally ups and downs of fortune.

The 9th and 10th legions were on the left, and discharged a volley of spears at the Atrebates, who happened to be facing them. Breathless and exhausted with running, and many of them now wounded, the Atrebates were quickly driven down to the river, and when they tried to cross it our soldiers with their swords attacked them at a disadvantage and destroyed a large number. Crossing the river themselves without hesitation and pushing forward up the steep slope, they renewed the fight when the enemy began to resist once more, and again put them to flight. Meanwhile in another part of the field, on a front facing in a slightly different direction, the 11th and 8th legions engaged the Viromandui, drove them down the hill, and were now fighting right on the river banks. By this time, however, the Roman camp was almost entirely exposed in front and on the left, and the 12th and 7th legions, which were posted fairly close together on the right, were attacked by the whole force of the Nervii, led in a compact mass by their commander-in-chief Boduognatus. Some of them began to surround the legions on their right flank, while the rest made for the hill-top where the camp stood.

At the same time, the Roman cavalry and light-armed troops, routed by the first attack, were in the act of retreating into the camp, when they found themselves face to face with the Nervii and took to flight again in a different direction.

The servants, too, who from the back gate on the summit of the hill had seen our victorious troops cross the river, and had gone out to plunder, on looking back and seeing the enemy in the camp immediately ran for their lives. Meanwhile shouting and din arose from the drivers coming up with the baggage, who rushed panic-stricken in every direction. With the army were some auxiliary cavalry sent by the Treveri, a people with a unique reputation for courage among the Gauls. When these horsemen saw the Roman camp full of the enemy, the legions hard pressed and almost surrounded, and the non-combatants, cavalry, slingers, and Numidians scattered and stampeding in every direction, they decided that our case was desperate, and, riding off home in terror, reported that the Romans were utterly defeated and their camp and baggage captured.

After addressing the 10th legion Caesar had gone to the right wing, where he found the troops in difficulties. The cohorts of the 12th legion were packed together so closely that the men were in one another's way and could not fight properly. All the centurions of the 4th cohort, as well as a standard-bearer, were killed, and the standard was lost; nearly all the centurions of the other cohorts were either killed or wounded, including the chief centurion Publius Sextius Baculus, a man of very great courage, who was so disabled by a number of severe wounds that he could no longer stand. The men's movements were slow, and some in the rear, feeling themselves abandoned, were retiring from the fight and trying to get out of range. Meanwhile the enemy maintained unceasing pressure up the hill in front, and were also closing in on both flanks. As the situation was critical and no reserves were available, Caesar snatched a shield from a soldier in the rear (he had not his own shield with him), made his way into the front line, addressed each centurion by name, and shouted encouragement to the rest of the troops, ordering them to push forward and open out their ranks, so that they could use their swords more easily. His coming gave them fresh heart and hope; each man wanted to do his best under the eyes of his commander-in-chief, however desperate the peril, and the enemy's assault was slowed down a little.

Noticing that the 7th legion, which stood close by, was likewise hard put to it, Caesar told the military tribunes to join the two legions gradually together and adopt a square formation, so that they could advance against the enemy in any direction. By this manoeuvre the soldiers were enabled to support one another, and were no longer afraid of being surrounded from behind, which encouraged them to put up a bolder resistance. Meanwhile the two legions which had acted as a guard to the baggage at the rear of the column, having received news of the battle, had quickened their pace, and now appeared on the hill-top, where the enemy could see them; and Labienus, who had captured the enemy's camp, and from the high ground on which it stood could see what was going on in ours, sent the 10th legion to the rescue. The men of the 10th, who could tell from the flight of the cavalry and the non-combatants how serious things were, and what peril threatened the camp, the legions, and their commander-in-chief, strained every nerve to make the utmost speed.

Their arrival so completely changed the situation that even some of the Roman soldiers who had lain down, exhausted by wounds, got up and began to fight again, leaning on their shields. The non-combatants, observing the enemy's alarm, stood up to their attack, unarmed as they were; and the cavalry, anxious to wipe out the disgrace of their flight, scoured the whole battlefield and tried to outdo the legionaries in gallantry. But the enemy, even in their desperate plight, showed such bravery that when their front ranks had fallen those immediately behind stood on their prostrate bodies to fight; and when these too fell and the corpses were piled high, the survivors still kept hurling javelins as though from the top of a mound, and flung back the spears intercepted by their shields. Such courage accounted for the extraordinary feats they had performed already. Only heroes could have made light of crossing a wide river, clambering up the steep banks, and launching themselves on such a difficult position.

So ended this battle, by which the tribe of the Nervii was almost annihilated and their name almost blotted out from the face of the earth. On hearing the news of it, their old men, who had been sent away with the women and children into tidal creeks and marshes,[1] decided that nothing could stop the victorious Romans or protect their conquered tribe, and with the consent of all the survivors they sent envoys to Caesar and surrendered. In describing the calamity that had befallen their state, they asserted that they had three councillors left out of six hundred, and scarcely five hundred men capable of bearing arms out of sixty thousand. Caesar, wishing to let it be seen that he showed mercy to unfortunate suppliants, took great care to protect them from harm, confirmed them in possession of their territories and towns, and commanded their neighbours to refrain from injuring their persons or property, and to make their dependants do likewise.

The Atuatuci, who were coming in full force to help the Nervii,[2] on hearing of their defeat turned back without halting and went home. Abandoning their other

1. See above, page 82.
2. See above, page 82. The Atuatuci were descended from the Cimbri and Teutoni, who on their march towards the Roman Province and Italy deposited on the left bank of the Rhine the cattle and baggage that they could not take with them, with six thousand men to guard it. After the destruction of their fellow-countrymen [102–101 B.C.] these settlers struggled for many years with the neighbouring peoples, sometimes attacking them, at other times defending themselves against attack, until at length all the tribes made peace with them and allowed them to make their home in the district where they now live.

strongholds and fortified refuges, they collected all their possessions into one town of great natural strength. It was surrounded by very high and precipitous rocks, except at one point where there was a gently sloping approach not more than two hundred feet wide. This place the garrison had fortified with a double wall of great height, on top of which they now fixed heavy stones and beams sharpened to a point.

On the arrival of the Roman army the Atuatuci at first made a series of sorties from their fortress and engaged in skirmishes; but when they found themselves enclosed by an earthwork twelve feet high, with a circuit of five miles and redoubts at frequent intervals, they stayed inside. The Romans formed a line of mantlets and constructed a siege-terrace. When they began to erect a siege-tower at some distance, the defenders on the wall at first made abusive remarks and ridiculed the idea of setting up such a huge apparatus so far away. Did those pygmy Romans, they asked, with their feeble hands and muscles,[1] imagine that they could mount such a heavy tower on top of a wall? But when they saw the tower in motion and approaching the fortress walls, the strange, unfamiliar spectacle frightened them into sending envoys to ask Caesar for peace. The envoys said they were forced to the conclusion that the Romans had divine aid in their warlike operations, since they could move up apparatus of such height at such a speed. 'We place ourselves and all we have at your disposal,' they continued, 'and make only one request: if in your clemency and kindness, of which we have often heard, you decide to spare us, do not deprive us of our arms. Almost all our neighbours are hostile, being jealous of our bravery, and if we have to surrender our arms we cannot defend ourselves against them. We would rather suffer any

1. All the Gauls are inclined to be contemptuous of our short stature, contrasting it with their own great height.

fate at your hands, if it must be so, than be tortured to death by men whom we are used to ruling.' To this appeal Caesar replied that he would spare the tribe – not because they deserved it, but because it was his habit to be merciful – provided they surrendered before the battering-ram touched the wall, but that he could not consider any terms of surrender unless they handed over their arms. He would do for them what he had done for the Nervii: he would forbid their neighbours to molest in any way a people who had submitted to Rome. After making a report to their countrymen, the envoys came again to say that they were ready to obey. A large quantity of arms was thrown from the wall into the moat that lay in front of the fortress, the piles reaching nearly to the top of the wall and of the siege-terrace – although it appeared afterwards that they had about a third of their arms hidden inside. They opened the gates and were at peace for that day.

In the evening Caesar ordered the Roman soldiers in the fortress to leave it and had the gates closed, to prevent the men from doing any injury to the inhabitants during the night. But the enemy clearly had a preconcerted plan. Thinking that after their capitulation our pickets would either be withdrawn altogether or at any rate relax their vigilance, they equipped themselves with the arms that they had kept hidden, or with shields made of bark or wickerwork, hastily covered with skins to meet the emergency, and soon after midnight their whole force suddenly made a sortie at the point where our fortifications appeared easiest to scale. The alarm was quickly given by fire-signals, in accordance with orders issued beforehand, and troops hastened up from the nearest redoubts. The Atuatuci struggled with the ferocity that was to be expected of brave men fighting a forlorn hope against an enemy who had the advantage of position and could hurl down missiles from an earthwork and towers, and knowing that courage was the one thing which could save them. About four thousand were killed and the rest driven back into the fortress. Next day the gates, now undefended, were smashed open and the soldiers let in; and Caesar sold all the inhabitants of the place by auction in one lot. The purchasers reported that the number of persons included in the sale was fifty-three thousand.

About the same time Caesar was informed by Publius Crassus, whom he had sent with one legion against the Veneti and the other tribes on the Atlantic seaboard,[1] that all these had been subjected to Roman rule. These various operations had brought about a state of peace throughout Gaul, and the natives were so much impressed by the accounts of the campaigns which reached them, that the tribes living beyond the Rhine sent envoys to Caesar promising to give hostages and obey his commands. Being in a hurry to get away to northern Italy and Illyria, he told them to come again at the beginning of the following summer, and after quartering the legions for the winter, some in the territories of the Carnutes, Andes, and Turoni, the rest among tribes living near the scene of that year's fighting, he set out for Italy. On the receipt of his dispatches at Rome a public thanksgiving of fifteen days was decreed to celebrate his achievements – a greater honour than had previously been granted to anyone.

§ 5 UNSUCCESSFUL CAMPAIGN IN THE ALPS (57 B.C.)

WHEN Caesar was starting for Italy, he sent Servius Galba with the 12th legion and a detachment of cavalry to the territories of the Nantuates, Veragri, and Seduni, which extend from the frontier of the Allobroges, the Lake of Geneva, and the Rhone, to the high Alps. His object was to

1. The Venelli, Osismi, Coriosolites, Essuvii, Aulerci, and Redones.

open up the route over the Alps, by which traders travelled only at great risk and on payment of heavy tolls. Galba was authorized to quarter his legion in the district for the winter, if he thought it necessary. After he had won several victories and taken a number of enemy fortresses, and all the tribes had sent envoys and given hostages, he made peace. He then decided to quarter two cohorts among the Nantuates, and to winter with the remainder in a village of the Veragri called Octodurus, situated in a rather narrow valley and completely surrounded by very high mountains. The village was divided by a river into two parts, one of which he let the natives keep, while the other, which he made them evacuate, was assigned to his cohorts and fortified with a rampart and trench.

Several days had been spent in this encampment, and Galba had ordered grain to be brought in, when suddenly he was informed by his patrols that during the night all the Gauls had quitted the part of the village allotted to them, and that the surrounding heights were occupied by an immense multitude of the Seduni and Veragri. Various reasons had led the Gauls to form the sudden resolution of renewing hostilities and overpowering the Romans. In the first place, they despised the numerical weakness of the legion, which was under strength owing to the detachment of the two cohorts and a number of individuals who had been sent out in search of supplies. Secondly, they had the advantage of position, being able to run down and hurl their javelins into the valley beneath, and thought they would carry all before them at their very first charge. They also resented having their children torn from them and kept as hostages, and were convinced that the Romans were not merely seeking to open up communications, but intended to occupy the Alpine heights permanently and to annex the district to the neighbouring Province.

The work of entrenching the camp was not yet quite

completed, nor had a sufficient stock of grain and other supplies been laid in, because after the enemy's submission and surrender of hostages Galba did not think there was any reason to fear an outbreak of hostilities. On receiving the news, therefore, he at once called a council of war and invited opinions. The danger was as serious as it was sudden and unexpected: nearly all the heights were seen to be already swarming with armed men, and neither relief nor supplies could be brought up, because the roads were cut. Several members of the council were inclined to think the case hopeless, and advised that they should abandon the baggage, force their way out, and try to reach a place of safety by retracing their steps. But the majority decided to reserve this plan as a last resort, and in the meantime to defend the camp and await developments.

After a short interval, which barely gave time for posting the troops and carrying out the measures decided on, the enemy ran down from all sides at a given signal and began to hurl stones and spears at the rampart. At first, while our soldiers were still fresh, they resisted bravely, every missile they threw from their commanding position finding its mark, and ran to the relief of any part of the camp that was stripped of defenders and seen to be in danger. But what told against them was that the enemy, when exhausted by prolonged fighting, could retire from the battle and be relieved by fresh troops, which our men could not do on account of their small numbers; not only had tired men to stay in the fighting line, but even the wounded had to remain at their posts without any chance of respite.

After more than six hours' continuous fighting the Romans were at the end of their strength and had scarcely any weapons left to throw, while the enemy was pressing them harder than ever and took advantage of their exhausted state to break through the palisade and fill up the trenches. The situation was as bad as it could be; and Baculus – the chief centurion who was disabled by several wounds in the battle with the Nervii [1] – came running to Galba with Gaius Volusenus Quadratus, a military tribune and a man of sound judgment and great courage, and told him that their only hope of escape was to try their last resource – a sortie through the enemy's lines. Accordingly Galba summoned the centurions and immediately sent them to explain the new plan to the troops. They were to cease offensive action for a time, merely using their shields to intercept the enemy's missiles. When they had had time to recover from their exertions, the signal would be given to break out of the camp; then they would have to rely on their courage to save their lives. These orders were duly carried out. Suddenly they charged out from all the gates, without giving the enemy a chance of realizing what was happening or of preparing to meet their onset. It was a complete reversal of fortune: the Gauls who had counted on capturing the camp were surrounded and cut off. Of the forces that had taken part in the attack – known to number over thirty thousand – more than a third were killed; the rest fled in terror and were not allowed to halt even on the mountain heights. Having thus routed and disarmed the entire host, the Romans retired within the shelter of their fortifications, and after this success Galba did not want to take any more risks. The action which circumstances had compelled him to take was something that had never been contemplated when he was sent there to winter, and there was an alarming scarcity of corn and other supplies. Next day, therefore, he burnt all the buildings in the village and started to hasten back to the Province. No enemy barred his way or delayed his march, and he conducted the legion safely through the territory of the Nantuates into that of the Allobroges, where he spent the winter.

1. See above, page 86.

CHAPTER III

THE FIRST REBELLION (56 B.C.)

§ I THE FIGHT ON THE ATLANTIC COAST (56 B.C.)

WITH the completion of these operations Caesar had every reason to think that Gaul was pacified: the Belgae were overpowered, the Germans driven out, and the Seduni defeated in the Alps. He had therefore set out in the winter for Illyria, desiring to extend his acquaintance with the countries under his command by visiting the tribes of that district, when war suddenly broke out again in Gaul. The occasion of the outbreak was the action of young Publius Crassus, who with the 7th legion occupied the winter camp nearest the Atlantic, in the territory of the Andes. As food was scarce in that region, he sent a number of auxiliary officers and military tribunes to the neighbouring peoples to seek a supply of corn and other provisions. Among others, Titus Terrasidius was sent to the Essuvii, Marcus Trebius Gallus to the Coriosolites, Quintus Velanius and Titus Sillius to the Veneti.

The Veneti are much the most powerful tribe on this coast. They have the largest fleet of ships, in which they traffic with Britain; they excel the other tribes in knowledge and experience of navigation; and as the coast lies exposed to the violence of the open sea and has but few harbours, which the Veneti control, they compel nearly all who sail those waters to pay toll. They were the first to take action against the Romans by detaining Sillius and Velanius and any others they could catch, hoping by this to recover the hostages they had given to Crassus. Their neighbours followed their example with the impulsive haste that characterizes the actions of the Gauls, and detained Trebius and Terrasidius with the same motive. Hurriedly dispatching envoys to one another, their leaders pledged the various tribes to take no separate action but to share alike whatever fortune might befall them. They urged the other tribes to preserve their inherited liberties and not submit to the Roman yoke, and quickly gained the adherence of all the maritime peoples, who sent a joint embassy calling upon Crassus to return their hostages if he wanted to recover his officers.

When Caesar was informed of these events by Crassus he was far away from Gaul, and therefore instructed his subordinates to use the time that must elapse before his arrival in building warships on the river Loire, which flows into the Atlantic, enlisting crews in the Province, and procuring seamen and captains. These orders were promptly attended to, and Caesar rejoined his troops as soon as the campaigning season started. On learning of his arrival and the Roman preparations, the Veneti and the other tribes, realizing the gravity of the crime they had committed in detaining and imprisoning envoys – an office that all nations had always held sacred and inviolable –, began to make ready for war on a scale commensurate with the seriousness of their peril, paying particular attention to the provision of equipment for their ships. Their hopes of success were increased by the confidence they placed in the natural strength of their country. They knew that the roads were intersected by tidal inlets, and that sailing would be difficult for us on account of our ignorance of the waterways and the scarcity of harbours; and they felt sure that our armies would be prevented by shortage of grain from staying there very long. And even if all their expectations were disappointed, they had a strong fleet, while we had no ships available and were unacquainted with the shoals, harbours, and islands of the coast on which we should have to fight; and sailing in a wide ocean was clearly a very different matter from sailing in a land-locked sea like the Mediterranean. Having resolved to fight, they fortified their strongholds, stocked them with corn from the fields, and assembled as many ships as possible on the coast of Venetia, where it was generally thought that Caesar would open hostilities. They secured the alliance of various tribes in the neighbourhood[1] and of the Morini and Menapii, and summoned reinforcements from Britain, which faces that part of Gaul.

In spite of the difficulties Caesar had several strong reasons for undertaking this campaign: the unlawful detention of Roman Knights, the revolt and renewal of hostilities by enemies who had submitted and given hostages, the large number of tribes leagued against him, and above all the danger that if these were left unpunished others might think themselves entitled to follow their example. Knowing, too, that nearly all the Gauls were fond of political change and quickly and easily provoked to war, and that all men naturally love freedom and hate servitude, he thought it advisable to divide his forces and distribute them over a wider area before more tribes could join the coalition. Accordingly he sent Labienus with some cavalry into the country of the Treveri, near the Rhine. His orders were to make contact with the Remi and the other Belgic tribes and to see that they remained loyal; and if the Germans, whom some of the Gauls were said to have summoned to their assistance, should attempt to force a passage across the river in boats, to stop them. Publius Crassus was instructed to march to Aquitania with twelve legionary cohorts and a strong force of cavalry, in order to prevent the dispatch of reinforcements to the Celtic Gauls and the formation of an alliance between such powerful peoples. Sabinus was sent with three legions against the Venelli, Coriosolites, and Lexovii, to keep that section of the rebels isolated. The young Decimus Brutus was placed in command of the fleet, including the Gallic ships that Caesar had ordered the Pictones, Santoni, and other tribes in the conquered areas to

1. The Osismi, Lexovii, Namnetes, Ambiliati, and Diablintes.

provide. Brutus' orders were to sail as soon as possible for Venetia. Caesar himself marched there with the land forces.

Most of the Veneti's strongholds were so situated on the ends of spits or headlands that it was impossible to approach them by land when the tide rushed in from the open sea, which happens regularly every twelve hours; and they were also difficult to reach by sea, because at low tide the ships would run aground on the shoals. For these reasons the strongholds were hard to attack. Sometimes the Romans made them untenable by building huge dykes, which both kept the sea away and enabled the besiegers to get on a level with the top of the walls; but as soon as the defenders saw that their position was hopeless, they would bring up numbers of ships, of which they had an unlimited supply, transfer all their property to them, and retire to neighbouring strongholds equally well situated for defence. They found it easy to pursue these tactics during most of the summer, because our ships were weather-bound and sailing was very hazardous in that vast, open sea, where the tides were high and harbours almost non-existent.

The Gauls' own ships were built and rigged in a different manner from ours. They were made with much flatter bottoms, to help them to ride shallow water caused by shoals or ebb-tides. Exceptionally high bows and sterns fitted them for use in heavy seas and violent gales, and the hulls were made entirely of oak, to enable them to stand any amount of shocks and rough usage. The cross-timbers, which consisted of beams a foot wide, were fastened with iron bolts as thick as a man's thumb. The anchors were secured with iron chains instead of ropes. They used sails made of raw hides or thin leather, either because they had no flax and were ignorant of its use, or more probably because they thought that ordinary sails would not stand the violent storms and squalls of the Atlantic and were not suitable for such heavy vessels. In meeting them the only advantage our

ships possessed was that they were faster and could be pro-
pelled by oars; in other respects the enemy's were much better adapted for sailing such treacherous and stormy waters.
We could not injure them by ramming because they were
so solidly built, and their height made it difficult to reach
them with missiles or board them with grappling-irons.
Moreover, when it began to blow hard and they were running before the wind, they weathered the storm more easily;
they could bring to in shallow water with greater safety,
and when left aground by the tide had nothing to fear from
reefs or pointed rocks – whereas to our ships all these risks
were formidable.

After taking several strongholds Caesar saw that all his
labour was being wasted: capturing their strongholds did
not prevent the enemy from escaping, and he was not in a
position to cripple them. He decided, therefore, that he must
wait for his fleet to be assembled and brought up. Directly
it hove in sight, some two hundred and twenty enemy
ships, perfectly equipped and ready for immediate action,
sailed out of harbour and took up stations facing it. Neither
its commander Brutus nor the military tribunes and centurions in charge of the individual ships could decide what
to do or what tactics to adopt. They knew that no injury
could be inflicted on the enemy by ramming, and when they
tried erecting turrets they found that they were still over-
topped by the foreigners' lofty sterns and were too low to
make their missiles carry properly, while the enemy's fell
with great force. One device, however, that our men had
prepared proved very useful – pointed hooks fixed into the
ends of long poles, not unlike the grappling-hooks used in
sieges. With these the halyards were grasped and pulled
taut, and then snapped by rowing hard away. This of course
brought the yards down, and since the Gallic ships depended wholly on their sails and rigging, when stripped of
these they were at once immobilized. After that it was a

soldier's battle, in which the Romans easily proved superior, especially as it was fought under the eyes of Caesar and the whole army, so that any act of special bravery was bound to be noticed; all the cliffs and hills that commanded a near view of the sea were occupied by the troops. When the yards of an enemy ship were torn down in the manner described, two or three of ours would get alongside and the soldiers would make vigorous efforts to board it. When the natives saw what was happening, and after the loss of several ships could still find no answer to these tactics, they tried to escape by flight. They had already put their ships before the wind when suddenly such a dead calm fell that they could not stir. Nothing could have been more fortunate for us. It enabled us to complete the victory by pursuing and capturing the vessels one after another, and only a very few managed to make land when night came on after a battle that lasted from about ten o'clock in the morning until sunset.

This victory ended the war with the Veneti and all the other maritime tribes. For besides assembling all their men of military age, and indeed all the older men of any standing or reputation for good judgement, they had also concentrated every one of their ships; and now that all these were lost, the survivors had no refuge left and no means of defending their strongholds. So they surrendered themselves and all their possessions to Caesar. He resolved to make an example of them in order to teach the natives to be more careful in future about respecting the rights of ambassadors: he had all their councillors executed and the rest of the population sold as slaves.

While these events were taking place in the country of the Veneti, Sabinus arrived with the troops assigned to him in the territory of the Venelli. Their leader was Viridovix, the commander-in-chief of all the rebel tribes, from which he had raised a large army. Within a few days of Sabinus' arrival the Aulerci Eburovices and the Lexovii massacred their councillors because they would not sanction the policy of going to war, shut their gates, and joined Viridovix; and there had also assembled from all over Gaul a host of desperadoes and bandits, to whom the prospect of fighting and plunder was more attractive than farming and regular work. Sabinus refused to leave his camp, which was ideally situated, while Viridovix, who had encamped opposite him at a distance of two miles, led his troops out daily and offered battle. The Gauls began to despise Sabinus, and even some of his own troops made insulting remarks; in the end he so convinced the enemy of his timidity that they ventured close up to the rampart of the camp. The real reason for his inaction was his opinion that a subordinate ought not to engage such a large enemy force, especially in the absence of his commander-in-chief, without having either an advantage of position or some particularly favourable opportunity.

When everyone was fully persuaded that Sabinus was afraid, he selected from his auxiliaries a quick-witted Gaul, a man suitable for the purpose he had in mind, and induced him by liberal rewards and promises to go over to the enemy, explaining to him what he wanted done. The man came to them posing as a deserter, described the Romans' terror, and said that Caesar himself was hard pressed by the Veneti, and that Sabinus planned to steal out of his camp the very next night and go to his aid. On hearing this they all cried that the chance of scoring a success should not be missed: they must march on the camp. In coming to this decision they were influenced by several things – the recent hesitation of Sabinus, the assurances of the deserter, their lack of supplies, for which they had not made proper provision, the hope of a victorious outcome of the Veneti's campaign, and the general tendency of mankind to wishful thinking. They were so possessed by these ideas that they would not let Viridovix and the other leaders leave the assembly until they consented to their arming and making a dash for the camp. When they got their way they were exultant, thinking that victory was within their grasp, and advanced to the camp with faggots and brushwood for filling up the trenches.

The camp stood at the top of a gentle slope about a mile long. The Gauls ran up it, so that the Romans might have no time to recover from their surprise and arm themselves, and they were out of breath when they arrived. After addressing his men Sabinus gave the signal which they were eagerly awaiting: while the enemy were hampered by the loads they carried, he ordered a sudden sortie from two of the gates. Thanks to the favourable position of the camp, the enemy's unskilfulness and exhausted condition, our soldiers' courage, and the experience they had gained in previous battles, the very first charge made the Gauls turn tail. But they were in no condition to escape, and it was easy for our fresh troops to overtake them and to kill a large number; the remainder were rounded up by the cavalry, with the exception of a few who got clean away. Sabinus heard of the naval battle at the same time as his own victory was reported to Caesar, and all the rebel states immediately submitted to him. For while the Gauls are quick and impetuous in taking up arms, they have not the strength of character to stand up against reverses.

§ 2 VICTORIOUS CAMPAIGN IN AQUITANIA (56 B.C.)

ABOUT the same time Publius Crassus reached Aquitania. Knowing that he had to fight in a country where some years previously [78 B.C.] the general Lucius Valerius Praeconinus had been defeated and killed, and the proconsul

Lucius Manlius compelled to retreat with the loss of all his heavy equipment, he realized that he must proceed with extreme caution. Accordingly he arranged for a supply of provisions, raised auxiliaries and cavalry, and called up individually many men of proved courage from Toulouse, Carcassonne, and Narbonne, towns in the Province not far distant from Aquitania. He then marched into the territory of the Sotiates, who on hearing of his approach assembled a large force and sent on ahead their cavalry, in which they were very strong. They attacked our column on the march, first of all with the cavalry; when this was repulsed and pursued by ours, they suddenly unmasked their infantry, which was ambushed in a valley. The infantry renewed the action by falling upon our troops while they were in disorder, and a prolonged and fierce struggle ensued; for the Sotiates were emboldened by their past victories and thought that the fate of all Aquitania depended on their bravery, while our men wanted to show what they could do without their commander-in-chief and the other legions, and under a youthful leader. At length, exhausted by wounds, the enemy turned and fled. After killing a large number Crassus advanced on their town and marched straight to the assault. As the garrison offered a stout resistance, he moved up mantlets and towers. Against these they first attempted a sortie, and then tunnelled in the direction of the siege-terrace and the mantlets; the Aquitani excel in this work, as there are copper-mines and quarries in many parts of their country. But when they found that the vigilance of our troops prevented their effecting anything by this means, they sent envoys to Crassus asking him to accept their surrender. He consented, and at his command they handed over their arms.

While everyone's attention was occupied by these events, the king of the tribe, Adiatuanus, attempted a sortie from another part of the town with six hundred followers who were bound to him by a vow of loyalty. The Sotiates

call such persons *soldurii*. The friend to whom they attach
themselves undertakes to share with them all the good things
of life, on the understanding that, if he meets with a violent
end, they shall either share his fate or make away with
themselves; and within the memory of man none has yet
been known to refuse to die when the friend to whom he
had sworn allegiance was killed. Shouts arose from the
nearest part of the fortifications, and the soldiers ran to
arms. After a hard fight Adiatuanus was driven back into
the town; but in spite of what had happened he prevailed
on Crassus to let him surrender on the same terms as the
rest.

After receiving the arms and hostages Crassus started for
the country of the Vocates and Tarusates. The natives
were now thoroughly alarmed, hearing that a town well
protected both by its situation and by fortifications had
fallen within a few days of our army's arrival. They
therefore sent envoys to their neighbours on every
side, made promises of mutual loyalty, exchanged hostages,
and mobilized their troops. They even sent to the nearest
tribes of northern Spain, and obtained from them reinforcements and generals, whose arrival enabled them to take the
field with large forces under commanders of great prestige
– men who had served throughout the Spanish war under
Quintus Sertorius and were reputed military experts. Following Roman practice they occupied carefully chosen
positions, entrenched a camp, and took measures to intercept our convoys of supplies. Crassus' own forces were so
small that they could not very well be divided, whereas the
enemy could scour the countryside and block the roads, and
at the same time leave an adequate guard in camp. Finding
that this made it difficult to bring up grain and other supplies, and that the enemy's numbers were increasing daily,
he thought he had better lose no time in bringing them to
a decisive action. On referring the question to a council of

war he found that all the others were of the same opinion, and therefore determined to fight the next day.

At daybreak he brought out all his forces and deployed them in two lines, with the auxiliaries in the centre, and waited to see what plan of action the enemy would adopt. Although the Gauls, with their great numerical superiority and illustrious military record, had every confidence in the result of an engagement, they thought an even safer way would be to gain a bloodless victory by obstructing the roads and cutting off the army's supplies; and if a shortage of food compelled the Romans to retreat, their idea was to attack them on the march, when they would be hampered by the presence of the transport and dispirited by having to fight with their packs on their backs. Their leaders approved these plans, and when the Romans deployed their troops the Gauls remained in camp. Crassus took note of this; and as the enemy's reluctance to fight gave the impression that they were afraid, and increased the fighting spirit of his own men, who were all heard saying that the camp should be attacked without delay, he delivered the customary address and complied with their unanimous desire by advancing to the assault. Some filled up the trenches, others drove the defenders from the rampart and entrenchments with a rain of missiles, while the auxiliaries, in whose fighting quality Crassus had little confidence, supplied the rest with stones and weapons and brought up sods for making a bank of earth, and so made a convincing show of fighting. The enemy, too, put up a determined and brave resistance, and the javelins that they hurled down from their elevated position did good execution. Meanwhile some cavalrymen who had ridden round the camp reported to Crassus that the back of it was not so carefully fortified, and offered easy access. Crassus asked his cavalry officers to encourage their men by promises of liberal rewards to co-operate in a manoeuvre that he desired to execute. Under their guidance the cohorts that had been left to guard the Roman camp, which were still fresh, were quickly led out and conducted by a long detour, so that they could not be seen from the enemy's camp, to the section of the defences referred to, while everyone's attention was concentrated on the fighting. Demolishing the fortifications, they gained a footing in the camp before the enemy could clearly see them or make out what was happening. On hearing the shouting at the back of the camp our soldiers felt their strength renewed, as generally happens when men have hopes of winning, and redoubled their efforts. The enemy, finding themselves completely surrounded, were overwhelmed with despair, and had no other thought than to throw themselves over the rampart and flee for their lives. Our cavalry pursued them over perfectly flat plains, and of the fifty thousand men known to have assembled from the Aquitani and Cantabri, barely a quarter escaped. It was late at night when the cavalry returned to camp.

On receiving news of this battle most of the Aquitanian tribes[1] surrendered to Crassus and sent hostages of their own accord. Only a few of the most distant tribes, relying on the approach of winter to save them, neglected to follow their example.

§ 3 INDECISIVE CAMPAIGN AGAINST THE MORINI (56 B.C.)

ABOUT the same time, although the summer was nearly over, Caesar marched against the Morini and Menapii. While peace was established throughout the rest of Gaul, they remained in arms and had never sent envoys to sue for

1. Including the Tarbelli, Bigerriones, Ptianii, Vocates, Tarusates, Elusates, Gates, Ausci, Garunni, Sibulates, and Cocosates.

peace; and he thought that a short campaign would suffice to conquer them. He found himself opposed by tactics quite different from those of the other Gauls. As they knew that the strongest tribes which had met Caesar in the field had been completely defeated, they took refuge with all their belongings in a region protected by a continuous belt of forests and marshes. On reaching the edge of the forests Caesar began to construct a camp. No enemy had yet been seen, and the men were working in scattered groups, when suddenly the Gauls rushed out to the attack from all parts of the forest. Our men hastily seized their arms and chased them back into it, but after inflicting heavy losses upon them pursued too far over rather difficult ground and themselves suffered a few casualties. Some days were then spent in felling trees in the forest. To prevent his soldiers' being surprised by flank attacks while they were unarmed, Caesar placed all the felled timber parallel with the enemy's line of retreat, piling it so as to form a rampart on both sides. In an incredibly short time a path was cleared for a considerable distance. But when the enemy's cattle and the tail end of their transport were already in our hands, while they were making for the denser parts of the forest, such bad weather came on that the work had to be stopped, and as the rain continued it became impossible to keep the soldiers under canvas any longer. Accordingly, after ravaging all the countryside and burning the villages and farms, Caesar withdrew his troops and quartered them in the countries of the Aulerci, the Lexovii, and the other tribes that had been recently in arms.

CHAPTER IV

REPULSE OF A GERMAN INVASION OF GAUL (55 B. C.)

§ I MASSACRE OF THE USIPETES AND TENCTHERI (55 B.C.)

IN the following winter, in which the consulship of Pompey and Crassus began, the German tribes of the Usipetes and Tenctheri crossed the Rhine in large numbers not far from its mouth. They were forced to migrate because for several years they had been subjected to harassing attacks by the Suebi and prevented from tilling their land.

The Suebi are far the largest and most warlike of the German nations. It is said that they have a hundred cantons, each of which provides annually a thousand armed men for service in foreign wars. Those who are left at home have to support the men in the army as well as themselves, and the next year take their turn of service, while the others stay at home. Thus both agriculture, and military instruction and training, continue without interruption. No land, however, is the property of private individuals, and no one is allowed to cultivate the same plot for more than one year. They do not eat much cereal food, but live chiefly on milk and meat, and spend much time in hunting. Their diet, daily exercise, and the freedom from restraint that they enjoy – for from childhood they do not know what compulsion or discipline is, and do nothing against their inclination – combine to make them strong and as tall as giants. They inure themselves, in spite of the very cold climate in which they live, to wear no clothing but skins – and these so scanty that a large part of the body is uncovered – and to bathe in the rivers. Traders are admitted into their country more because they want to sell their booty than because they stand in any need of imports. Even horses, which the Gauls are inordinately fond of and purchase at big prices, are not imported by the Germans. They are content with their home-bred horses, which, although undersized and ugly, are rendered capable of very hard work by daily exercise. In cavalry battles they often dismount and fight on foot, training the horses to stand perfectly still, so that they can quickly get back to them in case of need. In their eyes it is the height of effeminacy and shame to use a saddle, and they do not hesitate to engage the largest force of cavalry riding saddled horses, however small their own numbers may be. They absolutely forbid the importation of wine, because they think that it makes men soft and incapable of enduring hard toil. They regard it as the proudest glory of a nation to keep the largest possible area round its frontiers uninhabited, because it shows that many other peoples are inferior to it in military might. It is said, for example, that on one side of the Suebic territory the country is uninhabited for a distance of more than five hundred and fifty miles. On the other side their nearest neighbours are the Ubii, who were once – by German standards – a considerable and prosperous nation. They are somewhat more civilized than the rest of the Germans; for living on the Rhine close to the frontier of Gaul, where traders visit them regularly, they have adopted Gallic customs. The Suebi, after repeated attempts to oust them from their home by force of arms, found them too numerous and strong to be dispossessed, but compelled them to pay tribute and greatly reduced their pride and power.

The Usipetes and Tenctheri were in the same case. For many years they withstood the Suebi's pressure, but eventually were driven from their country, and after wandering for three years in many parts of Germany reached the Rhine in the territory of the Menapii, who had lands, farmhouses, and villages on both banks of the river. Terrified by the arrival of such a multitude, the Menapii abandoned their dwellings on the German bank and placed outposts on the Gallic bank to prevent the emigrants from crossing. The Germans tried every expedient; but not having boats with which to force a passage, and being unable to cross by stealth because of the Menapian pickets, they pretended to return to their home country, and marched in that direction for three days. Then they turned back again, and re-covering the whole distance in a single night, their cavalry made a surprise attack on the unsuspecting Menapii, who, on being informed by their patrols of their enemy's departure, had fearlessly recrossed the Rhine and returned to their villages. The Germans slaughtered them, seized their boats, crossed the river before the Menapii on the Gallic side knew what was afoot, took possession of all their farmhouses, and lived on their provisions for the rest of the winter.

These events were reported to Caesar. The unstable character of the Gauls made him anxious – for they are easily induced to form new plans and generally welcome political change – and he thought it better to place no reliance on them. It is a custom of theirs to stop travellers, even against their will, and to question them about what they have heard by chance or by inquiry on this or that subject; and in the towns a crowd will gather round traders and demand to know what country they have come from and what they have learnt there. Such hearsay reports often induce them to make momentous decisions, which they are bound to repent immediately afterwards, since they credulously swallow unconfirmed rumours, and most of their informants invent such answers as they think will please them. Caesar was aware of this habit, and not wishing to find himself faced with a dangerous war, set out to rejoin his army earlier in the season than usual. On his arrival he found that his suspicions were correct: a number of tribes had sent embassies to the Usipetes and Tenctheri, inviting them to go farther afield than the Rhineland and promising to supply all their requirements. This attractive prospect had induced the Germans to range over a wider area, and they had now reached the country of the Eburones and Condrusi, dependants of the Treveri. Caesar thought it advisable to say nothing to the Gauls about the information he had received. Summoning their leaders, therefore, he addressed them in soothing and reassuring terms, and told them to furnish cavalry for the campaign which he proposed to conduct against the Germans.

After arranging for his corn supply and making his selection of the cavalry, he marched towards the district where the invading Germans were said to be. He was a few days' march away, when envoys arrived from them with the following message: 'We Germans are not taking aggressive action against the Roman People, but we are ready to fight if provoked. For it is our traditional custom to resist any attacker and to ask no quarter. We wish to say, however, that we have come into Gaul not from choice but because we were expelled from our homes. If you Romans desire our friendship, we can be of service to you. Either grant us land to live in or let us keep what we have won by the sword. The only people whose superiority we acknowledge are the Suebi, with whom the gods themselves cannot compete. There is no one else on earth that we cannot conquer.'

Caesar made what he considered a suitable reply to this oration, but the upshot of his remarks was that there could be no friendship between him and the Germans if they remained in Gaul. He said that it was not reasonable for men who had been unable to protect their own territory to expect to occupy other people's. There was no land available in Gaul which he could justly assign to them, particularly in view of their large numbers; but they might settle if they chose in the country of the Ubii, whose ambassadors were then with him, complaining of the wrongs done them by the Suebi and asking for assistance. He would order the Ubii to admit them. The German envoys said that they would refer Caesar's reply to their countrymen for consideration, and return in three days; in the meantime they asked him not to move his camp any nearer. But Caesar refused this request also. He knew that a large detachment of their cavalry had been sent across the Meuse[1] some days before to the country of the Ambivariti, in search of corn and plunder; and he thought that they must be expecting these back, and that this was their reason for trying to gain time.

When Caesar was not more than twelve miles from the Germans their envoys returned according to agreement, and meeting him on the march earnestly begged him to advance no farther. On Caesar's refusing to comply, they asked him to send word to the cavalry which had gone in advance of the column, forbidding them to engage in battle, and also requested leave to send an embassy to the Ubii. They said that if the Ubian chiefs and council would swear to keep faith with them, they would avail themselves of the offer that Caesar had made, and asked for three days to complete the necessary negotiations. Caesar believed that all these suggestions had the same object as their previous manoeuvre – to obtain a further three days' delay to give time for the return of the German cavalry from their foray. However, he said that he would restrict his advance that day to four miles – the distance that was necessary to get

1. The Meuse rises in the Vosges mountains, in the country of the Lingones, and flows into the Rhine some seventy-five miles from the sea. The Rhine rises in the country of the Lepontii in the Alps, and flows swiftly for a long distance through the lands of the Helvetii, Sequani, Triboci, Nemetes, Mediomatrici, and Treveri. As it nears the sea it divides into several channels, forming a number of very large islands (many of them inhabited by wild barbarian tribes, some of whom are supposed to live on fish and birds' eggs), and discharges itself by several mouths into the North Sea.

water. On the next day, if as many of them as possible would assemble at his halting-place, he would give their requests a formal hearing. In the meantime he sent orders to the officers who had gone on in front with the whole cavalry force that they were not to attack the enemy, and, if attacked themselves, were to remain on the defensive until he approached with the main army. But when the enemy caught sight of our cavalry, five thousand strong, although they themselves had not more than eight hundred horse – those who had crossed the Meuse to get corn having not yet returned – they immediately charged. Our men, who thought themselves safe from attack because the enemy's envoys had only just left Caesar and had asked for a truce for that day, were at first thrown into disorder. When they rallied, the German horsemen, following their usual practice, jumped down, unhorsed a number of our men by stabbing their horses in the belly, put the rest to flight, and kept them on the run in such a panic that they did not stop until they came in sight of the marching column of infantry. In this engagement seventy-four of our cavalrymen were killed, including Piso, a gallant Aquitanian of very good family, whose grandfather had been king of his tribe and had been granted the title of 'Friend' by the Roman Senate. He went to the assistance of his brother, who was cut off by some of the Germans, and succeeded in rescuing him; but his own horse was wounded and threw him. As long as he could, he resisted with the utmost bravery, but eventually was surrounded and fell covered with wounds. When his brother, who by this time had got well away from the fight, saw what had happened, he galloped straight up to the enemy and let them kill him too.

After this treacherous and unprovoked attack by an enemy who had asked for peace, Caesar dismissed all further thought of giving audience to their envoys or accepting any overtures. At the same time he thought it would be sheer madness to wait till they were reinforced by the return of their cavalry. The Gauls were so scatter-brained that even this single German success had no doubt made a great impression upon them, and they must not be given time to concert plans. He told his generals and quaestor of his decision, and, not wanting to lose a single day in bringing the enemy to battle, marched forward. The next morning he had a great stroke of luck. Still pursuing their policy of treachery and deceit, a large deputation of Germans, comprising all their leaders and elder men of note, came to visit him in his camp. Their ostensible object was to apologize for attacking the day before in contravention of the agreement that they themselves asked for; but they also hoped to hoodwink Caesar into granting an extension of the truce. Caesar was delighted that they had put themselves in his power, and ordered them to be detained, while he himself marched his whole army out of camp, with the cavalry bringing up the rear because he thought it had been demoralized by its recent defeat.

With the soldiers formed in three parallel columns, ready for wheeling into line of battle, he made a rapid march of eight miles and reached the enemy's camp before they realized his intention. The speed of his advance and the absence of their leaders combined to throw them into a sudden panic; they had no time to think what to do or to arm themselves, and were too distracted to decide whether it was best to march out against Caesar, to stay and defend the camp, or to flee for their lives. The Roman soldiers could tell that they were afraid by their cries and hurried movements, and, spurred on by the recollection of the previous day's treachery, burst into the camp. Those of the Germans who were quick enough in seizing their weapons resisted for a time, fighting under cover of their wagons and baggage. But there was also a great crowd of women and children in the camp – for they had brought all their families with them when they left home and crossed the Rhine. These began to flee in all directions, and were hunted down by the cavalry which Caesar sent out for the purpose. Hearing cries behind them and seeing that their people were being massacred, the Germans threw down their arms, deserted their standards, and rushed out of the camp. When they reached the confluence of the Moselle and the Rhine, they realized that they could flee no farther. A large number were killed, and the rest plunged into the water and perished, overcome by the force of the current in their terror-stricken and exhausted state. The Romans returned to camp without a single fatal casualty, and with only a very few wounded, although a grim struggle had been anticipated against an enemy four hundred and thirty thousand strong. Caesar gave the prisoners detained in camp leave to depart, but as they were afraid of being killed or tortured by the Gauls whose lands they had ravaged, they said they wished to remain with him. They were allowed to retain their liberty.

§ 2 THE FIRST CROSSING OF THE RHINE (55 B.C.)

On the conclusion of the German war Caesar thought it advisable for several reasons to cross the Rhine. His strongest motive was to make the Germans less inclined to come over into Gaul by giving them reason to be alarmed on their own account, and showing them that Roman armies could and would advance across the river. Another consideration was that the cavalry division which the Usipetes and Tenctheri sent across the Meuse in quest of plunder and corn,[1] having taken no part in the battle, had retired over the Rhine after the rout of their fellow-countrymen,

1. See above, page 112.

entered the territory of the Sugambri, and joined forces with them; and when Caesar sent an embassy to the Sugambri to demand the surrender of men who had made war on him and on Gaul, they answered that the Rhine was the limit of Roman sovereignty: if Caesar held that the Germans had no right to cross into Gaul against his wishes, how could he claim any dominion or authority beyond the Rhine? A third reason was that the Ubii – the only people in Germany who had sent envoys to Caesar, entered into alliance with him, and given hostages – were earnestly entreating him to come and defend them from the oppression of the Suebi, or, if the public business with which he was occupied made that impossible, merely to bring his army across the river, which would suffice to deliver them from immediate danger and assure their security for the future. They said that by the defeat of Ariovistus, and by this latest victory, the Roman army had gained such renown and reputation, even among the most distant peoples of Germany, that the mere knowledge of their alliance with Rome would be enough to give them protection. They undertook to provide a large fleet of boats for the transportation of the army.

For these reasons Caesar had determined to cross the Rhine, but a crossing by means of boats seemed to him both too risky, and beneath his dignity as a Roman commander. Therefore, although the construction of a bridge presented very great difficulties on account of the breadth, depth, and swiftness of the stream, he decided that he must either attempt it or give up the idea of crossing. The method he adopted in building the bridge was as follows. He took a pair of piles a foot and a half thick, slightly pointed at the lower ends and of a length adapted to the varying depth of the river, and fastened them together two feet apart. These he lowered into the river with appropriate tackle, placed them in position at right angles to the bank, and drove them home with pile-drivers, not vertically, as piles are generally fixed, but obliquely, inclined in the direction of the current. Opposite these, forty feet lower down the river, another pair of piles was planted, similarly fixed together, and inclined in the opposite direction to the current. The two pairs were then joined by a beam two feet wide, whose ends fitted exactly into the spaces between the two piles forming each pair. The upper pair was kept at the right distance from the lower pair by means of iron braces, one of which was used to fasten each pile to the end of the beam. The pairs of piles being thus held apart, and each pair individually strengthened by a diagonal tie between the two piles, the whole structure was so rigid, that, in accordance with the laws of physics, the greater the force of the current, the more tightly were the piles held in position. A series of these piles and transverse beams was carried right across the stream and connected by lengths of timber running in the direction of the bridge; on these were laid poles and bundles of sticks. In spite of the strength of the structure, additional piles were fixed obliquely to each pair of the original piles along the whole length of the down-stream side of the bridge, holding them up like a buttress and opposing the force of the current. Others were fixed also a little above the bridge, so that if the natives tried to demolish it by floating down tree trunks or beams, these buffers would break the force of the impact and preserve the bridge from injury.

Ten days after the collection of the timber had begun, the work was completed and the army crossed over. Leaving a strong guard at each end of the bridge, Caesar marched into the territory of the Sugambri. Meanwhile a number of tribes sent envoys with requests for peace and friendship, which Caesar graciously granted, bidding them bring hostages. But the Sugambri, who as soon as the construction of the bridge was begun had been advised by the fugitive

Usipetes and Tenctheri to prepare for flight, had left their country with all their belongings and hidden themselves in forests and uninhabited districts. Caesar remained for a few days in their territory, burning all the villages and farm buildings and cutting down the crops, and then returned to the Ubii, to whom he promised help if they were molested by the Suebi. They informed him that the Suebi, on learning from their scouts that a bridge was under construction, had convened a council – their usual procedure in such cases – and sent out word in all directions that the people should abandon their towns and hide their wives and children and property in the forests. All men capable of bearing arms had been ordered to assemble in one place, almost exactly in the middle of their territory. There they were awaiting the Romans, and had determined to fight a decisive battle on the spot. On receiving this news Caesar recrossed the bridge into Gaul and destroyed it behind him. He had achieved all the objects for which he had come – to overawe the Germans, punish the Sugambri, and relieve the Ubii from the harassing pressure of the Suebi –, and after spending a total of eighteen days across the Rhine he considered that he had done all that honour or interest required.

CHAPTER V

THE INVASIONS OF BRITAIN
(55–54 B.C.)

§ I THE FIRST INVASION (55 B.C.)

IT was now near the end of the summer, and winter sets in early in those parts, because all that coast of Gaul faces north. Nevertheless, Caesar made active preparations for an expedition to Britain, because he knew that in almost all the Gallic campaigns the Gauls had received reinforcements from the Britons. Even if there was not time for a campaign that season, he thought it would be of great advantage to him merely to visit the island, to see what its inhabitants were like, and to make himself acquainted with the lie of the land, the harbours, and the landing-places. Of all this the Gauls knew next to nothing; for in the ordinary way traders are the only people who visit Britain, and even they know only that part of the coast which faces Gaul. And so, although he interviewed traders from all parts, he could not ascertain anything about the size of the island, the character and strength of the tribes which inhabited it, their manner of fighting and customs, or the harbours capable of accommodating a large fleet of big ships. In order to get this information before risking an expedition, he sent a warship in command of Volusenus, whom he considered a suitable man for the job. His orders were to make a general reconnaissance and return as soon as he could. Meanwhile Caesar marched the whole army into the country of the Morini, from which there was the shortest crossing to Britain, and ordered ships to assemble there from all the neighbouring districts, as well as the fleet that had been built the previous summer for the Venetian war. His design had become known in the meantime, and when the news was brought by traders to the Britons, envoys were sent by a number of tribes, offering to give hostages and submit to Rome. Caesar gave them audience, made them generous promises, and urged them to abide by their resolve. He then sent them home, accompanied by Commius, whom he had made king of the Atrebates after the conquest of that tribe – a man of whose courage, judgement, and loyalty he had a high opinion, and who was greatly respected in Britain. He instructed Commius to visit as many tribes as possible, to urge them to entrust themselves to the protection of Rome, and to announce his impending arrival. Volusenus reconnoitred the coast as far as he could without disembarking and putting himself into the power of the natives, which he dared not do, and returned four days later with his report.

While Caesar was waiting in the country of the Morini for his fleet to be assembled, a large section of the tribe sent envoys to apologize for their previous hostile action, pleading that they were foreigners and ignorant of Roman ways, and promising to obey his commands in future. Caesar thought this very fortunate. He did not want to leave an enemy in his rear; yet it would have been too late in the season to start another campaign, and the expedition to Britain was much more important than the conquest of these petty tribes. He therefore demanded a large number of hostages, and on their arrival accepted the submission of the Morini.

In due course about eighty transports, which Caesar considered sufficient to convey two legions, were obtained and assembled, and also a number of warships, which were assigned to the quaestor, the generals, and the officers of the auxiliary troops. Besides these there were eighteen transports at a point eight miles along the coast, which were prevented by a contrary wind from making the same harbour as the rest; these were allotted to the cavalry. The remainder of the army was entrusted to Sabinus and Cotta, with orders to march against the Menapii and those clans of the Morini which had not sent envoys. Another general, Publius Sulpicius Rufus, was ordered to hold the harbour and was given a force considered adequate for the purpose.

After the completion of these arrangements, Caesar took advantage of favourable weather and set sail about midnight, ordering the cavalry to proceed to the farther port, embark there, and follow him. As these conducted the operation too slowly, their transports were carried back to land by the tide. Caesar himself reached Britain with the first ships about nine o'clock in the morning, and saw the enemy's forces posted on all the hills. The lie of the land at this point was such that javelins could be hurled from the cliffs right on to the narrow beach enclosed between them and the sea. Caesar thought this a quite unsuitable place for landing, and therefore rode at anchor until three o'clock, in order to give the rest of the ships time to come up. Meanwhile he assembled the generals and military tribunes, and, telling them what he had learned from Volusenus, explained his plans. He warned them that the exigencies of warfare, and particularly of naval operations, in which things move rapidly and the situation is constantly changing, required the instant execution of every order. On dismissing the officers he found that both wind and tidal current were in his favour. He therefore gave the signal for weighing anchor, and after proceeding about seven miles ran his ships aground on an evenly sloping beach, free from obstacles.

The natives, on realizing his intention, had sent forward their cavalry and a number of the chariots which they are accustomed to use in warfare; the rest of their troops followed close behind and were ready to oppose the landing. The Romans were faced with very grave difficulties. The size of the ships made it impossible to run them aground except in fairly deep water; and the soldiers, unfamiliar with the ground, with their hands full, and weighed down by the heavy burden of their arms, had at the same time to jump down from the ships, get a footing in the waves, and fight the enemy, who, standing on dry land or advancing only a short way into the water, fought with all their limbs unencumbered and on perfectly familiar ground, boldly hurling javelins and galloping their horses, which were trained to this kind of work. These perils frightened our soldiers, who were quite unaccustomed to battles of this kind, with the result that they did not show the same alacrity and enthusiasm as they usually did in battles on dry land.

Seeing this, Caesar ordered the warships – which were swifter and easier to handle than the transports, and likely to impress the natives more by their unfamiliar appearance – to be removed a short distance from the others, and then to be rowed hard and run ashore on the enemy's right flank, from which position slings, bows, and artillery could be used by men on deck to drive them back. This manoeuvre was highly successful. Scared by the strange shape of the warships, the motion of the oars, and the unfamiliar machines, the natives halted and then retreated a little. But as the Romans still hesitated, chiefly on account of the depth of the water, the man who carried the eagle of the 10th legion, after praying to the gods that his action might bring good luck to the legion, cried in a loud voice: 'Jump down, comrades, unless you want to surrender our eagle to the enemy; I, at any rate, mean to do my duty to my country and my general.' With these words he leapt out of the ship and advanced towards the enemy with the eagle in his hands. At this the soldiers, exhorting each other not to submit to such a disgrace, jumped with one accord from the ship, and the men from the next ships, when they saw them, followed them and advanced against the enemy. Both sides fought hard. But as the Romans could not keep their ranks or get a firm foothold or follow their proper standards, and men from different ships fell in under the first standard they came across, great confusion resulted. The enemy knew all the shallows, and when they saw from the beach small parties of soldiers disembarking one by one, they galloped up and attacked them at a disadvantage, surrounding them with superior numbers, while others would throw javelins at the right flank of a whole group. Caesar therefore ordered the warships' boats and the scouting-vessels to be loaded with troops, so that he could send help to any point where he saw the men in difficulties. As soon as the soldiers had got a footing on the beach and had waited for all their comrades to join them, they charged the enemy and put them to flight, but could not pursue very far, because the cavalry had not been able to hold their course and make the island. This was the one thing that prevented Caesar from achieving his usual success.

The defeated enemy, as soon as they rallied after their flight, hastened to send an embassy to ask for peace, promising to give hostages and carry out Caesar's commands. With these envoys came Commius the Atrebatian, whom Caesar had sent on ahead to Britain.[1] When he had disembarked and was delivering Caesar's message to them in the character of an ambassador, the natives had arrested and bound him. Now, after the battle, they sent him back, and in asking for peace threw the blame for this proceeding on the common people, begging Caesar to pardon an error due to ignorance. Caesar reproached them for making war on him without provocation, after sending envoys to the continent of their own accord to sue for peace, but said that he would pardon their ignorance, and demanded hostages. Some of these they handed over at once; the rest they said would have to be fetched from a distance, and should be

1. See above, page 120.

delivered in a few days' time. Meanwhile they bade their men return to the fields, and the chiefs began to come from all parts to solicit Caesar's favour for themselves and their tribes. Peace was thus concluded.

On the fourth day after Caesar's arrival in Britain the eighteen transports on which the cavalry had been embarked[1] sailed from the northern port before a gentle breeze. When they were approaching Britain and were visible from the camp, such a violent storm suddenly arose that none of them could hold its course. Some were driven back to their starting-point; others, at great peril, were swept westwards to the south of the island. In spite of the danger they cast anchor, but as they were being filled with water by the waves, they were forced to stand out to sea into the darkness of night and return to the continent.

It happened to be full moon that night, at which time the Atlantic tides are particularly high – a fact unknown to the Romans. The result was that the warships used in the crossing, which had been beached, were waterlogged, and the transports, which were riding at anchor, were knocked about by the storm, without the soldiers' having any chance of interfering to save them. A number of ships were shattered, and the rest, having lost their cables, anchors, and the remainder of their tackle, were unusable, which naturally threw the whole army into great consternation. For they had no other vessels in which they could return, nor any materials for repairing the fleet; and, since it had been generally understood that they were to return to Gaul for the winter, they had not provided themselves with a stock of grain for wintering in Britain.

On learning of this accident, the British chiefs who had assembled after the battle to execute Caesar's commands, put their heads together. Knowing that Caesar had no cavalry, ships, or corn, and inferring the weakness of his forces

1. See above, pages 120–121.

from the small size of the camp, which was all the smaller because he had come without most of the heavy luggage, they decided that their best course was to renew hostilities, to hinder the legions from obtaining corn and other supplies, and to prolong the war into the winter. If this army was conquered or prevented from returning, they felt confident that no one would come across to invade Britain again. Accordingly, after renewing their promises of mutual loyalty, they slipped away one by one from the camp and secretly called up once more the men who had returned to the fields. Although Caesar had not yet heard of their intention, the disaster which had overtaken his fleet and the fact that they were no longer sending hostages led him to anticipate what was coming. He therefore prepared for anything that might happen. Corn was brought in daily from the fields, timber and bronze from the most severely damaged vessels were used to repair the others, and naval equipment was ordered to be sent from the continent. By the energetic efforts of the soldiers all but twelve ships were saved and rendered tolerably seaworthy.

While this work was proceeding, one legion, as usual, had been sent out to get corn – in this case the 7th. Nothing had yet occurred to raise any suspicion of a fresh attack, and some of the Britons were still working in the fields, while others were actually going backwards and forwards to the camp. Suddenly the guards on duty at the gates reported to Caesar that an unusually large cloud of dust was visible in the direction in which the legion had gone. Caesar guessed the truth – that the natives had hatched a new scheme – and ordered the cohorts on guard duty to set out with him in the direction indicated, two of the others to relieve them, and the rest to arm and follow immediately. After going some way he saw that the legion was hard pressed by enemy forces and holding its ground with difficulty, packed closely and pelted with missiles from all directions. For as the corn had already been cut everywhere except in one place, the enemy had expected that our men would go there and had hidden by night in the woods. Then, when the soldiers were scattered and busy cutting corn, with their arms laid down, they had made a sudden attack, killing a few and throwing the rest into confusion before they could form up, and also surrounding them with cavalry and chariots.[1]

The men of the 7th legion were unnerved by these tactics, and it was just at the right moment that Caesar came to their rescue. At his approach the enemy halted and the soldiers recovered from their alarm. But as he considered the situation too hazardous for attacking or engaging in battle, he stayed where he was, and after a short interval led the legions back to camp. While these events kept all our men occupied, the natives who were still in the fields made off.

There followed several days of continuous bad weather, which kept our men in camp and also prevented the enemy from attacking. During this time the natives sent messengers in all directions, who informed their people of the small numbers of our troops, and pointed out what a good opportunity they had of getting booty and liberating themselves for ever, if they could drive the Romans from their camp. By this means they quickly collected a large force of infantry and cavalry, which advanced towards the camp.

1. In chariot fighting the Britons begin by driving all over the field hurling javelins, and generally the terror inspired by the horses and the noise of the wheels are sufficient to throw their opponents' ranks into disorder. Then, after making their way between the squadrons of their own cavalry, they jump down from the chariots and engage on foot. In the meantime their charioteers retire a short distance from the battle and place the chariots in such a position that their masters, if hard pressed by numbers, have an easy means of retreat to their own lines. Thus they combine the mobility of cavalry with the staying-power of infantry; and by daily training and practice they attain such proficiency that even on a steep incline they are able to control the horses at full gallop, and to check and turn them in a moment. They can run along the chariot pole, stand on the yoke, and get back into the chariot as quick as lightning.

Caesar foresaw that what had happened before would happen again: even if the enemy were beaten, their speed would enable them to escape out of harm's way. Nevertheless, having luckily obtained about thirty horsemen whom Commius had brought across, he drew up the legions in battle-formation in front of the camp. Before the engagement had lasted long the enemy were overpowered and took to flight. The Romans pursued as far as their strength enabled them to run, killing a number of the fugitives, and then set fire to all the buildings over a wide area and returned to camp.

The same day envoys came to Caesar to sue for peace. He demanded twice as many hostages as before, and ordered these to be brought to the continent, as the equinox was close at hand and he thought it better not to expose his damaged ships to the dangers of a voyage in wintry weather. Taking advantage of a favourable wind he set sail shortly after midnight, and the whole fleet reached the continent safely.

Two transports, however, failed to make the same harbours as the rest and were carried a little farther south. When about three hundred soldiers had disembarked from these two ships and were pushing towards the camp, the Morini, whom Caesar had compelled to make peace before setting out for Britain, thought they saw a chance of obtaining booty and surrounded them, at first with only a small force, bidding them lay down their arms if they did not want to be killed. The Romans formed a ring and defended themselves, but in a short time the shouts of their assailants brought some six thousand natives to the spot. On hearing what was happening Caesar sent all the cavalry to their aid. Meanwhile the soldiers held the enemy's attack, fighting with the utmost bravery for over four hours, and killed a number of them at the cost of only a few men wounded. As soon as the cavalry came in sight the Morini threw down their arms and fled, suffering very heavy casualties.

The next day Caesar sent Labienus against the rebellious Morini with the legions that had returned from Britain. As the marshes in which they had taken refuge the previous year were now dry, the natives had nowhere to retreat to, and nearly all fell into Labienus' hands. Sabinus and Cotta, however, who had led their legions into the territory of the Menapii, had to content themselves with destroying all the crops, cutting the corn, and burning the buildings, because all the inhabitants had concealed themselves in very dense forests. They then returned to Caesar, who arranged for all the legions to winter in Belgic territory. There he received the promised hostages from only two British tribes; the remainder neglected to send them.

On the conclusion of these campaigns and the receipt of Caesar's dispatches, the Senate decreed a public thanksgiving of twenty days.

§ 2 THE SECOND INVASION (54 B.C.)

IN the consulship of Lucius Domitius and Appius Claudius, when Caesar was leaving his winter quarters as usual to go to Italy, he ordered the generals placed in command of the legions to have as many ships as possible built during the winter, and the old ones repaired. He specified the dimensions and shape of the new ships. To enable them to be loaded quickly and beached easily he had them made slightly lower than those which we generally use in the Mediterranean – especially as he had found that owing to the frequent ebb and flow of the tides the waves in the Channel were comparatively small. To enable them, however, to carry a heavy cargo, including a large number of animals, they were made somewhat wider than the ships we use in other waters. They were all to be of a type suitable for both sailing and rowing – an arrangement which was greatly facilitated by their low freeboard. The materials required for fitting them out were to be imported from Spain.

On the completion of the assizes in northern Italy Caesar set out for Illyria, because he heard that the Pirustae were making damaging raids over the frontier of that province. On his arrival he ordered the tribes to levy troops and appointed a place for their assembly. When they heard this news the Pirustae sent representatives to say that their government was not responsible for what had happened, and that they were ready to make full reparation for the damage. He accepted their explanation and ordered them to deliver hostages by a certain day, failing which he would make war on them. The hostages were punctually delivered in obedience to his orders, and he then appointed arbitrators to assess the damage sustained by the various communities and fix the reparation.

After disposing of this matter and holding his assizes in Illyria, Caesar returned to Italy and from there went to rejoin the army. On his arrival he made a tour of all the winter camps, and found that, in spite of a serious shortage of materials, the men had worked with such enthusiasm that they had built and equipped six hundred vessels of the type described, and twenty-eight warships. These would all be ready for launching in a few days. Caesar congratulated the soldiers and the officers who had superintended the work, gave them further instructions, and ordered all the ships to be assembled at Portus Itius, the starting-point for the easiest crossing to Britain – a run of about thirty miles. Leaving a sufficient number of troops to carry out this task, he took four legions, unencumbered by a baggage train, and eight hundred cavalry, and set out for the country of the Treveri, because they would not attend the annual councils of chieftains or submit to his authority, and were alleged to be making overtures to the Germans across the Rhine.

The Treveri have much the most powerful cavalry in Gaul, and also a considerable force of infantry. Their territory, it will be remembered, borders on the Rhine. Two rivals were struggling there for supremacy – Indutiomarus and Cingetorix. As soon as news came of Caesar's approach with the legions, Cingetorix presented himself, assured Caesar that he and all his followers would remain loyal to the Roman alliance, and explained the position of affairs among the Treveri. Indutiomarus, however, began to prepare for war, raising forces of cavalry and infantry, and hiding those too young or too old to fight in the huge forest of the Ardennes, which stretches from the Rhine through the middle of the Treveran country to the frontier of the Remi. Some of the other leaders of the tribe, who were friends of Cingetorix, were alarmed by the approach of the Roman army, and since it was not in their power, they said, to help their country, they came to Caesar and petitioned for their personal safety. Indutiomarus was now afraid of being completely isolated, and sent to Caesar to say that the reason why he had not wanted to leave his followers and wait upon him was that by remaining he had a better chance of keeping the tribe loyal. If all the men of rank left the country, the common people in their ignorance might fall into error. In this way he had kept control of his countrymen, and with Caesar's permission would come to his camp and place himself and the tribe under his protection. Caesar understood his motive in saying this, and knew what deterred him from prosecuting his original design. Nevertheless, to avoid having to waste the summer there after making all preparations for a campaign in Britain, he told Indutiomarus to present himself with two hundred hostages, including his son and all his relations, who were mentioned by name. When these were brought, Caesar reassured him and urged him to remain loyal. But he also summoned the other leaders of the tribe and called on them individually to support Cingetorix. He thought that Cingetorix deserved this help, and that it was important to do all he could to increase the power of a man who had proved himself so devoted a friend. This abatement of his influence provoked Indutiomarus to bitter resentment, which greatly inflamed the hostility that he already felt towards the Romans.

After settling this matter Caesar proceeded with the legions to Portus Itius. He found that sixty ships which were built in the country of the Meldi had been driven out of their course by a storm and had returned to their starting-point. All the rest were completely equipped and ready for sea. Four thousand cavalry from all parts of Gaul assembled at the port, and the leaders of all the tribes. Caesar had decided to leave behind only a few of these who had proved their loyalty, and to take all the rest with him as hostages, because he was afraid of a rising in Gaul during his absence.

Among the Gallic leaders was Dumnorix the Aeduan.[1] He was one whom Caesar was particularly determined to keep with him, because he knew him to be a political intriguer, ambitious, bold, and very influential with the Gauls. Moreover, Dumnorix had said in the Aeduan council that Caesar had offered to make him king of the tribe – a statement that was much resented by the Aedui, although they dared not protest to Caesar or ask him to give up the idea. Caesar learnt these facts from some Gauls in whose house he had lodged. Dumnorix began by begging hard to be allowed to stay at home, saying that he was unused to sailing and afraid of the sea, and also that he was debarred from leaving the country by religious duties. When he found that there was no hope of altering Caesar's deter-

1. See above, pages 40, 43, 48–51.

mination not to leave him behind, he began to intrigue with the other chiefs, taking them aside one by one, urging them to remain on the continent, and working on their fears. He said that Caesar had an ulterior object in thus stripping Gaul of all her leading citizens: he shrank from killing them under the eyes of their countrymen, but his purpose was to put them all to death when he had got them across to Britain. He pledged his word to work with the others for what they saw to be the interest of Gaul, and called on them to take an oath to the same effect.

When these facts were reported to Caesar by a number of informants, he decided that in view of the high regard which he had for the Aedui he ought to do everything possible to restrain Dumnorix and deter him from pursuing his design; and as the man's obsession was clearly increasing, it must be put beyond his power to do any injury to Caesar or to Roman interests. For between three and four weeks the army was delayed at the port because the north-west wind – the prevailing wind at all seasons on that coast – made it impossible to sail; and in the meantime Caesar took measures to make Dumnorix behave himself, but at the same time to obtain information about any plans he might form. At length, taking advantage of favourable weather, Caesar ordered the infantry and cavalry to embark. But while everyone's attention was occupied with this operation, Dumnorix took some Aeduan horsemen out of the camp without Caesar's knowledge and started for home. On hearing of this Caesar postponed the sailing. Letting everything else wait, he sent a strong detachment of cavalry to pursue him and bring him back; if he showed fight and refused to obey, their orders were to kill him, since Caesar thought that a man who flouted his authority under his very eyes could not be expected to behave rationally behind his back. On being summoned to return Dumnorix began to resist, sword in hand, begging his followers to protect him, and shouting over and over again that he was a free man and a citizen of a free state. In obedience to Caesar's orders he was surrounded and killed, and all the Aeduan horsemen returned to the Roman camp.

Caesar then set sail, leaving Labienus on the continent with three legions and two thousand cavalry, with orders to guard the ports, provide for a supply of corn, watch events in Gaul, and act as circumstances from time to time might require. Caesar took with him five legions and the remaining two thousand cavalry, and putting out about sunset was at first carried on his way by a light south-westerly breeze. But about midnight the wind dropped, with the result that he was driven far out of his course by the tidal current and at daybreak saw Britain left behind on the port side. When the set of the current changed he went with it, and rowed hard to make the part of the island where he had found the best landing-places the year before. The soldiers worked splendidly, and by continuous rowing enabled the heavily laden transports to keep up with the warships. When the whole fleet reached Britain about midday, no enemy was to be seen. Caesar discovered afterwards from prisoners that, although large numbers had assembled at the spot, they were frightened by the sight of so many ships [1] and had quitted the shore to conceal themselves on higher ground.

Caesar disembarked his army and chose a suitable spot for a camp. On learning from prisoners where the enemy were posted, he left ten cohorts and three hundred cavalry on the coast to guard the fleet and marched against the Britons shortly after midnight, feeling little anxiety about the ships because he was leaving them anchored on an open shore of soft sand. The fleet and its guard were put under

1. Including those retained from the previous year and the privately-owned vessels built by individuals for their own use, over eight hundred were visible simultaneously.

the command of Quintus Atrius. A night march of about twelve miles brought Caesar in sight of the enemy, who advanced to a river with their cavalry and chariots, and tried to bar his way by attacking from a position on higher ground. Repulsed by his cavalry they hid in the woods, where they occupied a well-fortified post of great natural strength, previously prepared, no doubt, for some war among themselves, since all the entrances were blocked by felled trees laid close together. Scattered parties made skirmishing attacks out of the woods, trying to prevent the Romans from penetrating the defences. But the soldiers of the 7th legion, locking their shields together over their heads and piling up earth against the fortifications, captured the place and drove them out of the woods at the cost of only a few men wounded. Caesar forbad them to pursue far, however, because he did not know the ground, and because he wanted to devote the few remaining hours of the day to the fortification of his camp.

The next morning he sent out a force of infantry and cavalry in three columns to pursue the fleeing enemy. They had advanced some way and were in sight of the nearest fugitives, when dispatch-riders brought news from Atrius of a great storm in the night, by which nearly all the ships had been damaged or cast ashore; the anchors and cables had not held, and the sailors and their captains could not cope with such a violent gale, so that many vessels were disabled by running foul of one another. Caesar at once ordered the legions and cavalry to be halted and recalled. He himself went back to the beach, where with his own eyes he saw pretty much what the messengers and the dispatch described. About forty ships were a total loss; the rest looked as if they could be repaired at the cost of much trouble. Accordingly he called out all the skilled workmen from the legions, sent to the continent for more, and wrote to tell Labienus to build as many ships as possible with the troops under his command. Further, although it was a task involving enormous labour, he decided that it would be best to have all the ships beached and enclosed together with the camp by one fortification. This work, although it was continued day and night, took some ten days to complete. As soon as the ships were hauled up and the camp strongly fortified, Caesar left the same units as before to guard them, and returned to the place from which he had come. On arriving there he found that larger British forces had now been assembled from all sides by Cassivellaunus, to whom the chief command and direction of the campaign had been entrusted by common consent. Cassivellaunus' territory is separated from the maritime tribes by a river called the Thames, and lies about seventy-five miles from the sea.[1] Previously he had been continually at war with the

---

1. The interior of Britain is inhabited by people who claim, on the strength of an oral tradition, to be aboriginal; the coast, by Belgic immigrants who came to plunder and make war – nearly all of them retaining the names of the tribes from which they originated – and later settled down to till the soil. The population is exceedingly large, the ground thickly studded with homesteads, closely resembling those of the Gauls, and the cattle very numerous. For money they use either bronze, or gold coins, or iron ingots of fixed weights. Tin is found inland, and small quantities of iron near the coast; the copper that they use is imported. There is timber of every kind, as in Gaul, except beech and fir. Hares, fowl, and geese they think it unlawful to eat, but rear them for pleasure and amusement. The climate is more temperate than in Gaul, the cold being less severe.

The island is triangular, with one side facing Gaul. One corner of this side, on the coast of Kent, is the landing-place for nearly all the ships from Gaul, and points east; the lower corner points south. The length of this side is about 475 miles. Another side faces west, towards Spain. In this direction is Ireland, which is supposed to be half the size of Britain, and lies at the same distance from it as Gaul. Midway across is the Isle of Man, and it is believed that there are also a number of smaller islands, in which according to some writers there is a month of perpetual darkness at the winter solstice. Our inquiries on this subject were always fruitless, but we found by accurate measurements with a water-clock that the nights are shorter than on the continent. This side of Britain, according to the natives' estimate, is 665 miles long. The third side faces north; no land lies opposite it, but its eastern corner points roughly in the direction of Germany. Its length is

other tribes, but the arrival of our army frightened them into appointing him their supreme commander.

The British cavalry and charioteers had a fierce encounter with our cavalry on the march, but our men had the best of it everywhere and drove them into the woods and hills, killing a good many, but also incurring some casualties themselves by a too eager pursuit. The enemy waited for a time, and then, while our soldiers were off their guard and busy fortifying the camp, suddenly dashed out of the woods, swooped upon the outpost on duty in front of the camp, and started a violent battle. Caesar sent two cohorts – the first of their respective legions – to the rescue, and these took up a position close together; but the men were unnerved by the unfamiliar tactics, and the enemy very daringly broke through between them and got away unhurt. That day Quintus Laberius Durus, a military tribune, was killed. The attack was eventually repulsed by throwing in some more cohorts. Throughout this peculiar combat, which was fought in front of the camp in full view of everyone, it was seen that our troops were too heavily weighted by their armour to deal with such an enemy: they could not pursue them when they retreated, and dared not get separated from their standards. The cavalry, too, found it very dangerous work fighting the charioteers ; for the Britons would generally give ground on purpose, and after drawing them some

---

estimated at 760 miles. Thus the whole island is 1,900 miles in circumference.

By far the most civilized inhabitants are those living in Kent (a purely maritime district), whose way of life differs little from that of the Gauls. Most of the tribes in the interior do not grow corn but live on milk and meat, and wear skins. All the Britons dye their bodies with woad, which produces a blue colour, and this gives them a more terrifying appearance in battle. They wear their hair long, and shave the whole of their bodies except the head and the upper lip. Wives are shared between groups of ten or twelve men, especially between brothers and between fathers and sons; but the offspring of these unions are counted as the children of the the man with whom a particular woman cohabited first.

distance from the legions would jump down from their chariots and fight on foot, with the odds in their favour. In engaging their cavalry our men were not much better off: their tactics were such that the danger was exactly the same for both pursuers and pursued. A further difficulty was that they never fought in close order, but in very open formation, and had reserves posted here and there; in this way the various groups covered one another's retreat, and fresh troops replaced those who were tired.

Next day the enemy took up a position on the hills at a distance from the camp. They showed themselves now only in small parties and harassed our cavalry with less vigour than the day before. But at midday, when Caesar had sent three legions and all the cavalry on a foraging expedition under his general Gaius Trebonius, they suddenly swooped down on them from all sides, pressing their attack right up to the standards of the legions. The legionaries drove them off by a strong counter-attack, and continued to pursue until the cavalry, emboldened by the support of the legions which they saw close behind them, made a charge that sent the natives flying headlong. A great many were killed, and the rest were given no chance of rallying or making a stand or jumping from their chariots. This rout caused the immediate dispersal of the forces that had assembled from various tribes to Cassivellaunus' aid, and the Britons never again joined battle with their whole strength.

On learning the enemy's plan of campaign, Caesar led his army to the Thames in order to enter Cassivellaunus' territory. The river is fordable at one point only, and even there with difficulty. At this place he found large enemy forces drawn up on the opposite bank. The bank was also fenced by sharp stakes fixed along the edge, and he was told by prisoners and deserters that similar ones were concealed in the river-bed. He sent the cavalry across first, and then at once ordered the infantry to follow. But the infantry went with such speed and impetuosity, although they had only their heads above water, that they attacked at the same moment as the cavalry. The enemy was overpowered and fled from the river-bank.

Cassivellaunus had now given up all hope of fighting a pitched battle. Disbanding the greater part of his troops, he retained only some four thousand charioteers, with whom he watched our line of march. He would retire a short way from the route and hide in dense thickets, driving the inhabitants and cattle from the open country into the woods wherever he knew we intended to pass. If ever our cavalry incautiously ventured too far away in plundering and devastating the country, he would send all his charioteers out of the woods by well-known lanes and pathways and deliver very formidable attacks, hoping by this means to make them afraid to go far afield. Caesar was thus compelled to keep the cavalry in touch with the column of infantry, and to let the enemy off with such devastation and burning as could be done under the protection of the legionaries – tired as they often were with marching.

During this march envoys arrived from the Trinovantes, about the strongest tribe in south-eastern Britain. Mandubracius, a young prince of this tribe, had gone over to the continent to put himself under Caesar's protection, having fled for his life when his father the king of the Trinovantes was killed by Cassivellaunus. The envoys promised to surrender and obey Caesar's commands, and asked him to protect Mandubracius from Cassivellaunus and send him home to rule his people as king. Caesar demanded forty hostages and grain for his troops, and then allowed Mandubracius to go. The Trinovantes promptly sent the required number of hostages and the grain.

When they saw that the Trinovantes had been protected against Cassivellaunus and spared any injury on the part of the Roman troops, several other tribes[1] sent embassies and surrendered. From them Caesar learnt that he was not far from Cassivellaunus' stronghold,[2] which was protected by forests and marshes, and had been filled with a large number of men and cattle. He marched to the place with his legions, and found that it was of great natural strength and excellently fortified. Nevertheless, he proceeded to assault it on two sides. After a short time the enemy proved unable to resist the violent attack of the legions, and rushed out of the fortress on another side. A quantity of cattle was found there, and many of the fugitives were captured or killed.

While these operations were proceeding in his territory, Cassivellaunus sent envoys to Kent ordering the four kings of that region, Cingetorix, Carvilius, Taximagulus, and Segovax, to collect all their troops and make a surprise attack on the naval camp. When these forces appeared the Romans made a sortie, in which without suffering any loss they killed a great many of them and captured Lugotorix, a leader of noble birth. On receiving news of this action, Cassivellaunus, alarmed by so many reverses, by the devastation of his country, and above all by the defection of his allies, sent envoys to Caesar to obtain terms of surrender, employing Commius as an intermediary. Caesar had decided to return to the continent for the winter, for fear any sudden rising should break out in Gaul. The summer, too, was nearly over, and he knew that the Britons could easily hold out for the short time that remained. Accordingly he granted Cassivellaunus' request for terms, demanding hostages, fixing an annual tribute to be paid by the Britons to the Roman government, and strictly forbidding Cassivellaunus to molest Mandubracius or the Trinovantes.

1. The Cenimagni, Segontiaci, Ancalites, Bibroci, and Cassi.
2. The Britons apply the term 'strongholds' to densely wooded spots fortified with a rampart and trench, to which they retire in order to escape the attacks of invaders.

As soon as the hostages were delivered he led the army back to the coast, where he found the ships repaired. He had them launched, and as he had a large number of prisoners, and some of the ships had been destroyed by the storm, decided to make the return voyage in two trips. It happened that of all these large fleets, which made so many voyages in this and the preceding year, not a single ship with troops on board was lost, while very few of the vessels coming over empty from the continent[1] reached their destination, nearly all the rest being forced back to land. After waiting a long time for them in vain, Caesar was afraid of being prevented from sailing by the approaching season of the equinox, and so had to pack the men more tightly than usual on the ships he had. The sea becoming very calm, he set sail late in the evening and brought all the fleet safely to land at dawn.

1. i.e. those which had returned to Gaul after landing troops in Britain, and sixty that Labienus had built after the start of the expedition.

CHAPTER VI

THE SECOND REBELLION
(54–53 B.C.)

§ I DESTRUCTION OF SABINUS' ARMY BY THE EBURONES
(54 B.C.)

THE harvest that year in Gaul was a poor one on account of drought. Accordingly, after beaching the ships and holding a council of Gallic leaders at Samarobriva, Caesar was compelled to change his previous method of quartering the army for the winter, and distribute the legions among a larger number of tribes. One was sent to the Morini under the general Gaius Fabius, another to the Nervii under Quintus Tullius Cicero, a third to the Essuvii under Lucius Roscius. A fourth, under Labienus, was ordered to winter in the country of the Remi near the frontier of the Treveri, and three more were placed in Belgic territory under the quaestor Marcus Crassus and the generals Lucius Munatius Plancus and Gaius Trebonius. One of the legions recently raised in the country north of the Po, and a further detachment of five cohorts, were sent under the command of Sabinus and Cotta to the Eburones, who live principally between the Meuse and the Rhine, and were at that time ruled by Ambiorix and Catuvolcus. This wide distribution Caesar thought would be the easiest way of meeting the shortage of corn. In fact, however, the quarters of all the legions except that under Roscius, which had been sent to a perfectly quiet and peaceful district, were within a hundred miles of one another. Caesar determined to stay in Gaul himself until he knew that all the troops had reached their destinations and fortified their camps.

In the land of the Carnutes was a man of noble birth

called Tasgetius, whose ancestors had been kings of the tribe. In recognition of his merit and devotion – for in all the campaigns his services had been exceptionally valuable – Caesar had placed him upon the throne of his ancestors. In the third year of his reign he was assassinated by enemies with the avowed approval of many members of the tribe. The crime was reported to Caesar, and, as the number of persons implicated was large, he feared lest they might instigate the tribe to revolt. Accordingly he at once transferred Plancus to the country of the Carnutes from his quarters among the Belgae, with orders to stay there for the rest of the winter, and to arrest and send to him those whom he found to be responsible for Tasgetius' death. Meanwhile Caesar heard from all the generals and quaestors in command of the legions that they had reached their quarters and completed the fortification of their camps.

About a fortnight later an open revolt was suddenly started by the Eburonians Ambiorix and Catuvolcus. They had waited on Sabinus and Cotta at the frontier of their kingdom and brought a supply of grain to the Roman camp, but were then induced by a message from Indutiomarus the Treveran to call their subjects to arms. Making a sudden attack on a party collecting wood, they came with a large force to assault the camp. The legionaries quickly armed and mounted the rampart, and some Spanish horsemen who were sent out by one of the gates were victorious in a cavalry engagement. The Eburones realized that they had no hope of success, and retired from the attack; then they shouted aloud, after the manner of their nation, for someone from our side to go out and parley with them, declaring that they had something to say which concerned us as well as themselves, and which they hoped might bring the conflict to an end.

Gaius Arpineius, a Roman Knight and a friend of Sabinus, was sent to confer with them, accompanied by a

Spaniard named Quintus Junius, who had already been employed by Caesar on many missions to Ambiorix. They were addressed by Ambiorix in the following terms: 'I admit,' he said, 'that I am greatly indebted to Caesar for the services which he has rendered me. It was he who relieved me of the tribute that I used to pay to my neighbours the Atuatuci, and restored to me my son and my brother's son, who, when sent to them as hostages, had been enslaved and kept in chains. In attacking your camp I acted against my better judgement and my own wishes. I was constrained by my subjects – for I am not an absolute ruler: the people have as much power over me as I have over them. And the reason why the tribe took up arms was because it could not oppose the movement in which all the Gauls suddenly leagued themselves together. The insignificance of my power clearly proves the truth of what I say: I am not so ignorant as to imagine that my army by itself is strong enough to defeat the Romans. The whole of Gaul is united in this attempt, and they have arranged to attack all the camps to-day simultaneously, so that the legions shall not be able to help one another. It would have been difficult for us to refuse help to our fellow-countrymen, especially as we knew that their object was the recovery of our national liberty. But having now discharged the duty which patriotism required of me, I remember what I owe to Caesar for his favours, and I urge and implore Sabinus, as my friend and host, to consider his own and his soldiers' safety. A large force of German mercenaries has crossed the Rhine and will be here in a couple of days. It is for you to decide whether you will withdraw your troops from the camp before the neighbouring tribes can find out what you are doing, and take them either to Cicero, who is less than fifty miles away, or to Labienus – a somewhat greater distance. I swear to grant them safe-conduct through my territory. In so doing I am acting in the interests of my people, who will be relieved from the burden of the camp in their midst, and at the same time repaying Caesar for his kindness.' After making this speech Ambiorix retired.

These remarks were reported by Arpineius and Junius to the generals, who heard them with surprise and alarm; and although the suggestion came from an enemy, they did not think it ought to be disregarded. The most disquieting thing was that it really did seem scarcely credible that an obscure and insignificant tribe like the Eburones could have dared of its own initiative to make war on Rome. Accordingly the matter was referred to a council of war, where it was hotly debated. Cotta and many of the military tribunes and first-grade centurions thought that they ought not to take any hasty step or leave the camp without Caesar's authority. 'We can resist any number of Gauls,' they said, 'and a large force of Germans into the bargain, in this fortified camp. We have proof of that; for the men put up a very brave resistance against the enemy's first attack, and indeed took the offensive and inflicted heavy loss upon them. We are not short of grain, and before we run short help will come from the nearest camps and from Caesar. In any case, what could be more irresponsible or unsoldierly than to follow the advice of an enemy in a matter of prime importance?' In reply to this Sabinus insisted that it would be too late to do anything when the Gauls had assembled in greater numbers, reinforced by the Germans, or when some disaster had occurred in the other camps that were within reach. 'We have only a short time to decide,' he said, 'and as for Caesar, I think he must have started for Italy. Otherwise, the Carnutes would not have resolved on the murder of Tasgetius, nor would the Eburones, if Caesar had been in Gaul, have held us in such contempt as to attack the camp. It is irrelevant to say that the suggestion comes from the enemy. It is the facts of the case that I am looking at. The Rhine is close by, and the Germans are bitterly resentful of

Ariovistus' death and of our victories in earlier campaigns. Gaul is blazing with indignation at all the humiliations she has suffered by being brought under Roman dominion, and at the eclipse of her former military prestige. And it is inconceivable that Ambiorix would have taken such action without being sure of his ground. My policy is safe either way. If nothing serious is afoot, we shall make our way to the nearest legion without any risk; if the Gauls are united and in league with the Germans, our only chance of escape is to act quickly. As to the plan recommended by Cotta and the others who differ from me, what would be the result of adopting it? It may or may not involve immediate danger; it certainly means a long blockade and the threat of starvation.'

After these divergent views had been put forward, Cotta and the centurions continued to oppose Sabinus vigorously. 'Have your own way, then, if you will,' cried Sabinus, raising his voice so that many of the soldiers could hear. 'I am not more afraid of death than the rest of you. The men will understand: if disaster follows, it is you, Cotta, that they will hold responsible. If you would give your consent, by the day after to-morrow they would have reached the nearest camp, and would have their comrades by their side to share the fortune of war with them, instead of remaining isolated like outcasts and exiles, to be massacred or to die of starvation.' The officers rose from their places, laid hold of the two generals, and implored them not to persist in a dispute which must gravely imperil the army. 'Whether we go or stay,' they said, 'there is no real difficulty, if only we all agree on one course of action; but if we go on quarrelling, there is no chance of escape.' The debate dragged on till midnight, but at last Cotta, greatly distressed, gave in. Sabinus' plan was adopted, and it was announced that they would march at dawn. The soldiers stayed up for the rest of the night, each man going through his kit to see what he could take with him, and how much of his winter equipment must be abandoned. They thought of every possible argument to persuade themselves that there was no danger in going, and considerable danger in remaining, and tired themselves so much with loss of sleep that the actual peril was increased. At daybreak they started out, apparently quite convinced that the enemy who had suggested the plan was the best of friends – for they went in a long, straggling column, encumbered with a very heavy load of baggage.

Hearing the sound of voices in the night, the Gauls knew that the soldiers were awake, and concluded that they were leaving the camp. They therefore placed two ambushes at a likely place some two miles away in the woods, where they were screened from observation, and there awaited the Roman column. When the greater part of it had descended into a large defile, they suddenly appeared at either end, harassed the rearguard, prevented the head of the column from climbing the hill which led out of the defile, and forced the soldiers to fight on very unfavourable ground. Sabinus, having failed to foresee what might happen, now got excited and ran to and fro arranging the cohorts; but even this he did nervously and in a way which showed that he was at his wits' end – as generally happens to those who are compelled to make decisions when a battle has actually begun. Cotta, however, who had foreseen the possibility of a surprise attack on the march, and for that reason had opposed the idea of leaving the camp, did everything possible to save the army – calling upon the men and encouraging them as their commander-in-chief might have done, and fighting in the ranks like any soldier. As the length of the column made it difficult for the generals to attend to everything personally and to see what was required in every part of the field, they passed word along to abandon the baggage and form a circle. Although this measure cannot be condemned in such circumstances, it had unfortunate results: it discouraged the soldiers and increased the enemy's ardour for the fight, because it clearly indicated an extremity of fear and desperation. It inevitably meant, too, that men were everywhere leaving their units and running to the baggage to look for their most cherished possessions and pull them out, amid a hubbub of shouting and cries.

The enemy, for their part, showed no lack of resource. Their leaders passed word along the whole line that no one was to leave his post; all the plunder that the Romans left would be theirs, and should be kept for them alone; so they must realize that everything depended on victory. The Gauls were equal to our troops in fighting quality, and superior in numbers. Yet our men, although their general had failed them and fortune deserted them, relied on their courage to save them, and every time a cohort charged, a large number of the enemy fell. Seeing this, Ambiorix ordered his men to throw their javelins without going too close, and to give ground before the Roman charges; being lightly armed and trained by daily practice to execute such manoeuvres, they would still be able to inflict heavy casualties. As soon as the Romans began to retire to their main body, they were to give chase. These instructions were carefully obeyed. Whenever a cohort made a charge out of the circle, the enemy retreated at full speed. A temporary gap was bound to be left in the circle, so that the unit which stood next was exposed to missiles on its right flank; and when the cohort began to return to its original place, it was surrounded by the Gauls who had fallen back and by the nearest of those who had remained in position. If the Romans tried simply holding their ground in the circle, there was no scope for any courageous effort, and they were huddled together too closely to avoid the javelins that the huge Gallic host rained upon them. Yet, notwithstanding all the disadvantages that they had to contend with, and in spite of heavy losses, they still held out, and throughout a fight that lasted for a considerable part of the day – from dawn till two o'clock – did nothing to be ashamed of. In this battle Titus Balventius, who the previous year had been chief centurion of his legion, a brave and highly-respected man, had both his thighs pierced by a javelin; another centurion of the same rank, Quintus Lucanius, was killed in a very courageous attempt to rescue his son, who had been surrounded; and Cotta himself, while engaged in cheering on each cohort and company, was wounded by a sling-stone which struck him full in the face.

Sabinus was so much alarmed by these events that on catching sight of Ambiorix, who was addressing his troops at some distance, he sent his interpreter Gnaeus Pompeius to ask for quarter for himself and his soldiers. In response to this appeal Ambiorix said that Sabinus might speak to him if he wanted. He hoped that his men could be induced to spare the Roman soldiers' lives; in any case Sabinus himself should come to no harm – that much he would personally guarantee. Sabinus proposed to the wounded Cotta that they should withdraw from the fight and together confer with Ambiorix, who he hoped could be induced to spare them and the troops. But Cotta refused to go to an enemy who had not laid down his arms, and would not budge from his resolve. Sabinus ordered the military tribunes who were with him at the moment, and the first-grade centurions, to follow him. On approaching Ambiorix he was told to lay down his arms. He obeyed, and commanded the others to do the same. While he was discussing terms with Ambiorix, who purposely prolonged the conversation, he was gradually surrounded, and then killed. At this the Gauls raised their customary shout of triumph, and with a loud yell charged and broke our ranks. Cotta fell fighting where he stood, and most of the soldiers with him. The survivors retreated into the camp from which they had come. Lucius

Petrosidius, the standard-bearer of the legion, seeing himself beset by a large crowd of Gauls, threw his eagle inside the rampart and died fighting heroically outside the camp. The rest had hard work to withstand the enemy's onslaught till nightfall; in the night, seeing that all hope was gone, every single man committed suicide. A few who had escaped from the battle made their way by scarcely distinguishable woodland tracks to Labienus' camp, and told him what had happened.

§ 2 ATTACK BY THE NERVII ON CICERO'S WINTER CAMP (54 B.C.)

ELATED by his victory, Ambiorix at once started with his cavalry for the country of the Atuatuci, which bordered on his kingdom, marching day and night without a halt. His infantry had orders to follow. Explaining to the Atuatuci what had occurred, he roused them to arms. The next day he reached the Nervii, and urged them not to lose the chance of freeing themselves for ever and avenging the wrongs they had suffered at the hands of the Romans. Two generals, he told them, were killed, and a large part of the Roman army annihilated; it would be easy to surprise and destroy Cicero's legion in its winter quarters. He promised to aid them in this enterprise, and easily persuaded them to undertake it. Accordingly the Nervii hastened to send messengers to the tribes under their rule,[1] and, raising as large a force as they could, swooped down on Cicero's camp before he had received news of Sabinus' death. Like him, Cicero could not help being taken by surprise: some soldiers who had gone into the woods to get firewood and timber for building fortifications were cut off by the

1. The Ceutrones, Grudii, Levaci, Pleumoxii, and Geidumni.

unexpected arrival of the enemy's cavalry. Then a large-scale attack on the legion was begun by the Eburones, Nervii, and Atuatuci, accompanied by their allies and satellites. The soldiers rushed to arms and mounted the rampart. A very hard day's fighting ensued, because the enemy staked all their hopes on swift action, and were confident that success in that engagement would assure them final victory.

Cicero immediately wrote to Caesar, and offered large rewards to the couriers if they succeeded in delivering his letter; but all the roads were guarded, and they were intercepted. During the night, the timber that had been collected for the defence works was used to build towers, as many as a hundred and twenty of these being run up with incredible speed, and all defects in the fortifications were made good. Next day the enemy, considerably reinforced, renewed their attack on the camp and filled up the trench, while the Romans resisted with the same determination. Similar attacks followed day after day, and work had to be continued throughout the night, so that even the sick and the wounded could get no sleep. Everything necessary for repelling the next day's assault was got ready by night, including large numbers of siege-spears and stakes charred at the point. The towers were provided with additional storeys, and with wicker breastworks surmounted by a crenellated top. Cicero himself, though in very poor health, would not rest even at night, until a crowd of soldiers actually went to him and by their remonstrances made him take care of himself.

At length a number of the Nervian leaders and chieftains, who had some claim to consider themselves friends of Cicero, and therefore entitled to speak to him, asked for an interview. Their request was granted, and they told him the same as Ambiorix had told Sabinus – that the whole of Gaul was in arms, the Germans had crossed the Rhine, and the camps of Caesar and the other generals were being attacked.

They also described the death of Sabinus, and, to prove the
truth of their account, pointed to the presence of Ambiorix
with their army. 'You are mistaken,' they continued, 'if
you expect any help whatever from troops who know that
they are in extreme peril themselves. However, we have no
quarrel with Cicero or the Roman People, except that we
object to the establishment of winter camps in our country,
and do not want it to become a regular practice. As far as
we are concerned, you can leave the camp without being
molested, and go where you please without fear.' By way
of reply, Cicero contented himself with saying that it was
not the habit of the Roman people to accept any terms
from an armed enemy. If they would lay down their arms,
and send an embassy to Caesar to ask for terms, he would
support their request, and hoped that Caesar in his justice
would grant it.

After this disappointment the Nervii surrounded the
camp with a rampart ten feet high and a trench fifteen feet
wide. They had learnt something of the art of entrenchment by observing our methods in previous years, and also
got hints from prisoners belonging to our army whom they
had taken. But as they lacked the proper tools for the work,
they had to cut the sods with their swords, and remove the
earth with their hands and in their cloaks. From this one
could get some idea of their great number: in less than three
hours they completed a fortified line three miles in circumference, and during the next few days set to work, under the prisoners' instruction, to erect towers high enough
to overtop the rampart of the camp, and to make
grappling-hooks and sappers' huts.

On the seventh day of the siege a great gale sprang up,
and the enemy began slinging moulded bullets of red-hot
clay and hurling incendiary darts at the huts in the camp,
which, as is usual in Gaul, were thatched. The huts quickly
caught fire, and the strong wind spread the flames

throughout the camp. The enemy raised a loud cheer, as if victory were now a certainty, and began to move up their towers and sappers' huts and to scale the rampart with ladders. The defenders showed the greatest courage and coolness. They were surrounded by scorching heat and pelted with a hail of missiles, and knew that all their baggage, containing everything they possessed, was being burnt. Yet not a single man deserted his post on the rampart, and hardly anyone even turned his head to look at what was happening; every man fought in this great crisis with the utmost energy and heroism. This was by far the worst day's fighting for them; nevertheless, it ended in their killing and wounding more of the enemy than on any other day, because the Gauls were crowded in a tightly packed mass at the very foot of the rampart, and those at the back prevented the front ranks from retreating. When the fire had died down a little, one of the enemy's towers was pushed right up to the rampart at one point. The centurions of the 3rd cohort retired from the spot where they were stationed, withdrew all their men, and then made signs and called to the Gauls to come inside if they liked; but not one of them dared to move. They were then driven from their position on the tower by a volley of stones from every direction, and the tower was itself set on fire.

In the legion were two very brave centurions named Titus Pullo and Lucius Vorenus, both of them nearly qualified for the first grade. They were always disputing which was the better soldier, and every year the competition for promotion set them quarrelling. When the fighting at the entrenchment was at its height, Pullo cried: 'Why hesitate, Vorenus? What better opportunity do you want to prove your courage? To-day shall decide between us.' With these words he advanced outside the fortification, and rushed into the thickest place he could see in the enemy's line. This brought Vorenus too over the rampart, hastening after his

rival for fear of what everyone would think if he lagged behind. Pullo stopped a short way from the Gauls, hurled his
spear, and transfixed one of them who was running forward from the ranks. The man fainted from the wound, and
his comrades covered him with their shields, at the same
time showering missiles upon Pullo and preventing him
from advancing farther. His shield was pierced by a javelin,
which stuck in his sword-belt; and as the blow knocked his
scabbard out of place, he could not get his hand quickly to
his sword when he tried to draw it, and was surrounded by
the enemy while unable to defend himself. His rival Vorenus
ran up to rescue him in his distress, and all the Gauls immediately left Pullo, who they thought had been mortally
wounded by the javelin, and turned upon Vorenus. Vorenus drew his sword, and fighting hand to hand killed one of
his assailants and drove the rest back a little; but pressing on
too eagerly he stumbled down a steep slope and fell. It was
now his turn to be surrounded, but Pullo came to his aid;
both of them escaped unhurt, and after killing a number of
the enemy returned to camp covered with glory. Thus
Fortune played with them in their struggle for pre-
eminence: bitter rivals though they were, each helped and
saved the other, so that it could not be decided which was
the more deserving of the prize of valour.

Day by day the peril and hardship of the siege increased,
especially as so many of the men were incapacitated by
wounds that few were now available for the defence. As
the situation became worse, Cicero made still more frequent attempts to get a letter through to Caesar. Some of
the messengers were detected at once and tortured to death
under the eyes of the soldiers. There was one Nervian in
the camp, a man of good birth named Vertico, who had
deserted to Cicero at the start of the siege and served him
very faithfully. This man induced his slave, by the promise
of freedom and a large reward, to carry a dispatch to Caesar.

He took it tied round a javelin, passed through his fellow-countrymen's lines without exciting any suspicion, and reached Caesar, who learnt from him the perils that surrounded Cicero and his legion. On receiving the dispatch in the late afternoon, Caesar at once sent a messenger to his quaestor Marcus Crassus, whose camp was twenty-four miles away in the country of the Bellovaci, ordering him to march at midnight with his legion and join him with all speed. Accordingly, Crassus left his camp with the messenger. Another message was sent to Fabius, bidding him march his legion into the country of the Atrebates, through which Caesar would have to pass on his way to Cicero's camp. He also directed Labienus to bring his legion to the frontier of the Nervii, if he could do so without risk. As the remaining legions were a long way off, Caesar did not think it advisable to wait until they could be assembled; but he collected about four hundred cavalry from the nearest camps.

The next morning, on learning from Crassus' scouts that he was approaching, Caesar set out about nine o'clock and marched twenty miles. He directed that Crassus, with the legion which he was bringing with him, should take charge of everything left behind at Samarobriva – the heavy baggage, the hostages furnished by various tribes, the state papers, and the whole of the grain that had been collected to last through the winter. Fabius and his legion, in accordance with their orders, joined Caesar on the march without much delay. As for Labienus, he had heard the bad news about the destruction of Sabinus and the fifteen cohorts; all the forces of the Treveri were close upon him, and he feared the consequences of a departure from his camp which must look like a flight: the enemy would be sure to attack, and he doubted his ability to resist, especially as he knew that they were elated by the recent Gallic victory. Accordingly he wrote back to Caesar saying that it would be very dangerous for him to move his legion from its quarters; he described in detail what had happened in the country of the Eburones, and told him that the whole army of the Treveri, infantry and cavalry, had taken up a position three miles from his camp.

Caesar approved of Labienus' decision. Although this meant that he had only two legions instead of the three he had expected, he thought that the only possible way to save the situation was to act quickly. He proceeded by forced marches to the territory of the Nervii, and there learnt from prisoners what was happening in Cicero's camp, and how critical the position was. He then induced one of his Gallic horsemen, by the promise of a large reward, to convey a letter to Cicero, which he wrote in Greek characters, for fear it might be intercepted and his plans become known to the enemy. If he was unable to get into the camp, the man was to tie the letter to the thong of a javelin and throw it in over the rampart. The letter informed Cicero that Caesar was on the way with some legions and would be there shortly, and told him to keep up a bold front. The Gaul was afraid to enter the camp, and therefore threw the javelin in, according to his instructions. It happened to stick in one of the towers, where it remained unnoticed for two days. Then a soldier saw it, pulled it out, and took it to Cicero, who after reading it paraded the troops and read it aloud, to their great joy. By this time the smoke of burning buildings was visible in the distance, which dispelled all doubt about the approach of the legions.

On hearing the news from their patrols, the Gauls raised the siege and marched to meet Caesar with all their forces, about sixty thousand men. With the help of Vertico – the man already mentioned – Cicero again found a Gaul to carry a dispatch to Caesar, in which he advised him to march warily and carefully, because the enemy had left the camp and diverted all their forces to oppose him. When the dispatch reached him, about midnight, Caesar informed his troops of its contents and told them to summon up their courage for a battle. At daybreak he broke up the camp, and had advanced about four miles, when he saw the Gallic host on the other side of a wide valley with a stream running through it. It would have been very risky to fight on unfavourable ground with such a small force; and knowing that Cicero was now released from blockade, he felt that he had no cause for anxiety, and had better take his time. He therefore halted and made a fortified camp on the most advantageous site he could find. The camp would have been small in any case, since he had barely seven thousand men and no heavy baggage; but he reduced its size still further by making the camp roads narrower than usual, so that his forces would seem contemptibly small. At the same time he sent out scouts in all directions to find the most convenient place for crossing the valley.

Some cavalry skirmishes took place that day near the stream, but the two armies maintained their positions. The Gauls were awaiting the arrival of larger forces. Caesar hoped, by feigning fear, to entice them on to his own ground, and so to be able to fight in front of his camp on his own side of the valley; or, failing that, to cross the valley and the stream with less risk by reconnoitring the available routes beforehand. At dawn the enemy's cavalry came up to the camp and engaged the Roman horse. Caesar ordered them to give ground voluntarily and fall back into the camp, and told the legionaries to increase the height of the rampart all round and block up the gateways; in doing so they were to run about as much as possible and pretend to be afraid. By these feints the enemy were induced to cross the valley and form up in a disadvantageous position. After Caesar had enticed them still nearer by withdrawing his men from the rampart, they threw javelins from all directions over the fortifications, and sent heralds round with orders to announce that anyone, Gaul or Roman, who liked to come over and join them might safely do so before nine o'clock; after that, no one would be admitted. They were so contemptuous of the Roman army, that when they found the gateways blocked and thought they could not break in that way – though actually the barricades were shams, consisting of a single thickness of sods – they began to fill up the trenches and make openings in the palisade with their bare hands. Suddenly, while the infantry made sorties from all the gates, Caesar sent out the cavalry. The Gauls fled so precipitately that not a single one stayed to strike a blow; many were killed, and all the rest threw away their arms.

Caesar was afraid to pursue too far, because there were woods and marshes in the way, and because he saw that he would incur serious losses by abandoning his position. As it was, he joined Cicero the same day without having suffered any casualties. He saw with astonishment the towers, sappers' huts, and earthworks constructed by the Gauls, and, when Cicero's legion was paraded, found that not one man in ten remained unwounded. He was thus able to realize how grave the peril had been, and with what resolution the defence had been conducted. He gave Cicero the high praise he deserved, congratulated the whole legion, and spoke individually to the centurions and military tribunes who were mentioned by Cicero as having specially distinguished themselves. Obtaining from prisoners more precise information about the fate of Sabinus and Cotta, he paraded the legion next day, described the disaster that had taken place, and reassured the men. The defeat, he said, was due to the blundering rashness of the general, and they had no reason to be upset about it, since with the help of Providence their valour had avenged it; the enemy's triumph had been short, and there was no need for them to be depressed any longer.

§ 3 WIDESPREAD REVOLTS IN NORTHERN AND CENTRAL GAUL (54–53 B.C.)

THE news of Caesar's success was brought to Labienus by the Remi with extraordinary speed. He was more than fifty-five miles from Cicero's camp, and it was after two o'clock in the afternoon when Caesar reached it; yet before midnight some of the Remi were shouting at the camp gates, announcing the victory and offering their congratulations. When the news reached the Treveri, Indutiomarus, who had intended to attack Labienus' camp on the following day, fled home in the night with all his forces. Caesar sent Fabius back to his camp with his legion, and decided to winter himself with three legions in separate camps near Samarobriva, and in view of the serious disturbances that had occurred to remain with the army throughout the winter. Since the disaster in which Sabinus met his death became generally known, nearly all the tribes had been discussing warlike projects, sending messengers and embassies in all directions, trying to find out one another's plans and see who would take the initiative, and holding meetings at night in deserted spots. All through the winter Caesar had scarcely a moment's respite from anxiety: he was continually receiving some report about plans for revolt. The quaestor Roscius, for example, whom he had placed in command of the 13th legion, reported that large forces belonging to the tribes called Aremorican had assembled to attack him and had been within eight miles of his camp, but on hearing of Caesar's victory had made off with a haste that suggested an army in flight.

Caesar summoned the leading men of each tribe, and partly by intimidation, letting them know that he was aware of what was going on, partly by persuasion, succeeded in keeping a large part of the country obedient. The government of the Senones, however, a very powerful tribe with great influence over the others, tried to kill their king Cavarinus, whom Caesar had set on his ancestral throne in succession to his brother Moritasgus, who occupied it at the time of Caesar's arrival in Gaul. When Cavarinus got wind of their intention and fled, they pursued him as far as the frontier, dethroned him, and banished him. On receiving a deputation sent to justify their action, Caesar ordered the whole of the tribal council to appear before him; but they disregarded his command. The fact that someone had been bold enough to take the initiative in hostile action made a deep impression on the ignorant natives, and produced such a profound change in their attitude that nearly every tribe was suspected by Caesar of disloyalty. Almost the only exceptions were the Aedui, whom he always held in special esteem for their long-standing record of unbroken loyalty, and the Remi, who had earned similar regard by their recent services in the Gallic campaigns. Perhaps there is nothing very surprising in their readiness to revolt; among many other reasons, tribes which were considered the bravest and most warlike in the world naturally felt bitter resentment at the complete loss of this reputation which submission to Roman rule entailed.

Indutiomarus and the Treveri were particularly active. All through the winter they never ceased sending embassies across the Rhine, intriguing with the German tribes, promising them money, and assuring them that the great losses which the Roman army had sustained had left only a small part of it in existence. Not a single German tribe, however, could be induced to cross the river; they said that they had twice had experience of the Roman arms – in the campaign of Ariovistus, and at the time of the migration of the Tenctheri – and did not intend to tempt fortune again. In spite of this disappointment Indutiomarus proceeded to raise and drill troops, to procure horses from the neighbouring states, and by large rewards to entice exiles and condemned criminals from all over Gaul to join him. Indeed, he soon acquired such prestige in the country by these measures, that embassies poured in from all quarters, requesting his favour and alliance either for tribal governments or for individuals. From these unsolicited overtures he inferred that he would have no lack of volunteers when he began to advance beyond his own frontier. In one direction were the Senones and Carnutes, incited to revolt by their consciousness of guilt, while on another side the Nervii and Atuatuci were preparing to attack the Romans. So he gave notice of a muster in arms. This is the customary method of opening hostilities in Gaul. A law, common to all the tribes alike, requires all adult males to arm and attend the muster, and the last to arrive is cruelly tortured and put to death in the presence of the assembled host. At this meeting Indutiomarus declared his son-in-law Cingetorix a public enemy and confiscated his property. Cingetorix was the leader of the rival party, and had remained faithful to Caesar since putting himself under his protection.[1] Indutiomarus next announced to the assembly that his aid had been invoked by the Senones, the Carnutes, and several other tribes: he intended in due course to march to their country, ravaging the territory of the Remi on his way, but would first attack Labienus' camp. He then gave the necessary orders.

Labienus was safe in a camp well protected both by its situation and by fortifications, and felt no anxiety for himself or his legion; his only concern was not to lose any opportunity of scoring a success against the enemy. Accordingly, when Cingetorix and his relatives told him what Indutiomarus had said in the assembly, he sent messages to all the neighbouring tribes, calling upon them to supply contingents of cavalry by a certain date. Meanwhile

1. See above, pages 130–31.

Indutiomarus came prowling round the camp nearly every day with all his cavalry, either to reconnoitre its position or to get into conversation with the soldiers; and usually all the horsemen tried to frighten them by throwing javelins over the rampart. Labienus kept his men within the entrenchment and did all he could to confirm the enemy's belief that they were afraid.

Each day as he moved up to the Roman lines Indutiomarus showed greater contempt for his adversary. Eventually Labienus brought into the camp, in a single night, the cavalry which he had summoned from all the neighbouring tribes, and by setting a guard succeeded so well in keeping all his men inside, that there was no means by which the news could get abroad or be carried to the Treveri. Indutiomarus came up to the camp as usual and spent the greater part of the day there, his cavalrymen throwing javelins and shouting insults to provoke the soldiers to fight. They got no reply, and towards evening, when they felt like it, went off in scattered groups. Suddenly Labienus sent out all his cavalry through two of the gates. He gave strict orders that as soon as the enemy were scared off and put to flight – as he foresaw they would be – every man was to look for Indutiomarus, and not strike a blow at anyone else until they saw him killed. For he was anxious that they should not give him time to escape by going in pursuit of the others. He set a big price on his head, and to make doubly sure sent some cohorts to support the cavalry. Fortune aided the plan that human foresight had devised. With every man after him, and him alone, Indutiomarus was caught and killed in the very act of fording a river, and his head brought back to camp. On their way back the cavalry pursued and killed as many as they could, and all the forces which had assembled from the Eburones and the Nervii departed when they heard the news. This success made Gaul a little quieter for the time being.

Caesar had many reasons, however, for expecting still more serious disturbances before long. He therefore charged three of his generals, Marcus Silanus, Gaius Antistius Reginus, and Titus Sextius, with the duty of raising fresh troops. He also sent a message to Pompey – who, though vested as proconsul with military command, was remaining for political reasons in the neighbourhood of Rome – requesting him to mobilize the recruits from northern Italy whom he had sworn in during his consulship, and to send them out to him. Caesar considered it very important, with a view to making a permanent impression upon the tribesmen, to let it be seen that the man-power of Italy was sufficient not only to repair speedily any loss sustained in the field, but actually to increase the size of the expeditionary force. Pompey acceded to this request from motives of patriotism as well as of friendship, and Caesar's officers promptly enlisted further recruits, so that before the end of the winter three legions were formed and brought to Gaul, making double the number of the cohorts lost under Sabinus. This large reinforcement, and the speed with which it was effected, showed what Roman organization and resources were capable of.

After the death of Indutiomarus his command was transferred by the Treveri to members of his family, who persisted in trying to obtain the support of the nearest German tribes by promises of money. Failing in this, they made overtures to more distant tribes, a number of which consented. The alliance was confirmed by an exchange of oaths, and hostages were given as security for the payment of the money. Ambiorix also was admitted as a partner to the league. Caesar was informed of these intrigues, and saw warlike preparations going on all around. The Nervii, Atuatuci, and Menapii, together with all the tribes of German origin on the west bank of the Rhine, were in arms; the Senones refused to attend at his bidding, and were concerting plans with the Carnutes and others of their neighbours; and the Treveri were sending embassy after embassy to obtain German aid. He therefore decided that he must take the field in advance of the usual season.

Accordingly, before the winter was over, he assembled the four nearest legions and made an unexpected attack on the country of the Nervii. Before they could either concentrate their forces or flee, a large number of cattle and prisoners were captured and handed over as booty to the soldiers; the country was ravaged, and the Nervii forced to surrender and give hostages. After this quick success Caesar took the legions back into winter quarters. In the early spring he convoked the usual Gallic council, which was attended by all those summoned except the Senones, Carnutes, and Treveri. He regarded their non-appearance as the first step towards an armed revolt, and in order to make it clear that he considered its suppression of paramount importance, he decided to transfer the meeting to Lutetia, a town of the Parisii. They inhabited a territory adjoining that of the Senones, and a generation before had united with them to form one state; but they appeared to have had no hand in the present policy of the Senones. After announcing his decision from the platform in his camp, Caesar started with his legions the same day and made his way by forced marches to the country of the Senones.

On learning of his approach, Acco, the ringleader of the conspiracy, ordered the population to gather in their strongholds. Before they had time to complete this operation they heard that the Romans were at hand. The Senones had no choice but to abandon their project and send envoys to ask Caesar's pardon. These were introduced by the Aedui, under whose protection their tribe had been from ancient times. Caesar willingly pardoned them at the request of the Aedui and accepted their excuses; for he thought that the summer should be devoted to the impending war, and not wasted in holding an inquest. He ordered them, however, to provide a hundred hostages, whom he entrusted to the custody of the Aedui. The Carnutes, too, sent envoys and hostages while Caesar was in the district, pleading their cause with the support of the Remi, whose dependants they were, and received the same reply. Caesar then completed the business of the council and requisitioned cavalry from the various tribes.

Now that this part of Gaul was tranquillized, Caesar devoted all his energies to the war against the Treveri and Ambiorix. He bade Cavarinus accompany him with the cavalry of the Senones, lest his hasty temper or the hatred that he had earned should cause trouble in the tribe. Then, since he felt certain that Ambiorix did not intend to fight a battle, he cast about to discover what other plans he might have. Close to the Eburones, and protected by a continuous line of marshes and forests, dwelt the Menapii, the only Gallic people who had never sent envoys to Caesar to sue for peace. He knew that Ambiorix was united to them by ties of hospitality, and also that, through the agency of the Treveri, he had formed an alliance with the Germans. He thought it advisable to deprive Ambiorix of these allies before attacking him directly, for fear desperation should make him hide among the Menapii or join the tribes beyond the Rhine. Therefore, after sending the baggage of the entire army to Labienus' camp in the country of the Treveri and ordering two legions to proceed there too, he started himself for the territory of the Menapii with five legions in light marching order. The Menapii did not collect any troops, but relying on the protection of the terrain took refuge with all their belongings in the forests and marshes. Caesar put Fabius and the quaestor Marcus Crassus in command of detachments, and the three columns advanced with the aid of hastily constructed causeways, burning farms and villages, and taking a large number of

cattle and prisoners. By this means the Menapii were compelled to send envoys to sue for peace. Caesar took the hostages they offered, and told them that he would treat them
as enemies if they admitted Ambiorix or his agents into
their territory. With this warning, he left Commius the
Atrebatian with a force of cavalry to keep the Menapii
under surveillance, while he marched against the Treveri.

Meanwhile the Treveri had collected large forces of infantry and cavalry, and were preparing to attack Labienus
and the single legion which was wintering in their
territory. They were within two days' march of his camp,
when they heard of the arrival of the two legions dispatched
to him by Caesar, and, encamping at a distance of fifteen
miles, they decided to wait for reinforcements from the
Germans. Apprised of their intention, Labienus hoped that
their imprudence would give him some opportunity of
bringing them to action. He left five cohorts to guard the
baggage, marched against the enemy with the other twenty-
five and a strong force of cavalry, and entrenched a camp a
mile away from them. Between the two camps was a river
with steep banks, difficult to cross; Labienus had no intention of crossing it himself, and did not think the enemy
would. The Gauls' hope of being reinforced was increasing
daily, and Labienus purposely let the soldiers hear him say
that, since the Germans were said to be approaching, he
would not jeopardize their safety and his own by remaining,
but would break up the camp next morning at dawn. This
remark was soon reported to the enemy, since among the
large number of Gallic horsemen it was only natural that
there should be some who sympathized with their fellow-
countrymen's cause. At night Labienus summoned the military tribunes and first-grade centurions, and explained his
plans; then, to help in making the enemy think they were
afraid, he ordered the camp to be broken up with more
noise and disturbance than is customary with Roman

armies, and so made his departure resemble a flight. This also was reported to the Gauls by their patrols before daybreak; for the camps were very close together. They urged one another not to let the hoped-for prize slip from their grasp: to wait for German aid when the Romans were panic-stricken would mean unnecessary delay, and with such a large army it would be disgraceful to shrink from attacking a mere handful of men, especially men who were running away and hampered by baggage. Accordingly, when the rearguard of the Roman column had barely got outside the entrenchment, they boldly began to cross the river and join battle in an unfavourable position. Labienus had expected this, and enticed them all across by continuing to advance slowly, keeping up the pretence that he was marching away. Then, sending the baggage a short distance ahead and parking it on a piece of rising ground, he said to the soldiers: 'Here is your chance. You have got the enemy where you wanted them – in a bad position, where they are not free to manoeuvre. Fight as bravely under me as you often have under the commander-in-chief; imagine that he is here, watching the battle in person.' With these words he bade the units turn to face the enemy and form line of battle, sent a few squadrons of cavalry to protect the baggage, and posted the rest on the flanks. The men at once raised a shout and launched their spears. The enemy were amazed to see the army that they thought to be in flight advancing to the attack. They had not the courage to face its charge; directly the lines met, they turned tail and made for the nearest woods. Labienus hunted them down with his cavalry, killing many of them and taking a number of prisoners, and a few days later had recovered his hold over the tribe; for the Germans who were coming to aid them returned home when they found the Treveri routed. The relatives of Indutiomarus who had instigated the revolt fled the country and went along with the Germans.

Cingetorix, who had remained loyal right from the outset, was invested with civil and military control of the tribe.

§ 4 THE SECOND CROSSING OF THE RHINE (53 B.C.)

AFTER marching from the country of the Menapii to that of the Treveri, Caesar determined to cross the Rhine for two reasons: first, because the Germans had sent the Treveri reinforcements to use against him; secondly, to prevent Ambiorix's finding an asylum in Germany. He therefore proceeded to build a bridge a little above the place where he had crossed before. As the method of construction was familiar to the soldiers from the previous occasion, they were able by energetic efforts to complete the task in a few days. Leaving a strong guard on the Gallic side of the bridge to prevent any sudden rising on the part of the Treveri, he led across the remainder of his forces, including the cavalry. The Ubii, who had previously given hostages and submitted, sent envoys to clear themselves by explaining that they had not broken their word: the aid sent to the Treveri did not come from their state. They begged him to spare them, and not to let an indiscriminate animosity against the Germans make the innocent suffer for the guilty; if he wanted more hostages they should be given. On investigating the matter he found that the reinforcements had been sent by the Suebi. He therefore accepted the Ubii's explanation, and made careful inquiry about the routes leading to the territory of the Suebi.

A few days later Caesar was told by the Ubii that the Suebi were concentrating all their forces and calling upon their subject tribes to furnish contingents of infantry and cavalry. Thereupon he arranged for a supply of grain, selected a suitable site for a camp, and directed the Ubii to remove their cattle and transfer all their possessions from the fields into their strongholds, hoping that the ignorant and uncivilized Germans might be induced by shortage of food to fight a battle on unequal terms. He also told the Ubii to keep sending scouts into Suebic territory and find out what the enemy were about. The Ubii carried out these instructions, and a few days later reported that on the receipt of reliable information about the Roman army all the Suebi had retired, with the whole of their forces and those which they had raised from their allies, to the farthest extremity of their country, where there was an immense forest called Bacenis, stretching far into the interior and forming a natural barrier between the Suebi and the Cherusci, which prevented them from raiding and damaging each other's territory. On the edge of this forest, they said, the Suebi had resolved to await the arrival of the Romans. Caesar was afraid that if he followed them into the forests he might run short of corn, since none of the Germans pay much attention to agriculture.[1] He therefore decided to advance no farther. However, so as not to let the natives think they had seen the last of him, he left the greater part of the bridge standing. In order to hold up any reinforcements which they might try to send to Gaul, after withdrawing his army he broke down the end that touched the Ubian bank for a distance of two hundred feet, and at the Gallic end erected a four-storeyed tower, posted a detachment of twelve cohorts to protect the bridge, and fortified the position with strong defence works. A young officer named Gaius Volcacius Tullus was placed in command of it.

1. See above, page 36.

§ 5 DEVASTATION OF THE COUNTRY OF THE EBURONES
(53 B.C.)

WHEN the crops were beginning to ripen Caesar set out
through the Ardennes to fight Ambiorix. He sent Lucius
Minucius Basilus in advance with all the cavalry, to see if
he could gain any advantage by travelling quickly and
striking at a favourable opportunity. Caesar told him to
forbid fires to be lighted in his camps, so as not to give the
enemy warning of his approach from a distance, and promised to follow him immediately.

Basilus duly carried out his instructions. Completing the
journey more quickly than anyone had thought possible,
he surprised a number of the Eburones working in the
fields, and following their directions hurried on to a place
where Ambiorix, guarded only by a few horsemen, was
said to be. Much depends on fortune, in war, as in all other
things. It was a lucky chance that enabled Basilus to catch
Ambiorix unprepared and off his guard, and to appear
on the scene before his approach was reported or even
rumoured. But by an equally great stroke of luck Ambiorix
escaped alive, although he lost all the military equipment
that he had with him, his carriages, and his horses. His
house was in a wood, like most Gallic houses – for they
generally choose sites near woods and rivers, to avoid
the heat. So, fighting in a confined space, his attend-
ants and friends were able to resist the attack of Basilus'
cavalry for a time. Meanwhile, one of them mounted
him on a horse, and his flight was covered by the wood.
In this way he was first brought into danger, and
then delivered from it, by the all-prevailing power of
fortune.

Ambiorix did not assemble his troops – either of set purpose, because he thought it better not to give battle, or

through lack of time, because his plans were upset by the sudden arrival of the Roman cavalry, which he assumed would be followed up by the rest of the army. At all events he sent out messengers through the countryside, bidding every man shift for himself. Some fled into the Ardennes, others into a continuous belt of marshes, while those who lived nearest the sea hid in places cut off from the mainland at high tide. Many left their own country and entrusted their lives and all their possessions to complete strangers. Catuvolcus, who as king of one half of the Eburones had joined in Ambiorix's enterprise, was now a weak old man, unable to face the hardships of war or flight; solemnly cursing Ambiorix for having suggested the plan, he poisoned himself with yew, a tree which is very common in Gaul and Germany.

The Segni and Condrusi, peoples of Germanic origin and generally counted as Germans, living between the Eburones and the Treveri, sent ambassadors to ask Caesar not to regard them as enemies and not to assume that all the Germans in Gaul were leagued together against him. They said that they had never thought of making war upon him, and had not sent any help to Ambiorix. After confirming their statements by interrogating prisoners, Caesar ordered them to bring to him any Eburonian fugitives who had come to their country; if they obeyed, he would respect their territory. He then separated his forces into three divisions and took all the heavy baggage to Atuatuca, a fortress situated about in the middle of the country of the Eburones, where Sabinus and Cotta had had their winter quarters. He had several reasons for selecting this place: the principal one was that the fortifications constructed in the previous year were still intact, which would save the soldiers the labour of building new ones. He left the baggage under the protection of the 14th legion, one of the three which he had recently brought from Italy, where they had been levied. He placed

this legion and the camp in charge of Cicero, assigning
him also two hundred cavalry.

After dividing the army, Caesar ordered Labienus to
advance with three legions towards the coast, into the region bordering on the country of the Menapii, and sent
Trebonius with three more to ravage the district lying on the
frontiers of the Atuatuci. He took the remaining three himself, and decided to march to the river Scheldt, which flows
into the Meuse, and to the western end of the Ardennes,
where he heard Ambiorix had gone with a small number
of cavalry. Before setting out he promised to return in a
week, when a distribution of rations to the legion left at
the fortress would be due. He asked Labienus and Trebonius
to return by the same date if the military situation allowed,
so that after holding a further discussion they might be
able to restart the campaign on new lines, in the light of what
they would have learnt by that time of the enemy's plans.

It has been explained that the Eburones had no regular
force assembled, no stronghold, and no garrison capable of
armed resistance: their population was scattered in all directions. Each man had installed himself in any remote glen,
any wooded spot, or impenetrable morass, that offered a
chance of protection or escape. These hiding-places were
known to the natives living in the neighbourhood, and
great care was needed to ensure the safety of the Roman
troops. So long as they kept together, they were in no
danger from a panic-stricken and scattered enemy; but
losses severe enough to weaken the army might easily be
sustained by the waylaying of individual soldiers, who were
tempted far afield by the hope of plunder, or got separated
from the rest because the ill-defined and half-concealed
paths through the woods were not practicable for columns
in close formation. The only way to make an end of the
business, and exterminate this race of criminals, would
have been to break up the army into a large number of

detachments which could be sent out separately. But it was safer to keep the companies in their regular formation, according to the established practice of the Roman army, although this meant that they could not injure the Gauls in such country. Even so, any men who strayed apart from the main body were liable to be ambushed and surrounded by some of the bolder spirits among them. In these difficult circumstances the most careful precautions were taken; Caesar thought it better to let the enemy off comparatively lightly, in spite of the men's burning desire for revenge, than to punish them severely at the cost of serious loss to his own troops. He sent messages to the neighbouring tribes, inviting them all to win booty for themselves by plundering the Eburones. He preferred to expose Gauls, instead of Roman legionaries, to the dangers of fighting in the forests, and also wanted to envelop the Eburones with a great multitude of men, in order to punish their heinous crime with total annihilation. Large numbers soon assembled from every side.

While the whole of the Eburonian territory was being plundered, it was getting near the day on which Caesar had intended to return to the legion left in charge of the baggage. At this moment an instance occurred of the important part played in war by accident, which can have far-reaching consequences. After the panic-stricken flight of the enemy, already described, there was no hostile force in the field to give the slightest occasion for alarm. But the Germans across the Rhine heard that the Eburones were being plundered, and that all comers were invited to share the spoil. Immediately a force of two thousand cavalry was raised by the Sugambri, who live close to the Rhine – the people who sheltered the fugitive Tenctheri and Usipetes.[1] They crossed the river on boats and rafts, some thirty miles below the place where Caesar's bridge had been

1. See above, pages 115–16.

built and the garrison left, entered the territory of the Eburones, caught a number of the scattered fugitives, and seized a quantity of cattle – a prize much sought after by these Barbarians. Lured on by the hope of more plunder, they advanced farther; for these born fighters and bandits were not to be stopped by marshes or forests. On asking their prisoners where Caesar was, they were told that he had started on a campaign some distance away, and that all the army had left the district. One of the prisoners added: 'Why go after this paltry, miserable loot, when you have the chance of making your fortunes right away? In three hours you can reach Atuatuca, where the Romans have stored all their property. The garrison is so small that they can't even man the wall, and not a man dare set foot outside the entrenchments.' The offer of such a chance decided the Germans. They hid the booty they had got, and guided by their informant made straight for Atuatuca.

Throughout the previous week Cicero had been most careful to keep the soldiers in camp according to Caesar's instructions, not allowing even a single servant to go outside the entrenchment. But on the seventh day he began to fear that Caesar would not keep his appointment; it was said that he had advanced a long way, and there was no news of his return. The soldiers, too, were grumbling at Cicero's patient acceptance of the situation: to be cooped up like this in camp, they said, was almost as bad as a blockade. With nine legions and a strong cavalry force in the field, and the enemy scattered and very nearly destroyed, he had no reason to expect a serious accident within three miles of his camp. Accordingly he sent five cohorts to get corn from the nearest fields, which were separated from the camp by only a single hill. With them there went, as a separate detachment, some three hundred men who had recovered from illness during the week,[1] and permission

1. A number of sick men had been left behind by the legions.

to accompany them was granted also to a large number of servants, who took out a great many of the animals that were being kept in the camp.

It happened that just at this moment the German cavalry appeared, and, riding right on without slackening speed, tried to break in by the back gate. As the view was obstructed by woods on that side, they were not seen until they were quite close to the camp – so close that the traders who had their tents at the foot of the rampart had no time to get away. The suddenness of the attack upset the soldiers, and the cohort on guard had difficulty in withstanding the first rush. The enemy spread out all round, trying to find a way in. The soldiers had hard work to defend the gates; elsewhere the lie of the land and the entrenchments gave protection. The whole camp was in a state of alarm; the men were asking one another the cause of the disturbance, and could not tell where to assemble or in which direction to advance. Some said the camp was already taken; others maintained that the Germans had come in triumph after destroying the Roman army and its commander-in-chief. Most of them were filled with strange superstitious fancies suggested by the spot on which they stood, and saw in imagination the disaster that had befallen Cotta and Sabinus, who perished not far from that same fort. Everyone was so paralyzed by fear that the Germans believed the prisoner had spoken the truth when he told them that there was no garrison in the camp. They strove hard to force their way in, calling on one another not to let such a piece of luck slip through their fingers.

Among the sick men left with the garrison was Baculus, who had served under Caesar as chief centurion of his legion, and has been mentioned in connexion with earlier engagements.[1] For five days he had been too ill to eat. Feeling anxious for his own and his comrades' safety, he

1. See above, pages 86, 93–4.

walked unarmed out of his tent, and, on seeing the enemy close at hand and the situation extremely critical, borrowed arms from the nearest soldiers and posted himself in the gateway. He was joined by the centurions of the cohort on guard, and for a time they fought together to hold the enemy's attack. Baculus was severely wounded and fainted, and the others just managed to save him by passing him back from hand to hand. This respite gave the rest of the troops time to recover courage enough to man the fortifications and make a show of defence.

Meanwhile the reaping-party, which had finished its work, heard the shouting at the camp. The horsemen hurried on, and discovered how serious the peril was. Out there in the open there was no fortification to shelter the frightened men – raw recruits without any experience –, and they turned to the military tribune and centurions, waiting to be told what to do; even the bravest were unnerved by the emergency. The Germans caught sight of the standards in the distance, and desisted from their attack on the camp. At first they thought it was the legions, returned from the distant expedition on which the prisoners said they had gone; but when they saw how small the force was, they regarded it with contempt and attacked from all sides. The servants ran forward to the nearest rising ground, from which they were quickly dislodged, and, by rushing to the standards round which the companies were formed up, increased the nervous soldiers' alarm. Since the camp was so near, some were for adopting a wedge-formation and making a quick dash through, feeling confident that, though a few might be surrounded and killed, the rest could escape. Others preferred to make a stand on the hill, and all take their chance together. The latter plan was rejected by the detachment of veterans which had gone out with the cohorts. The veterans, therefore, with words of mutual encouragement, advanced under their commander Gaius

Trebonius, a Roman Knight, broke right through the enemy, and reached the camp without a single casualty. Close behind them, in the gap made by their courageous charge, the servants and the cavalry got safely through. But those who had taken their stand on the hill showed that they had still learnt nothing of the art of war: they failed either to stick to the plan they had chosen of defending themselves on the high ground, or to imitate the swift and vigorous action which they could see had saved their comrades. Instead, in an attempt to regain the camp, they let themselves be caught in a bad position on low-lying ground. The centurions, some of whom had been promoted for gallantry from lower grades in other legions to the higher grades in this one, were determined not to forfeit the reputation they had won in previous actions, and fell fighting with the utmost courage. Some of the soldiers were saved by the centurions' brave stand, which made the enemy fall back, and – to their surprise – reached the camp in safety. The rest were surrounded by the enemy and killed.

As the Germans saw that the Roman troops had now manned the fortifications, they gave up hope of taking the camp by storm, and retired across the Rhine with the booty that they had hidden in the woods. Even after their departure, the defenders were still so frightened that Volusenus, who was sent ahead by Caesar with the cavalry and arrived that night in the camp, could not make them believe that Caesar was close at hand, with his army safe and sound. Fear had so completely possessed them all that they nearly took leave of their senses, and would have it that the whole army had been cut to pieces, and that the cavalry had managed to escape by flight: if the army were not destroyed, they maintained, the Germans would never have attacked the camp. The panic was eventually stopped by Caesar's arrival. He was well aware of the way things happen in war, and on his return made only one criticism – that the cohorts had been allowed to leave their post in the garrison: Cicero should have avoided running even the slightest risk. For the rest, he recognized that what had happened was largely the result of accident: it was a strange chance that had brought the enemy to the camp so suddenly, and a still stranger chance that had sent them away when they were almost masters of the rampart and gates. And the strangest thing of all was that, although their object in crossing the Rhine was to plunder Ambiorix's country, circumstances had led them to attack the Roman camp instead, and thus render Ambiorix the greatest service he could have desired.

Setting out once more to harass the Eburones, Caesar sent out in all directions a large force of cavalry that he had collected from the neighbouring tribes. Every village and every building they saw was set on fire; all over the country the cattle were either slaughtered or driven off as booty; and the crops, a part of which had already been laid flat by the autumnal rains, were consumed by the great numbers of horses and men. It seemed certain, therefore, that even if some of the inhabitants had escaped for the moment by hiding, they must die of starvation after the retirement of the troops. With such a large number of horsemen scouring the country in separate parties, it happened time and again that prisoners were taken who had just seen Ambiorix in flight; they would actually look round to see where he was, insisting that he was barely out of sight. This raised his pursuers' hopes of running him down, and so standing high in Caesar's favour. They took endless pains and made almost superhuman efforts. But they always seemed just to have missed what they so ardently desired; Ambiorix would escape by hiding in a wood or ravine, and under cover of night would make off in some new direction, escorted only by four horsemen – for to no one else did he dare entrust his life.

After ravaging the country in this way, Caesar withdrew his army – minus the two cohorts of Cicero's legion which had been lost – to Durocortorum, a town of the Remi, where he convened a Gallic council and held an inquiry into the conspiracy of the Senones and Carnutes. Acco, the instigator of the plot, was condemned to death and executed in the ancient Roman manner. Some others, who fled in fear of being brought to trial, were outlawed. Caesar then distributed the legions in winter quarters – two on the frontier of the Treveri, two among the Lingones, and the other six at Agedincum in the country of the Senones – and after provisioning them, since Gaul was quiet, set out for northern Italy as usual to hold his assizes.

CHAPTER VII

THE REBELLION OF
VERCINGETORIX (52 B.C.)

§ 1 THE OPENING STAGE (52 B.C.)

On his arrival in Italy Caesar was told of the assassination of Publius Clodius, and of a senatorial decree ordering all Italians of military age to be sworn in. He proceeded to enrol recruits in all parts of the Cisalpine Province. The news of these events soon reached Gaul; and the Gauls, drawing what they thought was the natural inference, invented a story that Caesar was detained by the disturbances in Rome, where political strife was so acute, they said, that he could not rejoin his army. The prospect of such a chance spurred them into action. They were already smarting under their subjection to Rome, and now began to plan war with greater confidence and boldness. The leading men arranged meetings at secluded spots in the woods, where they spoke bitterly of the execution of Acco and pointed out that the same fate might befall them next. They complained of the miserable condition of the whole country, and offered tempting rewards to induce some of their hearers to open hostilities and risk their lives for the liberty of Gaul. The first step, they said, was to contrive means of cutting Caesar off from his army before their plot was divulged. This could easily be done, because the legions would not dare to leave their winter quarters in the absence of their commander-in-chief, and he would not be able to reach them without an escort. In any case it was better to die in battle than to resign themselves to the loss of their ancient military glory and the liberty inherited from their ancestors. These discussions ended with a declaration by the Carnutes that they were prepared to face any danger for the common cause, and would undertake to strike the first blow. As it was not possible at the moment to give mutual guarantees by exchange of hostages, for fear their design should be betrayed, the Carnutes called upon the others to stack their military standards together – a most solemn rite, according to Gallic custom –, and to bind themselves by an oath not to desert them when once hostilities were begun. The Carnutes were warmly congratulated by the assembly; all present took the oath, and before separating fixed a date for the rising.

When the appointed day arrived, the Carnutes, led by two desperadoes named Gutuater and Conconnetodumnus, swooped down at a given signal on Cenabum, killed the Romans who had settled there for purposes of commerce – including Gaius Fufius Cita, a Roman Knight of high standing, whom Caesar had put in charge of the commissariat – and plundered their property. Tidings of these events sped swiftly to all the tribes of Gaul: for when anything specially important or remarkable occurs, the people shout the news to one another through the countryside and villages, and others in turn take up the cry and pass it on to their neighbours. Thus, on the present occasion, what happened at Cenabum at dawn was known before eight o'clock at night in the country of the Arverni, about a hundred and fifty miles away.

There, the lead given by the Carnutes was followed by Vercingetorix, a very powerful young Arvernian, whose father Celtillus had held suzerainty over all Gaul, and had been put to death by his compatriots for seeking to make himself king. Assembling his retainers, Vercingetorix had no difficulty in exciting their passions, and the news of what was afoot soon brought others out in arms. An effort to restrain him was made by his uncle Gobannitio and other chiefs, who thought the enterprise too risky, and he was expelled from the town of Gergovia. Undeterred, however, he went round the countryside raising a band of vagabonds and beggars. With these at his back he was able to win over all the Arvernians whom he approached. Calling upon them to take up arms for the freedom of Gaul, he assembled a large force and succeeded in expelling the opponents by whom, not long before, he had been driven out himself. He was proclaimed king by his adherents, and sent embassies in every direction adjuring the tribes to keep faith. In a short time he had secured the support of the Senones, Parisii, Cadurci, Turoni, Aulerci, Lemovices, Andes, Pictones, and all the other tribes on the west coast, who unanimously elected him commander-in-chief. Armed with this power, he ordered each tribe to give hostages, to bring a specified quota of troops at once, and to manufacture a specified quantity of arms by a certain date – paying particular attention to the cavalry arm. Himself a man of boundless energy, he terrorized waverers with the rigours of an iron discipline. Serious cases of disaffection were punished by torture and death at the stake, and even for a minor fault he would cut off a man's ears or gouge out one of his eyes, and send him home to serve as a warning to others of the severe chastisement meted out to offenders.

By this terrorism he quickly raised an army, part of which he sent into the territory of the Ruteni under a Cadurcan of great daring named Lucterius. Vercingetorix himself marched against the Bituriges, who at his approach sent envoys to their overlords the Aedui, asking for help to enable them to offer a more effective resistance. On the advice of the generals whom Caesar had left with the army, the Aedui sent cavalry and infantry to aid the Bituriges. When these reached the Loire, however, the boundary between the Bituriges and the Aedui, they halted, and after a few days turned back without venturing to cross it. The explanation they gave to the generals was that they were afraid of treachery on the part of the Bituriges, who, according to information they had received, had concerted a plan with the Arverni to cut them off on both sides if once they crossed the river. Whether they really acted for the reason they alleged, or from motives of treachery, I do not know for certain, and therefore do not feel justified in making a positive statement. On the departure of the Aedui, the Bituriges immediately joined forces with the Arverni.

By the time news of these events reached Caesar in Italy, the situation in Rome had improved, thanks to the resolute action of Pompey; and accordingly he set out for Gaul. On arriving he was faced with a difficult problem: how was he to rejoin his army? If he summoned the legions to the Transalpine Province, they would clearly have to fight a pitched battle on the march without him; and to travel across Gaul without an escort would mean risking his own life, since in the circumstances even the tribes that were apparently quiet could not be relied upon.

In the meantime Lucterius, the Cadurcan who had been sent to the Ruteni, induced them to join the Arverni. Advancing into the territories of the Nitiobroges and Gabali, he took hostages from both, and after assembling a strong force attempted to make a raid into the Province in the direction of Narbonne. Caesar decided that he must let everything else wait. Marching at once to the town, he reassured the frightened inhabitants and posted detachments of the garrison troops in the districts that lay near the point of attack.[1] He also ordered a part of the Provincial garrison and a fresh draft that he had brought from Italy to concentrate in the territory of the Helvii, which adjoins that of the Arverni.

These measures checked Lucterius and made him keep his distance, because he was afraid to venture into the area

1. The part of the Province inhabited by the Ruteni, Volcae Arecomici, and Tolosates, and the neighbourhood of Narbonne itself.

encircled by the Roman detachments. Accordingly Caesar joined the forces assembled in the country of the Helvii. The Cevennes mountains, which form a barrier between the Helvii and the Arverni, were at this season – the severest part of the winter – covered with very deep snow, and the passes blocked. But the soldiers cleared stretches of the path by shovelling away drifts up to six feet deep, and by prodigious exertions enabled Caesar to get across into the land of the Arverni. Taking them completely by surprise – for they thought that the Cevennes gave them as secure protection as a solid wall, since the passes had never been considered practicable even for single travellers at that time of year – Caesar ordered his cavalry to scour the widest possible area and frighten the Gauls as much as they could. Rumours and dispatches soon brought the news to Vercingetorix, and in the greatest alarm all his Arvernian supporters came running to him, begging him to save them from ruin and not to let their country be pillaged by the enemy; they had a right to claim protection, they said, since it was obvious that they were now bearing the brunt of the attack. In response to their entreaties he moved his camp from the country of the Bituriges and marched towards that of the Arverni.

But Caesar stayed there only two days, because he had anticipated Vercingetorix's move. Then, on the pretext of collecting reinforcements and cavalry, he went away, leaving the troops under the command of the young Brutus. He instructed him to send out the cavalry as far as possible in every direction, and announced that he would try not to be away from the camp longer than three days. After making these arrangements, to the great surprise of his escort he made his way post haste to Vienne. There he picked up some fresh cavalry which he had sent on some time before, and without stopping night or day pushed on through the country of the Aedui into that of the Lingones, where two

legions were wintering – for he thought it possible that the
Aedui might go so far as to make an attempt on his life,
and wished to forestall this by making all the speed he could.
Directly he arrived at the winter camp, he sent word to the
other legions, and had them all concentrated before the
news of his coming could reach the Arverni. When he did
get to know of it, Vercingetorix led his army back into the
country of the Bituriges, and from there marched to attack Gorgobina, a stronghold of the Boii, whom Caesar,
after defeating them in the battle with the Helvetii, had
established there under the suzerainty of the Aedui.

This move greatly embarrassed Caesar. If he kept the
legions all together until the end of the winter, and allowed
a people subject to the Aedui to be overpowered without
interference, it was only too likely that the whole of Gaul
would desert his cause, since it would be evident that his
friends could not look to him for protection. On the other
hand, if he withdrew the troops from their quarters so
early in the year, he might be hard put to it to supply them
with food, owing to the difficulties of transport. He thought
it better, however, to face any risk, rather than alienate all
his supporters by submitting to such a loss of prestige. Accordingly he asked the Aedui to send up supplies, and sent
forward a message to the Boii saying that he was on his way
to their relief, and urging them to remain loyal and resist
the enemy's attack courageously. Then, leaving two legions
at Agedincum with the heavy baggage of the entire army,
he set out for the country of the Boii.

The next day he reached Vellaunodunum, a stronghold
of the Senones, and in order to facilitate the movement of
supplies by ensuring that he left no enemy in his rear, laid
siege to it. In two days he had encircled it with entrenchments, and on the third day the garrison sent out envoys to
surrender. Caesar ordered them to deposit all their arms
in one place, bring out their horses, and give six hundred

hostages. As he wanted to complete his journey to Gorgobina as soon as possible, he left Trebonius to see to the
execution of these orders and himself set out for Cenabum,
in the territory of the Carnutes. The Carnutes, who had
only just heard of the siege of Vellaunodunum and expected
that it would last some time, were engaged in collecting
troops to send to the defence of Cenabum. Caesar reached
this town in two days, but by the time he had encamped in
front of it, it was too late to attack that day. He therefore
directed the necessary preparations to be made for an assault
on the next day, and as there was a bridge over the Loire
right under the town walls, and he was afraid that the inhabitants might escape under cover of night, he ordered two
legions to remain under arms all night. Shortly before midnight the people of Cenabum moved silently out of the
town and began to cross the river. Apprised of this by his
patrols, Caesar set the gates on fire and sent inside the
legions he had kept ready for action. The town was
captured, and all but a very few of the enemy taken
prisoner – for the narrow streets and bridge were blocked
by the crowd of fugitives. After plundering and burning
Cenabum, and distributing among his soldiers the booty
it contained and the prisoners, Caesar marched across the
Loire and made his way into the territory of the Bituriges.

At his approach Vercingetorix raised the siege of Gorgobina and marched to meet him. Caesar had laid siege to a
stronghold of the Bituriges called Noviodunum, which lay
upon his line of march, when envoys came to him from the
garrison, begging him to pardon them and spare their lives.
As he wanted to complete the campaign with the same
speed that had already brought him so many successes, he
granted their petition, ordering them to collect all their arms
in one place, bring out their horses, and furnish hostages.
A part of the hostages had already been delivered up, and
some centurions had been sent into the town with a small

party of soldiers to collect the arms and horses, when the cavalry preceding Vercingetorix's main body was seen in the distance. Directly the besieged townsmen caught sight of it and thought there was a chance of being relieved, they raised a cheer and began to snatch up their arms, shut the gates, and man the wall. The centurions inside the town, realizing from the cheering that some fresh scheme was afoot, seized the gates sword in hand and got their men away without a single casualty. Caesar ordered his Gallic cavalry out of camp and engaged Vercingetorix's horse; when the cavalry got into difficulties, he reinforced it with four hundred German horsemen whom he had kept with his army from the start of this campaign. Their charge overpowered the enemy, who were put to flight and fell back with heavy loss on their main body. Their defeat made the defenders of Noviodunum change their minds once more. Terror-stricken, they laid hands on those they thought responsible for instigating the people against the Romans, haled them off to Caesar, and surrendered. Noviodunum being thus disposed of, Caesar advanced on Avaricum, a very large and strongly-defended town situated in a particularly fertile part of the Biturigan country, as he felt sure that its capture would secure the submission of the whole tribe.

§ 2 SIEGE AND CAPTURE OF AVARICUM (52 B.C.)

AFTER this series of reverses at Vellaunodunum, Cenabum, and Noviodunum, Vercingetorix summoned his followers to a council of war and told them that their plan of campaign must be completely changed. 'We must strive by every means,' he said, 'to prevent the Romans from obtaining forage and supplies. This will be easy, since we are strong

in cavalry and the season is in our favour. There is no grass
to cut; so the enemy will be forced to send out parties to get
hay from the barns, and our cavalry can go out every day
and see that not a single one of them returns alive. What is
more, when our lives are at stake we must be prepared to
sacrifice our private possessions. Along the enemy's line of
march we must burn all the villages and farms within the
radius that their foragers can cover. We ourselves have
plenty of supplies, because we can rely upon the resources
of the people in whose territory the campaign is conducted;
but the Romans will either succumb to starvation or have
to expose themselves to serious risk by going far from their
camp in search of food. We can either kill them or strip
them of their baggage – which will be equally effective,
since without it they cannot keep the field. We should also
burn all the towns except those which are rendered impregnable by natural and artificial defences; otherwise they
may serve as refuges for shirkers among our own numbers,
and give the enemy the chance of looting the stores of
provisions and other property that they contain. You may
think these measures harsh and cruel, but you must admit
that it would be a still harsher fate to have your wives and
children carried off into slavery and be killed yourselves –
which is what will inevitably befall you if you are conquered.'

This proposal was unanimously approved, and in a single
day more than twenty of the Bituriges' towns were fired.
The same was done in the territory of the neighbouring
tribes, until fires were visible in every direction; and although this was a grievous sorrow to all the Gauls, they
found consolation in the thought that victory was practically assured and that they would soon repair the loss. In
a second joint council of war the question was debated
whether Avaricum was to be burnt or defended. The
Bituriges went down on their knees and implored the

representatives of the other tribes not to compel them to set fire with their own hands to a town that was almost the finest in Gaul, the chief defence and pride of their state. It could easily be held, they said, in view of its natural strength; for it was almost completely surrounded by river and marsh, in which there was only one narrow opening. Their petition was granted – Vercingetorix, though he opposed it at first, was at length prevailed upon by their entreaties and by the general sympathy felt for them – and a careful choice was made of officers to defend the town.

Following Caesar's march by easy stages, Vercingetorix selected for his encampment a spot sixteen miles from Avaricum protected by marshes and forests. By an organized liaison service he was informed hourly of events at Avaricum and transmitted his orders accordingly. He was constantly on the watch for parties going out for forage or corn, and by attacking them when they were isolated – for they were obliged to go far afield – he inflicted heavy losses, although they tried everything they could think of to baffle him, setting out at irregular intervals and by different routes.

Caesar encamped on the side of the town where there was a narrow gap in the marshes and watercourses surrounding it, and began to build a siege terrace, form lines of mantlets, and erect two towers upon the terrace; for the lie of the land made it impossible to invest the place. To maintain a supply of corn he kept importuning the Boii and the Aedui; but the Aedui were lukewarm and gave little help, while the Boii, a small and feeble tribe, had only slender resources, which were quickly exhausted. The troops were brought to such straits by the inability of the Boii to relieve them and the indifference of the Aedui, as well as by the burning of the granaries, that for several days they had no grain and saved themselves from starvation only by bringing in cattle from distant villages. Yet not a word were they heard to utter that was unworthy of Roman soldiers with successful campaigns to their credit. Indeed, when Caesar addressed the men of each legion at their work, and told them that if they found their privations unbearable he would abandon the siege, with one voice they begged him not to do so, saying that they had served under him for many years without suffering any humiliation or ever being forced to relinquish a task that they had set their hands to. They would feel it a humiliation to abandon the siege now, and would rather suffer any hardship than fail in avenging the Romans who had fallen victims to Gallic treachery at Cenabum. They said the same to their centurions and military tribunes, asking them to pass it on to Caesar.

The siege towers had already been moved close to the wall, when Caesar learnt from prisoners that Vercingetorix, having run out of forage, had moved nearer Avaricum, and had taken command in person of the cavalry and the light-armed infantry who regularly fought among the cavalry, in order to ambush the place where he expected our men would go the next day to forage. Accordingly Caesar set out silently at midnight and reached the enemy's camp in the morning. But they received speedy warning of his approach from their patrols, hid their wagons and baggage in the densest parts of the woods, and drew up all their forces on open rising ground. On hearing of this Caesar at once ordered his men to pile their packs and get their arms ready.

The hill that the enemy occupied had a gentle gradient at the bottom, and was almost surrounded by a marsh which was extremely difficult to negotiate, although only fifty feet wide. The Gauls had broken down the causeways leading over the marsh, and relying on the strength of their position refused to budge from the hill. Formed up in tribal groups, they held all the fords and the thickets that bordered the marsh, determined, if the Romans tried to force a passage, to overpower them by running down to the attack while they were stuck fast in the mud. Awaiting us at such a short distance, they looked as if they were prepared to fight a battle on more or less equal terms; but their position was so much stronger than ours that this show of courage was clearly a mere pretence. The legionaries were indignant at the enemy's daring to face them at such close range, and clamoured for the signal to attack. But Caesar pointed out how costly a victory would be in these conditions, how many brave men's lives must be sacrificed; when they showed such steadfast loyalty and were willing to face any danger for his honour, he would be guilty of the grossest injustice if he did not consider their lives before his own interests. After addressing them in this way to alleviate their disappointment, he led them back to camp the same day and proceeded to complete his preparations for the siege of the town.

On returning to his main body Vercingetorix was accused of treachery for having moved his camp nearer the Romans, for going off with all the cavalry, and for leaving such a large army without anyone in supreme command, with the result that the Romans had taken advantage of his departure to make a swift move against it. All this could not have happened by accident, they said, but must have been deliberately planned; evidently he would rather become king of Gaul by Caesar's favour than by the gift of his fellow-countrymen. To these charges Vercingetorix replied that he moved camp because he was short of forage, and they themselves had pressed him to do so; he went nearer the Romans because he had found a very favourable position, so well protected by nature that no defence works were required. 'I knew,' he continued, 'that the cavalry would not be missed on this marshy ground, whereas it was very useful in the place to which I took it. I purposely did not delegate the command to anyone when I went away,

for fear the person I chose might be induced by the enthusiasm of the rank and file to give battle; for I could see
that that was what they all desired, because they were soft
and incapable of prolonged exertion. If the arrival of the
Romans during my absence was an accident, it was a stroke
of luck for us; if it was the result of information conveyed
by a traitor, you ought to be grateful to him for enabling
you to see from your commanding position how weak
are their forces and how contemptible is their cowardice,
since they slunk back ignominiously to their camp without
daring to fight. I have no need to obtain from Caesar by
treachery the power that I can secure by victory – a victory
already in my grasp, and to be shared by the whole Gallic
people. You may take back the command you entrusted
me with, if you imagine that you are conferring a favour
on me when in reality you owe your lives to me. To satisfy
yourselves that what I say is true, hear what these Roman
soldiers have to say.' With these words he brought forward
some camp servants whom he had captured on a foraging
expedition some days previously and had subjected to the
tortures of chains and starvation. These he had carefully
primed beforehand with the answers they were to make
when questioned. They said that they were legionaries, and
that the hunger and want they had suffered made them steal
out of camp to see if they could find any corn or cattle in
the fields. The whole army, they added, was in the same
plight; every man was at the end of his strength and unfit
for work, and their commander had decided to raise the
siege in three days' time unless some progress was made.
'That,' cried Vercingetorix, 'is what you owe to me, whom
you charge with treachery. Thanks to me, without shedding
a drop of your own blood, you see a great and victorious
army almost destroyed by starvation; and when it is routed
and retreats in disgrace, I have taken good care that no
people shall admit it into their territory.'

The whole concourse cheered and clashed their weapons, as the Gauls are accustomed to do when they approve of what a speaker says. Vercingetorix was a great leader, they declared, his loyalty above suspicion, and no one could conduct the campaign with greater skill. They determined to send into Avaricum ten thousand men picked from all the contingents, not wishing to entrust the national cause to the Bituriges alone, because they realized that if the Bituriges saved the town the victory would be entirely theirs.

To baffle the extraordinary bravery of our troops the Gauls resorted to all kinds of devices; for they are a most ingenious people, and very clever at borrowing and applying ideas suggested to them. They pulled aside our wall-hooks with lassoes, for example, and when they had made them fast hauled them inside with windlasses. They made our terraces fall in by undermining, at which they were expert because they have extensive iron mines in their country and are thoroughly familiar with every kind of underground working. They had also equipped the whole circuit of the wall[1] with towers, furnished with platforms and

1. Gallic walls are always built more or less on the following plan. Balks of timber are laid on the ground at regular intervals of two feet along the whole line on which the wall is to be built, at right angles to it. These are made fast to one another by long beams running across them at their centre points, and are covered with a quantity of rubble; and the two-foot intervals between them are faced with large stones fitted tightly in. When this first course has been placed in position and fastened together, another course is laid on top. The same interval of two feet is kept between the balks of the second course, but they are not in contact with those of the first course, being separated from them by a course of stones two feet high; thus every balk is separated from each of its neighbours by one large stone, and so held firmly in position. By the addition of further courses the fabric is raised to the required height. This style of building presents a diversified appearance that is not unsightly, with its alternation of balks and stones each preserving their own straight lines. It is also very serviceable and well adapted for defending a town: the masonry protects it from fire, the timber from destruction by the battering-ram, which cannot either pierce or knock to pieces a structure braced internally by beams running generally to a length of forty feet in one piece.

protected by hides. They made frequent sorties by day and night, either to set fire to the terrace or to attack our soldiers at work. As our towers were raised higher by the material added each day to the terrace, they increased the height of theirs correspondingly by inserting floors between the upright posts forming the framework. They countermined the subterranean galleries that we were digging towards the walls, and prevented their continuation by throwing into them stakes sharpened and hardened in a fire, boiling pitch, and very heavy stones.

The besiegers were continually hampered, not only by these various devices, but also by incessant rain following a thaw. By unremitting toil, however, they overcame all these hindrances and in twenty-five days raised a terrace three hundred and thirty feet wide and eighty feet high. It was now almost touching the wall; and one night when Caesar was staying up as usual with the working-parties, urging them not to lose an instant, smoke was noticed rising from the terrace shortly before midnight. The enemy had dug a tunnel under it and set it on fire. At the same moment the Gauls raised a cheer all along the wall and came pouring out of two gates on either side of our towers. Others flung torches and dry wood on to the terrace from their position on the wall and dropped pitch and other inflammable material, so that it was hard to decide which points to defend or which attack to counter first. It was Caesar's practice, however, to have two legions on duty all night in front of the camp, while a larger number laboured at the works by shifts. So the defence was quickly organized; some checked the sorties while others pulled back the towers and made a gap in the terrace, and all the rest of the troops ran from the camp to extinguish the flames.

The fight went on everywhere throughout the remainder of the night, and the enemy's hope of victory was continually renewed, especially as they saw that the sheds used to protect the men who moved the towers were burnt and that it was not easy for our soldiers to advance without cover to help their comrades, while in their own ranks fresh men kept relieving those who were worn out. They felt that the fate of Gaul depended entirely on what happened at that moment, and performed before our eyes an exploit so memorable that I felt I must not leave it unrecorded. There was a Gaul standing before one of the gates and throwing into the flames, opposite one of our towers, lumps of tallow and pitch that were passed along to him. An arrow from a catapult pierced his right side and he fell dead. Another near him stepped over his prostrate body and took over his job. When he likewise was killed by the catapult, a third took his place, and so they went on. The post was not abandoned by the defenders until the fire on the terrace was extinguished, the Gauls repulsed all along the line, and the battle at an end.

The enemy had now tried everything without success, and the next day determined to abandon the town, a course to which Vercingetorix was urgently pressing them. By making the attempt when all was quiet at night they hoped to bring it off without serious loss; Vercingetorix's camp was not far away, and the continuous stretch of marshland that lay between the town and the Romans would hinder pursuit. They were already preparing to execute this plan the following night, when suddenly their wives came running out into the streets and tears threw themselves at the men's feet. 'Do not abandon us,' they begged, 'and the children who are yours as much as ours, to a cruel enemy. We cannot fly with you because we have not the strength.' When they saw that their minds were made up – for men who stand in extreme peril are generally too scared to feel pity – they started shrieking and gesticulating to the Romans to warn them of the men's intention. This frightened the Gauls into giving up the idea; for they were afraid that the Roman cavalry would have seized the roads before they could get away.

The next day Caesar completed the siege works which he had under construction and moved forward one of the towers. It began to rain heavily, and he thought this a good opportunity to attempt an assault, especially as he saw that the guards on the wall had been carelessly posted. He told the men to go about their work in a half-hearted fashion, and explained his plan to them. The legions were got ready for action, as far as possible under cover of mantlets, and Caesar, calling upon them to seize the chance of victory and reap at long last the fruit of all their toil, promised rewards to those who were first to mount the wall. He then gave the signal for the assault. The soldiers suddenly darted out everywhere and quickly lined the wall. Taken by surprise, and panic-stricken, the enemy were dislodged from the wall and towers, but re-formed in the market place and other open spaces in wedge-shaped masses, determined to fight a pitched battle against attackers from any direction. But when they saw the Romans occupying the entire circuit of the wall around them, and not a man coming down to meet them on level ground, they were afraid of being cut off from all chance of escape, and throwing down their arms ran without stopping to the farthest corners of the town. There, some were cut down by our infantry as they jammed the narrow gateways, and others by the cavalry after making their way out. None of our soldiers thought about making money by taking prisoners. They were exasperated by the massacre of Romans at Cenabum and the labour of the siege, and spared neither old men nor women nor children. Of the whole population – about forty thousand – a bare eight hundred who rushed out of the town at the first alarm got safely through to Vercingetorix. He took them in silently, late at night. Afraid that if numbers of them entered the camp together the compassion they would arouse among the rank and file of his army might cause a riot, he stationed his trusted friends and the tribal leaders some distance along the road, with orders to sort them out and convey them to the various parts of the camp allotted to each tribe at the start of the campaign.

The next day Vercingetorix called a council of war and encouraged his followers, telling them not to be unduly disheartened or upset by this reverse. 'The Romans have not won by superior courage or in fair fight,' he said, 'but by their expert knowledge of siegecraft, a special technique that we were unacquainted with. It is idle to expect invariable success in war. I personally was never in favour of defending Avaricum, as you yourselves can testify. It was the imprudence of the Bituriges and the too ready acquiescence of the rest that caused this setback. However, the successes that I shall soon gain will more than make up for it. I am working hard to bring over the tribes which are standing aloof from us. The whole of Gaul will then be united, and when we are all of one mind the entire world cannot stand against us. I have already nearly succeeded in this. Meanwhile it is only fair that you should do what I ask for the safety of us all – fortify the camp, so that we can more easily resist any sudden attack.'

This speech was well received by the Gauls, who were especially pleased to find that Vercingetorix had not lost heart after such a serious defeat, and faced them instead of hiding himself. They credited him with extraordinary foresight and prudence because, while there was still time, he had twice given them good advice about Avaricum – in the first place to burn it, later to evacuate it. And so, unlike most commanders, whose position is weakened by failure, Vercingetorix gained reputation with every day that followed the reverse. Their hopes were raised by his assurances that other tribes could be induced to join them. They even built a fortified camp – an unheard-of thing in Gaul. The shock had been so severe that, unused to hard work though they were, they felt they must submit to anything that was demanded of them.

Vercingetorix kept his promise and used every means he could think of to gain the adherence of the tribes outside the alliance. He tried to entice their chiefs by presents and offers of reward, employing the agents whom he thought best qualified for the purpose; some were personal friends of the chiefs, others were chosen for their powers of subtle speech. The refugees who came in after the fall of Avaricum were provided with arms and clothes, and to bring his army up to its former strength Vercingetorix called for reinforcements from the various tribes, fixing the precise number of each quota and the date by which it was to arrive at the camp. He also ordered all the archers who could be found (there were a very large number of them in Gaul) to be sent to him. By these measures he quickly repaired the losses at Avaricum, and Teutomatus [1] king of the Nitiobroges now joined him with a strong force of cavalry from his own tribe and some mercenaries whom he had raised in Aquitania.

§ 3 ROMAN REVERSE AT GERGOVIA (52 B.C.)

CAESAR stayed several days at Avaricum, where he found abundance of grain and other provisions, so that the troops were able to recover from their fatigue and undernourishment. It was now near the end of winter and the start of the campaigning season; and Caesar had just decided to march

1. Son of Ollovico, who was granted the title of 'Friend' by the Roman Senate.

against the enemy, in the hope of either manoeuvring them out of the marshes and forests or blockading them where they were, when some of the leading men of the Aedui came to ask for his help in a serious emergency. The situation, they said, was critical. Their old-established practice was to elect a single magistrate to hold sovereign power for a year. Now, however, there were two magistrates in office, each of whom claimed to have been legally appointed. One was Convictolitavis, a young man of wealth and distinction; the other was Cotus, a descendant of a very old house and a man with great personal influence and numerous family connexions, whose brother Valetiacus had held the same office the year before. The country had become an armed camp; both council and people were divided in their loyalty and each claimant was supported by his retainers. If the quarrel was kept up much longer it would mean civil war. The only way of preventing this was for Caesar to intervene and exert his authority.

It was most unfortunate for Caesar to have to leave the fighting front. But he knew what serious harm such disputes often cause. The Aedui were a powerful tribe, bound by the closest ties to Rome. He himself had done all in his power to strengthen them and had shown them every mark of favour; and now that there was a prospect of their coming to blows with each other, and a risk that the side which felt itself the weaker might call in help from Vercingetorix, he thought it was his first duty to prevent such a catastrophe. As Aeduan law forbade the chief magistrate to leave the country, and Caesar wished to avoid the appearance of violating this rule of its constitution, he decided to go there in person, and summoned the whole council and the two disputants to meet him at Decetia. Almost all the councillors assembled there, and informed Caesar that the announcement of Cotus' election had been made by his brother, the magistrate of the previous year, in the presence of a mere handful of people called together in secret, neither in the proper place nor at the proper time. It was further pointed out that Aeduan law forbade the election, not merely to the magistracy but even to a seat on the council, of a near relation of a person previously elected and still living. Caesar therefore made Cotus resign his claims, and told Convictolitavis, who had been appointed constitutionally, under the presidency of the priests and at a time when the magistracy was vacant, to continue in office.

After deciding the matter in this way, Caesar advised the Aedui to forget their disputes and quarrels and allow nothing to distract them from the war they had on hand. They might look forward to receiving from him the rewards they deserved when the conquest of Gaul was completed. In the meantime they must send him without delay all their cavalry, and ten thousand infantry to be distributed at various places for the protection of his convoys. He then divided his army into two parts. Four legions and a part of the cavalry were assigned to Labienus to lead against the Senones and Parisii. Caesar himself took the other six legions and the rest of the cavalry, and marched into the country of the Arverni towards Gergovia, following the course of the Allier. On learning this, Vercingetorix broke down all the bridges over that river and began to march along the opposite bank. The two armies were within sight of one another and Vercingetorix was generally encamped opposite Caesar, placing patrols to prevent the Romans from making a bridge anywhere and getting across. Thus Caesar found himself in a very difficult position: it looked as if his progress might be barred by the river for most of the summer, since it is not usually fordable until autumn. To get out of this impasse he encamped in a wooded spot opposite one of the bridges destroyed by the enemy, and next day stayed there in concealment with two legions, sending on the rest as usual with all the baggage, and breaking up some of the cohorts into companies so as to make it appear that the number of legions was unchanged. He ordered them to march on as far as they could, and when he had allowed enough time for them to reach their next encampment, he began to rebuild the bridge on the original piles, the lower parts of which were still intact. The work was quickly completed and the legions were taken across. Then, choosing a suitable site for a camp, Caesar recalled the other legions. When Vercingetorix heard of it, he was afraid of being compelled to fight a pitched battle, and therefore pushed on ahead by forced marches.

Five days' march brought Caesar to Gergovia, where on the day of his arrival he fought a cavalry skirmish and reconnoitred the position of the town. As it was situated on a high mountain and difficult of access on every side, he decided that it was hopeless to attempt an assault, and that it would be better not to start a siege until he had secured his food supply. Vercingetorix, who had encamped near the town, placed the various tribal contingents at short distances round his headquarters; they occupied all the mountain heights within view and presented a terrifying appearance. The chieftains whom he had chosen to form his council of war were summoned every morning at daybreak to exchange intelligence or make arrangements, and almost daily the cavalry were sent into action with archers dispersed among their ranks, to test each man's courage and fighting spirit. Opposite the town, there projected from the foot of the mountain a very steep hill of great natural strength. Once in possession of this, we should clearly be able to deprive the enemy of a considerable part of his water supply and restrict the movements of his foragers; but it was held by a fairly strong garrison. By starting out of camp at dead of night, however, Caesar dislodged the garrison before relief could come from the town, and making himself master of the position, installed two legions there in a camp connected with his larger camp by a double trench twelve feet wide, so that men could pass to and fro even singly, without fear of being surprised by the Gauls.

While these events were taking place at Gergovia, Convictolitavis, the Aeduan in whose favour Caesar had decided the dispute about the magistracy,[1] was bribed by the Arverni and entered into negotiation with certain young men of his tribe, chief among whom were Litaviccus and his brothers, members of a very illustrious family. He shared the money with them and bade them remember that they were free men and born to rule. It was the Aedui alone, he said, who hindered the Gallic victory which, but for them, would be certain. Their influence kept the other tribes loyal to Rome; and if they changed sides, the Romans would be unable to maintain their position in Gaul. 'It is true,' he went on, 'that I am under some obligation to Caesar – though the justice of my case was so apparent that he could hardly help deciding in my favour. But the cause of national liberty outweighs any such consideration. Why should we call Caesar in to adjudicate questions involving our rights and the interpretation of our laws? We do not expect him to submit questions of Roman law to our arbitration.' The young men soon yielded to the combined persuasions of Convictolitavis' eloquence and gold, and professed themselves ready to take the lead in the enterprise; but how to put it into execution required some thought, since they knew that it would be no easy task to induce the Aeduan people to take up arms against Rome. It was decided that Litaviccus should march at the head of the ten thousand men who were to be sent to Caesar as reinforcements, while his brothers hurried on ahead to Caesar; and the remainder of their programme was agreed upon.

On taking command of the army Litaviccus marched to a point within thirty miles of Gergovia, and then suddenly

1. See above, pages 198–9.

halted and paraded his troops. 'Soldiers,' he said with tears in his eyes, 'where are we going? All our cavalry and all our men of high rank have perished. Two of our leading citizens, Eporedorix and Viridomarus, have been accused of treason and put to death by the Romans without trial. Learn the facts from these men who have escaped from the actual scene of the massacre. I cannot bear to describe what has happened myself; for my brothers and all my other relations have been killed.' He then produced some men whom he had carefully coached, and they repeated to the troops the tale that he had already told. All the Aeduan cavalry, they said, had been butchered because it was alleged that they had entered into negotiation with the Arverni; they themselves had hidden among the crowd of soldiers and escaped while the slaughter was still going on. With shouts of indignation all the Aedui begged Litaviccus to consider what they were to do. 'It needs no consideration,' he replied. 'Obviously we must march straight to Gergovia and join the Arverni. After such a crime, can we doubt that the Romans are even now hastening here to kill us too? So if we have a spark of courage in us, let us avenge this foul murder by wiping out these ruffians.' With these words he indicated some Romans who had been travelling with him in reliance on his protection. The Gauls cruelly tortured and killed them and plundered a large quantity of grain and other supplies that they had with them. Litaviccus then sent messengers into every part of the Aeduan country and inflamed the people by the same propaganda about the massacre of cavalrymen and chiefs, calling on them to avenge their wrongs by doing the same as he had done.

The two Aeduans who were alleged to have been killed were serving in the contingent of Gallic cavalry, having been called up by a special summons from Caesar. Eporedorix was a young man of the noblest birth and very powerful in his own country; Viridomarus, a man of the same age and equally influential, though not of good birth, had been raised by Caesar, on Diviciacus' recommendation, from a humble position to the highest honour. They were rivals for power; and in the recent struggle for the magistracy Eporedorix had been a strong supporter of Convictolitavis, and Viridomarus of Cotus. On hearing of Litaviccus' project, Eporedorix came about midnight to inform Caesar of it, and begged him not to allow the misguided counsels of raw youths to detach the tribe from its friendship with Rome – which must happen if Litaviccus' army joined Vercingetorix, since neither their relations nor the tribal authorities could be indifferent to the safety of so many thousand men.

Caesar was much perturbed by the news that the Aedui were turning disloyal in spite of the special favour that he had always shown them. Without a moment's hesitation he started out with four legions in light marching order and all his cavalry. There was no time to reduce the size of the camp, since in such an emergency everything depended on prompt action, but he left Fabius to guard it with two legions. He ordered Litaviccus' brothers to be arrested, but found that he was just too late; they had already deserted to the enemy. Urged by Caesar to submit without complaint to the laborious march that the crisis necessitated, all ranks followed him with enthusiasm, and an advance of twenty-four miles brought him within sight of the Aeduan army. By sending forward the cavalry he forced them to halt and prevented them from resuming their march. Orders were given that no one was to kill any of them, and Eporedorix and Viridomarus, who were believed by the Aedui to have been put to death, were told to go to and fro among the cavalrymen and speak to their fellow-countrymen. As soon as the Aedui recognized them and realized that Litaviccus had imposed upon them, they stretched out their hands in token of surrender and throwing down their arms begged for quarter. Litaviccus escaped to Gergovia, accompanied by his retainers; for Gallic custom regards it as a crime, even in a desperate situation, for retainers to desert their lord.

Caesar sent a message to the Aeduan authorities informing them that by an act of grace he had spared men whom the laws of war entitled him to put to the sword; and after giving his army three hours' rest he started for Gergovia. When he had covered about half the distance he met a party of horse sent by Fabius, who told him that a dangerous situation had arisen. The enemy, they said, had assaulted the camp in full force, and, by continually sending in fresh troops to relieve their tired comrades, had exhausted our men, who on account of the size of the camp had to remain hard at work on the rampart without relief. Showers of arrows and every other kind of missile had wounded many of the defenders, but the artillery was of great use in helping them to hold out. The enemy had at length retired, and Fabius was now blocking up all but two of the camp gates, strengthening the rampart with breastworks, and preparing to meet a similar attack the next day. At this Caesar accelerated his march, and the soldiers made such exertions that they reached the camp before sunrise.

In the meantime Litaviccus' first messages reached the country of the Aedui. Without waiting for confirmation they accepted an idle rumour as an established fact, some excited by greed, others carried away by anger and impetuosity – the most striking characteristic of the Gallic race. All the Romans in their power were killed or enslaved and their property was plundered. Convictolitavis added fuel to the fire and goaded the people to frenzy, in the hope that if once they committed a serious crime they would be ashamed to return to reason. Marcus Aristius, a military tribune on his way to rejoin his legion, was ejected from the town of Chalon-sur-Saône with the promise of safe-conduct, and the Roman merchants living there were also compelled to leave. Directly they started the Gauls set on them and stripped them of all their baggage. As the Romans resisted, they continued harassing them all that day and the following night, and when many had been killed on both sides, called a larger number of their countrymen to arms.

Meanwhile news arrived that the whole Aeduan army was in Caesar's power. At this the tribal leaders came running to Aristius, saying that the government had no hand in what had occurred. They ordered an inquiry into the robberies, confiscated the property of Litaviccus and his brothers, and sent a deputation to make their excuses to Caesar. The object of these moves was to secure the release of their army. But the number of people involved in the outrages was large. Fascinated by the profits of the plunder, yet at the same time dreading retribution for their crimes, they began to make secret preparations for war and sent envoys to obtain the support of other tribes. Caesar understood this perfectly well, but answered the deputation in the most conciliatory terms: in spite of the ignorance and irresponsibility of the populace, he still felt the same goodwill towards the Aedui and would not judge them too harshly. Anticipating a widespread rising, however, and afraid of being surrounded by rebellious tribes, he began to consider how he could draw off from Gergovia and reunite the whole army without making his departure look like a flight occasioned by the fear of revolt.

He was still occupied with this problem when he thought he saw a chance of striking an effective blow. On going to inspect the defence works at the smaller of his two camps, he noticed that a hill within the enemy's lines was completely deserted, although previously they had been so thick upon it that the ground was scarcely visible. He inquired the reason for this surprising circumstance from the deserters who daily flocked to him. They all confirmed what he had already discovered from his patrols – that the heights adjoining this hill formed a ridge that was almost level, but narrow and wooded where it gave access to the farther side of the town. The Gauls, they said, were very anxious for the safety of this ridge, feeling sure that if they lost a second height in addition to the one already occupied by the Romans, it would be obvious to everyone that they were all but imprisoned and unable to get away or to send out foraging parties. So every man who could be spared had been summoned by Vercingetorix to fortify the ridge.

About midnight, therefore, Caesar sent several squadrons of cavalry in that direction with orders to scour the whole district and make as much disturbance as possible. At daybreak he had a large number of pack-horses and mules brought out of camp, unsaddled them, and ordered the drivers to put on helmets and ride round over the high ground masquerading as cavalry. A few cavalrymen who were sent with them were told to range over a wide area with the object of letting themselves be seen. All were to make a long circuit and converge upon the same place. These movements could be seen from the town, which commanded a view of the camp, but at such a distance it was impossible to make out with certainty what was going on. Next, a single legion was sent along the same line of heights by which the horsemen had gone, and after advancing a short way was stationed on lower ground, concealed in a wood. The Gauls now became even more alarmed, and the whole of their forces were transferred to the threatened ridge to aid in the work of fortification. When he saw their camps empty, Caesar told his soldiers to cover the crests of their helmets, hide their standards, and move across in small parties – so as not to attract the defenders' attention – from the larger to the smaller camp. He explained his plan to the generals in command of the various legions, warning them above all to keep their men well in hand, and not let them be tempted to advance too far by over-eagerness for battle or hope of plunder. He pointed out that their inferior position placed them at a disadvantage which could be remedied only by quick action: it was a case for a surprise attack, not a regular battle. He then gave the signal to advance, at the same time sending the Aedui up the hill by another route on the right.

The distance, as the crow flies, between the town ramparts and the point on the plain from which the ascent began was a little over a mile; but the turns that had to be made in order to ease the ascent increased its length. About half way up the Gauls had built a six-foot wall of large stones, which followed the contour of the mountain and was intended to impede any attack. All the lower part of the slope was left unoccupied, while the higher part, between this wall and the town ramparts, was covered with their camps, placed close together. Advancing at the signal, the Romans soon reached the wall, climbed over, and captured three of the camps – so quickly, that Teutomatus king of the Nitiobroges was surprised in his tent, where he was taking his siesta, and only just managed to escape, naked to the waist and riding a wounded horse, from the soldiers who entered in search of plunder.

As his purpose had now been achieved, Caesar ordered the recall to be sounded, and the 10th legion, which was with him, immediately halted. The other legions did not hear the trumpet, because a fairly wide hollow intervened; but the military tribunes and the generals did their best, in accordance with Caesar's orders, to hold them back. The soldiers, however, elated by the hope of a quick victory, by the enemy's flight, and by the recollection of their past triumphs, thought that nothing was too hard for their valour to achieve, and continued their pursuit until they got close to the ramparts and gates of the town. Then shouts came from every part of the fortress, and those of the defenders who were farthest away, alarmed by the sudden uproar, thought that the attackers were inside the gates, and rushed out. The married women threw clothes and money down from the ramparts, and leaning over with bared breasts and outstretched hands besought the Romans to spare them, and not to kill the women and children as they had done at Avaricum. Some were lowered from the rampart by their companions and gave themselves up to the soldiers. Lucius Fabius, a centurion of the 8th legion, who had said that day in the hearing of his men that he meant to win a reward such as Caesar had offered at Avaricum, by mounting the rampart before any other man, got three men of his company to hoist him up, and after clambering to the top himself, pulled up each of the others after him.

Meanwhile the Gauls who had assembled on the other side of the town to construct defence works had heard the shouting, and were recalled by a succession of messengers telling them that the town was in the Romans' hands. Their cavalry galloped up first, with the whole horde of infantry-men racing after them. Every man as he arrived took his stand under the ramparts and swelled the ranks of fighters. When a great crowd of them had gathered, the women who a moment before had been holding out their hands in supplication to the Romans began to appeal to their own folk, leaning over the wall with their hair flung loose in Gallic fashion, and bringing out their children for the men to see. It was an unequal struggle for the Romans, with both position and numbers against them; tired out with hurrying uphill and fighting a long engagement, they found it difficult to hold their own against troops just come fresh into action.

Seeing his men harassed on such unfavourable ground by continually increasing numbers, Caesar became anxious for their safety, and sent orders to Titus Sextius, the general left in charge of the small camp, to lead his cohorts out immediately and station them at the foot of the hill, facing the enemy's right flank, where he could cover the legions' retreat, if he saw them driven from their position, by frightening off their pursuers. Caesar also moved his own legion to a slightly more forward-position and there awaited the issue of the battle.

Fierce hand-to-hand fighting was in progress, the Gauls relying on their superior numbers and position, while our men trusted in their courage to see them through, when suddenly the Aedui, whom Caesar had sent up by another route on the right to create a diversion, appeared on our right flank. The similarity of their arms to those of the enemy gave our soldiers a bad fright; for although they could see that the newcomers had their right shoulders un-covered – the sign always agreed upon to mark friendly troops – they imagined that this was a ruse employed by the enemy to trick them. At the same moment the centu-rion Fabius and the others who had climbed with him on to the rampart were surrounded and killed, and their bodies pitched down. Marcus Petronius, another centurion of the same legion, tried to break down the gate, but was over-whelmed by a host of assailants, and realizing that he was a doomed man – he was already covered with wounds – shouted to the men of his company who had followed him: 'I can't save myself and you. It's my fault you're in this tight corner, because I was so keen to distinguish myself. So at least I'll help *you* to get away with your lives. Now's your chance: look after yourselves.' With these words he charged into the middle of the enemy, killed two of them, and forced the rest a short way back from the gate. The men still tried to rescue him. 'It's no use,' he cried, 'trying to save me. I've lost too much blood and haven't any strength left. So get away while you have the chance, and fall back to your legion.' So he went on fighting and a few moments later fell dead. But he had saved his men.

Harassed on every side, our men held their ground till they had lost forty-six centurions. When eventually they were driven back, the Gauls began to pursue relentlessly, but were checked by the 10th legion, which was posted in reserve on fairly level ground; and the 10th was in turn supported by the cohorts of the 13th under Sextius, which after leaving the small camp had moved forward to higher ground. As soon as they reached the plain, all the legions halted and re-formed facing the enemy, and Vercingetorix withdrew his men from the foot of the hill and led them within his entrenchments. Our losses that day amounted to nearly seven hundred.

The next day Caesar paraded the troops and reprimanded them for their rashness and impetuosity. They had decided for themselves, he said, to advance farther and attack the town, neither halting when the retreat was sounded nor obeying the military tribunes and generals who tried to restrain them. He stressed the disadvantage of an unfavourable position, explaining the motives which had dictated his action at Avaricum, when, although he had caught the enemy without their general or their cavalry, he preferred to sacrifice a certain victory rather than incur even light casualties by fighting on unfavourable ground. 'Much as I admire the heroism that you showed,' he went on, 'in refusing to be daunted by a fortified camp, a high mountain, and a walled fortress, I cannot too strongly condemn your bad discipline and your presumption in thinking that you know better than your commander-in-chief how to win a victory or to foresee the results of an action. I want obedience and self-restraint from my soldiers, just as much as courage in the face of danger.' He concluded his speech with words of encouragement, telling the men not to be upset by a reverse which was due to their unfavourable position, and not to the enemy's fighting quality.

As he had not changed his mind regarding the advisability of a retirement, Caesar then led the legions out of camp and formed line of battle in a strong position. Vercingetorix, however, still remained within his entrenchments and would not come down into the plain; and after a cavalry skirmish which resulted in favour of the Romans Caesar marched the army back into camp. After offering battle again the next day he decided that he had done enough to humble the conceit of the Gauls and restore the confidence of his own troops, and he therefore set out for the country of the Aedui. Still the enemy did not follow; and on the third day Caesar reached the river Allier, repaired a broken-down bridge, and marched his army across.

§ 4 VERCINGETORIX'S DEFEAT IN OPEN WARFARE
(52 B.C.)

AT the Allier the Aeduans Viridomarus and Eporedorix asked for an interview with Caesar and informed him that Litaviccus had gone with all the Gallic cavalry to try to seduce the Aedui from their allegiance; it was essential, they said, for them to get there before him in order to keep the tribe loyal. By this time Caesar had many proofs of the treachery of the Aedui, and felt sure that the result of letting these men go would be to make them revolt all the sooner. However, he thought it unwise to detain them, lest he should be accused of high-handed action or give an impression of being afraid. Before they went he briefly reminded them of his services to the Aedui – in what a feeble state they were when he received them into alliance, cooped up in their strongholds, stripped of their lands, deprived of all their allies, forced to pay tribute and submit to humiliating demands for hostages; and how he had not merely restored them to their previous position, but had raised them to a height of prosperity, prestige, and power that they had never reached before. Bidding them pass on this reminder to their countrymen he let them go.

Situated in a strategic position on the Loire was an Aeduan town called Noviodunum, to which Caesar had sent all his hostages from the various Gallic states, his stores of grain, public funds, a large part of his personal luggage and that of his troops, and numbers of horses that he had bought in Italy and Spain for use in the war. On reaching this town Eporedorix and Viridomarus heard the latest news about the Aedui – that Litaviccus had been received at Bibracte, one of their most important towns, and visited by the chief magistrate Convictolitavis and a large number of councillors; and that an official embassy had been sent to Vercingetorix to conclude a treaty of peace and alliance. This was too good a chance, they thought, to be missed. Accordingly they massacred the garrison of Noviodunum and the merchants who lived there, shared the money and horses, had all the hostages taken to the magistrates at Bibracte, and carried away as much grain as they had time to stow into boats, the rest being thrown into the river or burnt. The town itself they thought they could not possibly hold; so they burnt it to prevent its being of use to the Romans. Then they set about collecting troops from the neighbourhood, placing detachments and pickets along the Loire, and making demonstrations here and there with their cavalry to intimidate the Romans. In this way they hoped either to starve them out or to force them by stress of famine to retire into the Province. They were greatly encouraged in this hope by the swollen state of the river – the result of melting snow – which made it to all appearance quite unfordable.

Caesar decided that he must act quickly. If he had to build bridges, a battle might be forced upon him; and in that case it would be better to fight before enemy reinforcements arrived. The only alternative was to alter his whole plan of campaign and retire to the Province, a course which some of his frightened officers thought unavoidable. But there were many reasons against it. It was undignified and humiliating; the route was a difficult one leading over the Cevennes; above all he was anxious about the legions under command of Labienus, who was separated from him. Accordingly he made a series of extraordinarily long marches, by day and night, and astonished everyone by appearing on the bank of the Loire. The cavalry found a ford good enough for an emergency – all that was needed was for the men to be able to keep their shoulders and arms above water, so as to carry their shields and weapons. Cavalrymen waded in upstream to break the force of the current; and, as the shock of Caesar's appearance unnerved the enemy, the crossing was effected without loss. After provisioning the army with some grain and a quantity of cattle that were found in the neighbouring fields, he marched towards the country of the Senones.

Meanwhile Labienus, leaving the draft recently arrived from Italy at Agedincum to protect the baggage, started with his four legions for Lutetia, a town of the Parisii situated on an island in the Seine. When the Gauls knew of his approach, large forces assembled from the neighbouring tribes and the chief command was given to an Aulercan named Camulogenus, who although enfeebled by age was called out of retirement to this post of honour on account of his unrivalled knowledge of warfare. Camulogenus noticed a long stretch of marsh which drained into the Seine and rendered a wide area almost impassable. Encamping near by he prepared to prevent the Roman troops from crossing it. Labienus first tried, under cover of a line of mantlets, to make a causeway across the marsh on a foundation of fascines and other material. Finding this too difficult, he silently quitted his camp some time after midnight and retraced his steps to Metlosedum, a town of the Senones situated like Lutetia on an island in the river. He seized some fifty boats, quickly lashed them together to form a bridge, and sent troops across to the island. Such of the inhabitants as were left in the town – many had been called up to the war – were terrified by this unexpected attack and surrendered the place without a fight. After repairing a bridge recently broken down by the enemy, Labienus crossed to the right bank of the river, marched downstream to Lutetia, and encamped near it. The enemy, informed of this by refugees from Metlosedum, sent orders to burn Lutetia and destroy its bridges; they then moved from their position by the marsh and encamped on the left bank opposite Labienus.

By this time people were saying that Caesar had retreated from Gergovia and rumours were circulating about the insurrection of the Aedui and the success of the general Gallic rising. Gauls who got into conversation with Roman soldiers said that Caesar had been prevented from continuing his march across the Loire and compelled by famine to retire to the Province. The news of the Aeduan rebellion encouraged the Bellovaci, who had already been meditating revolt, to mobilize and make open preparations for war. Now that the situation was so much changed, Labienus saw that he must completely revise his plans; he no longer had any idea of making conquests or attacking, but was only concerned to get his army safely back to Agedincum. On one side he was threatened by the Bellovaci, reputed the bravest fighters in Gaul; on the other, Camulogenus had a well-equipped army ready for action; and Labienus' own legions were separated from their reserves and their baggage by a great river. Confronted suddenly

by such formidable difficulties, he realized that only resolute courage could save him. Towards evening he assembled
his officers. Urging them to execute his orders with energy
and care, he placed a Roman Knight in charge of each of
the boats which he had brought from Metlosedum, and
ordered them to move silently four miles downstream in
the early part of the night and wait for him there. He detailed to guard the camp the five cohorts which he considered least reliable in action, and told the remaining five of
the same legion to start upstream with all the luggage
shortly after midnight, making as much commotion as
possible. He also requisitioned some smaller boats, which
he sent in the same direction at high speed, with loud splash-
ing of the oars, and then himself moved quietly out of camp
with the other three legions and marched downstream to
the place where he had ordered the main flotilla to put in.

The enemy patrols posted all along the river were taken
by surprise, because a sudden heavy storm concealed the
approach of the legions, and both infantry and cavalry were
quickly ferried across under the superintendence of the
Knights in charge of the boats. Just before dawn the enemy
received several reports almost simultaneously – that there
was an unusual commotion in the Roman camp, that a
strong force was marching upstream, that the sound of oars
was audible from the same direction, and that a little way
downstream soldiers were being ferried across. This news
made them think that the Romans were crossing at three
different places and preparing for a general retreat in alarm
at the revolt of the Aedui. They therefore divided their own
troops into three sections. One section remained on guard
opposite the Roman camp; a small force was dispatched
towards Metlosedum with orders to advance upstream as
far as the boats had gone; and the remainder were led
against Labienus.

By dawn the whole of the three Roman legions had been

taken across and were in sight of the enemy. Labienus urged them to remember their long-standing tradition of courage and brilliant successes, and to imagine that Caesar, who had so often led them to victory, was present in person. He then gave the signal to attack. At the first onset the right wing, where the 7th legion was posted, drove back the enemy and put them to flight; on the left, where the 12th legion was, the enemy's front ranks were killed or disabled by missiles, but the rest put up a determined resistance, and it was clear that not a single one of them had any thought of flight. Camulogenus was there in person encouraging his men. The issue still hung in the balance, when the 7th legion, whose military tribunes had received a report of what was happening on the left wing, appeared in the enemy's rear and charged. Even then not a single Gaul gave ground; all of them, including Camulogenus, were surrounded and killed. The detachment left on guard opposite Labienus' camp, on hearing that a battle was being fought, went to lend a hand and occupied a hill, but could not withstand the charge of the victorious Romans, and joined their fleeing comrades. All who could not escape into woods or hills were killed by the cavalry. On the completion of this action Labienus returned to Agedincum, where he had left all the baggage, and then rejoined Caesar with his entire force.

The defection of the Aedui was the signal for a further extension of the war. They sent embassies into every part of Gaul and used all their influence, prestige, and money to induce other tribes to join them. The possession of the hostages whom Caesar had left in their keeping gave them another means of exerting pressure: by threatening to kill them they could intimidate tribes which hesitated. They asked Vercingetorix to visit them and arrange a plan of campaign, and when he came claimed the chief command for themselves. He refused their demand, and a pan-Gallic council was summoned at Bibracte. There was a full attendance of tribesmen from all parts.[1] The matter was referred to their decision and they unanimously confirmed the appointment of Vercingetorix. It was a bitter disappointment to the Aedui to have their claim to leadership rejected. They now realized how much worse off they were and regretted throwing away Caesar's friendship, but having once taken up arms they dared not break with the other tribes. It was with great reluctance that Eporedorix and Viridomarus – young men who regarded themselves as having a great future – took orders from Vercingetorix.

The various tribes were required to send hostages to Vercingetorix by a certain date, and the whole of the cavalry, numbering fifteen thousand, was ordered to concentrate immediately at Bibracte. He said that he would content himself with the infantry which he had in the previous campaign, and would not tempt fortune by fighting a pitched battle. With his great cavalry strength it would be quite easy to prevent the Romans from getting corn and forage. 'All you have to do,' he concluded, 'is to destroy your corn crops without hesitation and burn your granaries, knowing that this sacrifice will make you free men for ever, and rulers over others.' He then commanded the Aedui and the Segusiavi – a tribe living on the Provincial frontier – to supply ten thousand infantry, which together with eight hundred cavalry were placed under command of Eporedorix's brother and detailed to attack the Allobroges. At the same time, however, hoping that the memory of their recent defeat by Rome [61 B.C.] still rankled in the minds of the Allobroges, Vercingetorix tried to seduce them from their allegiance by sending secret agents and envoys, who offered bribes to their chiefs and promised the tribesmen that they should be made rulers of the whole Province. In

1. The chief absentees were the Remi and Lingones, who stuck to their alliance with Rome, and the Treveri, who remained neutral throughout because they lived at a distance and were harassed by German attacks.

another direction, the Gabali and the southernmost clans of the Arverni were sent to attack the Helvii, while the Ruteni and Cadurci were to devastate the country of the Volcae Arecomici. To meet these various assaults, a force of militiamen amounting to twenty-two cohorts had been raised in the Province itself by the general Lucius Caesar and was posted all along the threatened frontier. The Helvii, who chose to offer battle to the invaders advancing across their borders, were defeated with heavy loss, their chief magistrate Gaius Valerius Domnotaurus, son of Valerius Caburus, being among the casualties, and were compelled to take shelter behind the walls of their strongholds. The Allobroges posted a closely-linked chain of pickets along the Rhone and protected their frontier with great vigilance.

Meanwhile Caesar found a way of remedying his inferiority in cavalry. Since all the roads were blocked, and no reinforcements could be got from the Province or from Italy, he sent across the Rhine to the German tribes which he had subdued in previous campaigns, and obtained some of their cavalry, attended by the light infantrymen who always fought among them. As their horses were unsuitable for the service required of them, he mounted the Germans on horses requisitioned from the military tribunes and other Roman Knights serving with him, and from the time-expired volunteers.

During all this time the Gauls were concentrating the troops which had been operating in the country of the Arverni and the cavalry levied from all over Gaul. A large number of cavalry had now been assembled; and while Caesar was marching through the south-eastern part of the Lingones' territory into that of the Sequani, so as to be in a better position for reinforcing the Provincial troops, Vercingetorix established himself in three camps about ten miles from the Romans, summoned his cavalry officers to a council, and addressed them. 'The hour of victory,' he said, 'has come. The Romans are fleeing to the Province and abandoning Gaul. But although this will assure our liberty for the moment, for future peace and security we need more than that; otherwise they will return in increased force and continue the war indefinitely. So let us attack them on the march while they are encumbered with their baggage. If the whole column of infantry halts to come to the rescue, they cannot continue their march; if – which I feel sure is more likely – they abandon the baggage and try to save their own skins, they will be stripped of the supplies without which they cannot live, and disgraced into the bargain. As for their cavalry, not a man of them will dare even to stir outside the column; you ought to know that as well as I do. To encourage your men I will draw up all my troops in front of the camps and overawe the enemy.' The cavalrymen cried that they should all swear a solemn oath not to allow any man who had not ridden twice through the enemy's column to enter his home again or to see his wife, children, or parents. This proposal was approved and every man was duly sworn.

Next day their cavalry was divided into three sections, two of which made a demonstration on either flank of the Roman column while the third barred the way of the vanguard. Caesar also divided his cavalry into three sections and ordered them to advance against the enemy. Simultaneous engagements took place all along the column, which halted and formed a hollow square with the baggage inside. If Caesar saw the cavalry in difficulties anywhere or especially hard pressed, he moved up some of the infantry and formed line of battle, which hindered the enemy's pursuit and encouraged the cavalry by the assurance of support. At length the German horse gained the top of some rising ground on the right, dislodged some of the enemy, and chased them with heavy loss to a river where Vercingetorix's infantry was posted. At this the rest of his cavalry fled, afraid of being surrounded, and were cut down in numbers all over the field. Three Aeduans of the highest rank were brought to Caesar as prisoners: the cavalry commander Cotus, who had been Convictolitavis' rival at the recent election; Cavarillus, who after Litaviccus deserted the Roman cause had been placed in command of the Aeduan infantry; and Eporedorix, leader of the Aedui in their war with the Sequani before Caesar's arrival in Gaul [70–65 B.C.].

§ 5 SIEGE AND CAPTURE OF ALESIA (52 B.C.)

AFTER the rout of his cavalry Vercingetorix withdrew his troops from their position in front of the camps and marched straight for Alesia, a stronghold of the Mandubii, leaving orders for the heavy baggage to be packed up immediately and brought after him. Caesar, after removing the army's baggage with a guard of two legions to the nearest hill, followed the enemy as long as daylight lasted and killed some three thousand of their rearguard. The next day he encamped near Alesia. The Gauls were terrified by the defeat of their cavalry, the arm on which they placed the greatest reliance. Accordingly, after reconnoitring the position of the town, Caesar called on the soldiers to undertake the heavy task of investing it with siege works. It was clearly impregnable except by blockade; for it stood at a high altitude on top of a hill washed by streams on the north and south, and closely surrounded by other hills as high as itself on every side except the west, where a plain extended for some three miles. The whole of the slope below the town ramparts on the east was occupied by a camp crowded with Gallic troops, who had fortified it with a trench and a six-foot wall. The siege works that the

Romans were starting to make had a circumference of ten miles. Eight camps were placed in strategic positions, linked together by fortifications along which twenty-three redoubts were built. The redoubts were occupied in the daytime by pickets, to prevent a surprise attack at any point; at night strong garrisons bivouacked in them with sentries on duty.

During the construction of these works a hard-fought cavalry battle took place in the three-mile stretch of plain between the hills. Seeing his men in difficulties, Caesar reinforced them with the German cavalry and drew up the legions in front of their camps. Encouraged by their support the cavalry routed the enemy, whose flight was impeded by their own numbers. Hotly pursued by the Germans right up to the fortifications of Vercingetorix's camp, they got jammed in the narrow entrances and suffered heavy losses. Some let their horses go and tried to scramble over the trench and climb the wall. Caesar then ordered the legions posted in front of their camp ramparts to be moved forward a little, whereupon the Gauls inside the camp became as frightened as their fleeing cavalry, and expecting an immediate attack shouted a call to arms. Some in their terror rushed right into the town, and Vercingetorix had the town gates shut for fear the camp should be left unguarded. Before retiring the Germans killed many of the fugitives and captured a number of horses.

Vercingetorix now decided to send out all his cavalry in the night, before the Roman entrenchments were completed. He bade them go every man to his own country and impress for service all the men of military age. He pointed out how much they owed him and urged them to consider his safety; after all he had done for the cause of national liberty, they ought not to abandon him to the cruel vengeance of the enemy. Moreover, if they were slack in doing their duty, they would condemn eighty thousand picked men to perish with him. He had taken stock of the corn, he said, and by strict rationing would have enough for a month – even a little longer, if the ration were reduced. With these instructions the cavalry was sent out in silence through a gap in the entrenchments shortly before midnight. Vercingetorix now ordered all the garrison, on pain of death, to surrender to him all the corn they had, and proceeded to dole it out a little at a time; the large quantity of livestock which had been brought in by the Mandubii was shared out individually at once. All the troops posted outside the town were taken inside. In this way Vercingetorix prepared to continue the struggle until the arrival of reinforcements.

On being informed of this by deserters and prisoners, Caesar started to construct more elaborate siege works. He dug a trench twenty feet wide, which, having perpendicular sides, was as broad at the bottom as at the top. The other works were kept some six hundred and fifty yards behind this trench, to protect them against surprise attacks; for as such a vast extent of ground had to be enclosed, and it was difficult to man the whole circuit, there would be a danger of the enemy's swooping down in force on the lines at night, or hurling javelins in the daytime when the men were tied down to their work. At this distance, therefore, Caesar dug two trenches of equal depth, each fifteen feet wide, and filled the inner one, where it crossed the low ground of the plain, with water diverted from the streams. Behind the trenches a palisaded rampart twelve feet high was erected, strengthened by a battlemented breastwork, with large forked branches projecting where it joined the rampart to hinder the enemy if they tried to climb over. Towers were placed at intervals of a hundred and thirty yards along the entire circuit of fortifications.

Parties had to be sent out constantly in search of timber

and corn; and as this duty took them far afield, it seriously reduced the number of men available for the construction of the huge fortifications. Moreover, the Gauls tried many times to attack the works, making furious sorties from several of the town gates at once. Caesar decided, therefore, that he must strengthen them still further, to render them defensible by a smaller force. Accordingly tree trunks or very stout boughs were cut, and their tops stripped of bark and sharpened; they were then fixed in long trenches dug five feet deep, with their lower ends made fast to one another to prevent their being pulled up, and the branches projecting. There were five rows in each trench, touching one another and interlaced, and anyone who went among them was likely to impale himself on the sharp points. The soldiers called them boundary posts. In front of them, arranged in diagonal rows forming quincunxes, were pits three feet deep, tapering gradually towards the bottom, in which were embedded smooth logs as thick as a man's thigh, with the ends sharpened and charred, and projecting only three inches above ground. To keep the logs firmly in position, earth was thrown into the pits and trodden down to a depth of one foot, the rest of the cavity being filled with twigs and brushwood to hide the trap. These were planted in groups, each containing eight rows three feet apart, and they were nicknamed lilies from their resemblance to that flower. In front of these again were blocks of wood a foot long with iron hooks fixed in them, called goads by the soldiers. These were sunk right into the ground, and strewn thickly everywhere.

When these defences were completed, Caesar constructed a similar line of fortifications facing outwards instead of inwards. This line described a circuit of fourteen miles, running along the flattest ground that could be found, and its purpose was to hold off attacks from outside, so that, even if Vercingetorix's cavalry assembled a very large force, the troops defending the siege works could not be surrounded. To avoid the danger of having to send out foraging parties when the relieving force was near, every man was ordered to provide himself with a month's supply of corn and fodder.

Meanwhile the Gallic tribes convened a council of their leaders, who decided not to adopt Vercingetorix's plan of calling up everyone able to bear arms, as they were afraid that in such a vast mixed host they would be unable to control their contingents or keep them separate, or to organize an adequate supply of corn. They therefore demanded a specified number of men from each tribe as follows:

Aedui (with their dependent tribes[1])	35,000
Arverni (with their dependent tribes[2])	35,000
Sequani, Senones, Bituriges, Santoni, Ruteni, Carnutes	12,000 each
Bellovaci,[3] Lemovices	10,000 each
Pictones, Turoni, Parisii, Helvetii	8,000 each
Suessiones, Ambiani, Mediomatrici, Petrocorii, Nervii, Morini, Nitiobroges, Aulerci Cenomani	5,000 each
Atrebates	4,000
Veliocasses, Aulerci Eburovices	3,000 each
Rauraci, Boii	1,000 each
Aremorican tribes[4]	20,000

When eight thousand horse and about two hundred and fifty thousand infantry had been assembled in the country of the Aedui, a start was made with the task of reviewing and counting them and choosing officers. The chief command

1. Segusiavi, Ambivareti, Aulerci Brannovices, Blannovii.

2. Eleuteti, Cadurci, Gabali, Vellavii.

3. The Bellovaci did not send their full contingent, because they said they intended to fight the Romans on their own account and in their own way, and would not take orders from anyone. At the request of Commius, however, and in consideration of their friendship with him, they sent 2,000 men along with the other contingents.

4. i.e. all the maritime tribes – Coriosolites, Redones, Ambibarii, Caleti, Osismi, Veneti, Lexovii, Venelli.

of this relieving army was entrusted to Commius the Atrebatian,[1] the Aeduans Viridomarus and Eporedorix, and the Arvernian Vercassivellaunus, a cousin of Vercingetorix. With them were associated representatives of the various tribes, to act as an advisory committee for the conduct of the campaign. They all started for Alesia full of enthusiasm and confidence. Every single man believed that the mere sight of such an enormous host of infantry and cavalry would be enough to make the enemy turn tail, especially as he would be attacked on two fronts – for the besieged would sally out from the town at the same time as the relieving force came into view.

In Alesia, however, they knew nothing of these preparations; the time by which they had expected relief was past and their corn was exhausted. So they summoned an assembly and considered what their fate was to be. Among the various speeches that were made – some advising capitulation, others recommending a sortie while they still had the strength – the speech of Critognatus, a noble Arvernian whose opinion commanded great respect, deserves to be recorded for its unparalleled cruelty and wickedness. 'I do not intend,' he said, 'to make any comment on the views of those who advise "capitulation" – the name they give to the most shameful submission to enslavement; in my opinion they ought not to be regarded as citizens or allowed in the assembly. I will concern myself only with those who advocate a sortie. You all approve their suggestion, as showing that we have not forgotten our traditional courage. But it

1. In former years Commius had rendered Caesar loyal and useful service in Britain (see above, pages 120, 123, 139), and in return Caesar had ordered that his tribe should be immune from taxation and have its independence restored, and had made Commius suzerain over the Morini. But the whole Gallic people were so united in their determination to liberate themselves and recover their former military prestige, that they allowed no favours or recollection of friendship to influence them, and all devoted their energies and resources to the prosecution of the war.

is not courage, it is weakness, to be unable to endure a short period of privation. It is easier to find men who will voluntarily risk death than men who will bear suffering patiently. Even so, I would support their proposal – so much do I respect their authority – if it involved no loss beyond that of our own lives. But in making our decision we must consider all our fellow-countrymen, whom we have called to our aid. If eighty thousand of us are killed in one battle, what heart do you suppose our relatives and kinsmen will have when they are compelled to fight almost over our corpses? Do not leave them to continue the struggle alone when for your sakes they have counted their own danger as nothing, and do not by folly and rashness, or by lack of re-solution, ruin all Gaul and subject it to perpetual servitude. Because they have not come on the appointed day, do you doubt their loyalty or constancy to our cause? What? Do you suppose the Romans are working day after day on those outer fortifications to amuse themselves? Since our countrymen cannot get messengers through the cordon that is drawn round us, to assure you that they are coming soon, believe what the enemy are telling you by their actions: for it is the fear of their coming that keeps the Romans hard at work night and day. What counsel, then, have I to offer? I think we should do what our ancestors did in a war that was much less serious than this one [109–102 B.C.]. When they were forced into their strongholds by the Cimbri and Teutoni, and overcome like us by famine, instead of sur-rendering they kept themselves alive by eating the flesh of those who were too old or too young to fight. Even if we had no precedent for such an action, I think that when our liberty is at stake it would be a noble example to set to our descendants. For this is a life and death struggle, quite un-like the war with the Cimbri, who, though they devastated Gaul and grievously afflicted her, did eventually evacuate our country and migrate elsewhere, and left us free men,

to live on our own land under our own laws and in possession of our rights. The Romans, we know, have a very
different purpose. Envy is the motive that inspires them.
They know that we have won renown by our military
strength, and so they mean to instal themselves in our lands
and towns and fasten the yoke of slavery on us for ever.
That is how they have always treated conquered enemies.
You do not know much, perhaps, of the condition of distant peoples; but you need only look at the part of Gaul on
your own borders that has been made into a Roman province, with new laws and institutions imposed upon it,
ground beneath the conqueror's iron heel in perpetual
servitude.'

At the conclusion of the debate it was decided to send out
of the town those whom age or infirmity incapacitated for
fighting. Critognatus' proposal was to be adopted only as
a last resort – if the reinforcements still failed to arrive, and
things got so bad that it was a choice between that and sur-
rendering, or accepting dictated peace terms. So the Man-
dubian population, who had received the other Gauls into
their town, were compelled to leave it with their wives and
children. They came up to the Roman fortifications and
with tears besought the soldiers to take them as slaves and
relieve their hunger. But Caesar posted guards on the rampart with orders to refuse them admission.

Meanwhile Commius and the other commanders arrived before Alesia with the whole of their relief force and
encamped on a hill outside the Roman lines, not more than
a mile away. Next day they brought out their cavalry and
occupied all the plain – three miles long, it will be remembered. Their infantry was moved away a short distance and
posted on the slopes of the hill. As the town commanded a
view over the plain, the besieged saw the troops who had
come to their relief, and all crowding together in excitement rejoiced and congratulated one another on their

deliverance. Then they brought out their forces, posted them in front of the town, and filled the nearest trench with fascines and earth, ready for a sortie and all the perils it would entail.

Caesar placed the whole of his infantry along the two lines of entrenchments, so that in case of need every man could know his post and hold it. He then ordered out the cavalry to battle. The plain was visible from all the camps on the surrounding hill-tops, and the whole army was intently watching to see the result of the engagement. The Gauls had placed archers and light-armed infantrymen here and there among their cavalry, to support them if they had to give ground and to help them meet our cavalry charges. These took a number of our men by surprise and forced them to retire wounded from the battle. Feeling confident that their cavalry was winning, since it was obvious that our force was heavily outnumbered, the Gauls on every side – both the besieged and the relieving force – encouraged them with shouts and yells. As the action was taking place in full view of everyone, so that no gallant exploit and no act of cowardice could pass unnoticed, the thirst for glory and the fear of disgrace was an incentive to both sides. They had fought from midday till near sunset and the issue was still in doubt, when the German horse massed all their squadrons at one point, charged the Gauls, and hurled them back. When their cavalry broke and fled, the archers were surrounded and killed. The rest of our horsemen advanced from other points, pursued the fugitives right up to their camp, and gave them no chance of rallying. At this the Gauls who had come out of the town went back in, bitterly disappointed and now almost depairing of success.

After an interval of only one day, however, during which they prepared a great quantity of fascines, ladders, and grappling-hooks, the relieving army moved silently out of camp at midnight and advanced towards the entrenchments in the plain. Suddenly raising a shout to inform the besieged of their approach, they began to throw fascines into the trenches, drove the Romans from the rampart with arrows and stones discharged from slings or by hand, and employed every other method of assault. Meanwhile, hearing the distant shouting, Vercingetorix sounded the trumpet and led his men out of the town. The Roman troops moved up to the posts previously allotted to them at the entrenchments, and kept the Gauls at a distance with slingstones, bullets, large stones, and stakes which were placed ready at intervals along the rampart, while the artillery pelted them with missiles. It was too dark to see, and casualties were heavy on both sides. The generals Mark Antony and Gaius Trebonius, who had been detailed for the defence of this particular sector, reinforced the points where they knew the troops were hard pressed with men brought up from redoubts well behind the fighting line. As long as the Gauls were at a distance from the entrenchments, the rain of javelins which they discharged gained them some advantage. But when they came nearer they suddenly found themselves pierced by the 'goads' or tumbled into the pits and impaled themselves, while others were killed by heavy siege-spears discharged from the rampart and towers. Their losses were everywhere heavy, and when dawn came they had failed to penetrate the defences at any point. Afraid, therefore, of having their right flank turned by an attack from the camps on higher ground, they fell back upon their remaining troops. The besieged lost much time in bringing out the implements that Vercingetorix had prepared for the sortie and in filling up the first stretches of trench, and before they reached the main fortifications heard of the retreat of the relief force. So they returned into the town without effecting anything.

After this second costly repulse the Gauls held a council of war. By calling in men familiar with the ground they ascertained the positions of the higher camps and the nature of their defences. There was a hill on the north which had such a wide sweep that the Romans were unable to include it within the circuit of the siege works, and were compelled to place the camp there on a slight slope, in what would ordinarily be considered a bad position. It was garrisoned by two legions under the generals Gaius Antistius Reginus and Gaius Caninius Rebilus. After sending out scouts to reconnoitre the ground, the enemy commanders selected from their whole force sixty thousand men belonging to the tribes with the highest reputation for courage, secretly decided on their objective and plan of action, and ordered them to begin an attack at noon under Vercassivellaunus the Arvernian, one of their four generals and a relative of Vercingetorix. Leaving camp in the early evening, he almost completed his march before daybreak, and ordered his troops to rest under cover of the hill after their hard night's work. When he saw that it was getting on for midday, he marched towards the Roman camp referred to above, while at the same time the Gallic cavalry moved up to the fortifications in the plain and the rest of the army made a demonstration in front of their own camp.

On seeing these troop movements from the citadel of Alesia, Vercingetorix sallied out with the fascines, poles, sappers' huts, grappling-hooks, and other implements which he had prepared for the purpose. There was fighting simultaneously all over the field and the Gauls tried every expedient, concentrating on the weakest points of the defences. Distributed as they were along lines of such length, the Romans found it difficult to meet simultaneous attacks in many different places. They were unnerved, too, by the shouts they could hear behind them as they fought, which indicated that their lives were not in their own hands, but depended on the bravery of others. It is nearly always invisible dangers that are most terrifying.

Caesar found a good observation point, from which he

could follow the actions in every part of the field, and sent help where it was needed. Both sides realized that this was the time, above all others, for a supreme effort. The Gauls knew that unless they broke through the lines they were lost; the Romans, if they could hold their ground, looked forward to the end of all their hardships. The danger was greatest at the fortifications on the hill where Vercassivellaunus had been sent.[1] The unfavourable downward slope of the ground told heavily against the Romans. Some of the Gauls flung javelins, while others advanced to the attack with shields locked together above their heads, fresh troops continually relieving them when they were tired. All of them threw earth on to the fortifications, which enabled them to climb the rampart and covered the obstacles hidden in the ground. At length, when Caesar saw that his men were weakening and running short of weapons, he sent Labienus to their relief with six cohorts, telling him to remain on the defensive if possible; but if he could not hold the camp by any other means, he must withdraw some cohorts from their positions and counter-attack. Caesar himself visited other parts of the lines, urging the men to hold out: on that day, he said, on that very hour, depended the fruits of all their previous battles.

The besieged Gauls despaired at last of penetrating the huge fortifications in the plain and attempted to storm one of the steep ascents. Carrying there all the implements they had provided themselves with, they dislodged the defenders of the towers with a hail of missiles, filled the trenches with earth and fascines, and tore down the palisade and breastwork with their hooks. Caesar first sent some cohorts to the rescue under young Brutus, then others under the general Gaius Fabius; finally, as the struggle grew fiercer, he led up a fresh detachment in person. These troops renewed the fight and succeeded in repulsing the attack.

1. See above, page 230.

Caesar now started for the sector to which he had sent Labienus, taking four cohorts from the nearest redoubt, and ordering a part of the cavalry to follow him; another detachment was to ride round the outer lines and attack the enemy in the rear. Labienus, when he found that neither ramparts nor trenches could check the Gauls' furious onslaught, had fortunately been able to collect eleven cohorts from the nearest posts, and at this moment sent to tell Caesar that he considered the time for decisive action was at hand. Caesar put on speed to get there in time for the fight. The enemy knew that he was coming by the scarlet cloak which he always wore in action to mark his identity; and when they saw the cavalry squadrons and cohorts following him down the slopes, which were plainly visible from the heights on which they stood, they joined battle. Both sides raised a cheer, which was answered by the men on the rampart and all along the entrenchments. The Romans dropped their spears and fought with their swords. Suddenly the Gauls saw the cavalry in their rear and fresh cohorts coming up in front. They broke and fled, but found their retreat cut off by the cavalry and were mown down. Sedullus, chieftain and commander of the Lemovices, was killed, Vercassivellaunus was taken prisoner in the rout, seventy-four standards were brought in to Caesar, and only a few men of all the large army got back unhurt to their camp. When the Gauls in the town saw their countrymen being slaughtered in flight, they gave up hope and recalled their troops from the entrenchments. The relieving forces immediately fled from their camp; and if the Romans had not been tired out after a long day's work, during which they had been repeatedly summoned to the relief of hard-pressed comrades, the enemy's army might have been annihilated. As it was, a large number were taken or killed by the cavalry, which was sent in pursuit and came up with their rear soon after midnight. The survivors dispersed to their homes.

The next day Vercingetorix addressed an assembly. 'I did not undertake the war,' he said, 'for private ends, but in the cause of national liberty. And since I must now accept my fate, I place myself at your disposal. Make amends to the Romans by killing me or surrender me alive as you think best.' A deputation was sent to refer the matter to Caesar, who ordered the arms to be handed over and the tribal chiefs brought out to him. He seated himself at the fortification in front of his camp, and there the chiefs were brought; Vercingetorix was delivered up, and the arms laid down. Caesar set apart the Aeduan and Arvernian prisoners, in the hope that he could use them to regain the allegiance of their tribes; the rest he distributed as booty to the entire army, allotting one to every man.

He then went to the country of the Aedui and received their submission. Envoys from the Arverni waited upon him there, undertaking to obey any orders he gave, and were commanded to supply a large number of hostages. Some twenty thousand prisoners were restored to the Aedui and Arverni. Finally, the legions were distributed in winter quarters. Two legions and some cavalry were sent to the Sequani in charge of Labienus, with Marcus Sempronius Rutilus under him; two were placed under Fabius and Basilus among the Remi, to protect them from injury at the hands of their neighbours the Bellovaci; Reginus was sent to the Ambivareti, Titus Sextius to the Bituriges, and Caninius to the Ruteni, each with one legion; and Cicero and Sulpicius Rufus were quartered in Aeduan territory at Chalon-sur-Saône and Mâcon, to collect grain. Caesar himself decided to winter at Bibracte. When the results of this year's campaign were reported in his dispatches, a thanksgiving of twenty days was celebrated in Rome.

CHAPTER VIII

THE FINAL REBELLION
(52–51 B.C.)

§ 1 REVOLTS OF THE BITURIGES, CARNUTES, AND
BELLOVACI (52–51 B.C.)

THE whole of Gaul was now conquered. Caesar had
been fighting almost continuously since the summer
of the previous year, and after such gruelling work wanted
to recruit his soldiers' strength by a winter's rest. But he
heard that many of the tribes were plotting together and
concerting plans for a renewal of hostilities. His informants
pointed out the most probable explanation of this: the
Gauls all realized that they could not resist the Romans even
with the largest possible army, if it was concentrated in one
place, but thought that if a number of tribes made simultaneous attacks in different places, the Romans would not
have enough men or resources to meet them all in time.
Any tribe which had to suffer in consequence, it was argued,
must be prepared to accept its fate, if by delaying the enemy
it could enable the rest to assert their liberty.

Caesar did not want to let the Gauls be confirmed in this
idea. So leaving his quaestor Mark Antony in charge of his
headquarters at Bibracte, he set out with a cavalry escort
on the 29th of December to join the 13th legion – quartered
in the territory of the Bituriges not far from the Aeduan
frontier – and reinforced it with the 11th, which was nearest to it. He left two cohorts from each legion to guard the
baggage and led the rest into the most fertile part of the
Bituriges' country. This tribe possessed a number of towns
and an extensive territory – too big for the single legion
quartered among them to be able to prevent them from

plotting and planning war. Caesar's sudden march found them unprepared and scattered, tilling the fields without any thought of danger, and naturally they were caught by the cavalry before they could take refuge in the towns. They had not even the usual warning of a hostile invasion – the sight of burning buildings. For Caesar had commanded that nothing should be set on fire, in order to avoid giving the alarm, and to save the corn and hay, which he would need if he decided to advance far. The capture of thousands of prisoners threw the Bituriges into a panic, and those who managed to escape the first onset fled to the neighbouring tribes, either trusting to personal friends to take them in or hoping to be protected by the tribal authorities, since all alike were leagued together against the Romans. But they were disappointed; Caesar frustrated their design by making forced marches in every direction, which kept all the tribes so busy protecting themselves that they had no time to think about anyone else's safety. By this prompt action he confirmed the friendly tribes in their loyalty and frightened the waverers into accepting peace terms. When the Bituriges saw that his clemency offered them a chance of regaining his friendship, and that no punishment was inflicted on the neighbouring tribes which submitted and gave hostages, they availed themselves of the opportunity to follow the others' example.

As a reward to the soldiers for enduring such a hard campaign with the utmost patience and perseverance – marching through the short winter days over very bad roads in intolerable cold – Caesar promised each soldier a gratuity of two pounds in lieu of booty, and each centurion ten pounds. He then sent the legions back to their winter quarters and returned to Bibracte after an absence of forty days.

While he was engaged there in hearing cases, envoys came from the Bituriges, complaining that the Carnutes had attacked them and asking for help. At this, although he had been only eighteen days at Bibracte, he summoned the 14th and 6th legions – the two that were quartered on the Saône to procure corn[1] – and marched out to punish the Carnutes. When they heard that a Roman army was coming, they took warning from the fate that had befallen other tribes: abandoning their villages and towns, where they were living in small buildings hastily constructed to meet the immediate need of winter shelter (for their recent defeat had involved the loss of many of their towns), they fled in all directions. Caesar did not want to expose his men to the rigours of the weather, which was particularly bad just then, and therefore encamped at Cenabum, the capital of the Carnutes. Some of the legionaries were lodged in houses belonging to the Gauls, the rest were protected by shelters erected to cover the tents and hastily thatched. The cavalry and auxiliary troops, however, were sent out wherever the enemy was reported to have gone – a policy justified by its results, for they generally returned loaded with spoil. The Carnutes suffered from the severity of the winter, and were greatly terrified; driven from their homes, they dared not stay long anywhere, and the woods did not give them much shelter in such inclement weather. At length, after sustaining very heavy losses, they scattered among the tribes on their borders.

At this season, when campaigning was so difficult, Caesar thought it sufficient to prevent an attack by dispersing the enemy forces that were assembling; and he was now reasonably certain that no serious outbreak could occur there before the summer. So putting the two legions he had with him in charge of Trebonius, he installed them in quarters at Cenabum, and turned to the next matter requiring attention. Several deputations had come from the Remi, warning him that the Bellovaci – the best fighters in the whole of Gaul, surpassing even the rest of the Belgae – were mobilizing

1. See above, page 233.

in conjunction with their neighbours and concentrating troops under their own leader Correus and Commius the Atrebatian. Their intention, it was said, was to make a concerted attack on the Suessiones, who had been placed under the suzerainty of the Remi. Caesar considered that both honour and prudence required him to protect allies who had done Rome good service. He therefore called out the 11th legion again, instructed Gaius Fabius by letter to march his two legions into the territory of the Suessiones, and sent to Labienus for one of the two under his command. In this way, as far as the distribution of the winter quarters and military necessity allowed, he called on the legions by turns to share the labour of campaigning, while he himself never rested.

When these troops were assembled he marched against the Bellovaci, encamped in their territory, and sent squadrons of cavalry in all directions to take some prisoners, from whom he could discover the enemy's intentions. After executing his orders the cavalry reported that only a few men were found in the houses, and that these had not stayed behind to till the fields (for the whole country had been completely evacuated), but had been sent back to act as spies. Caesar asked the prisoners where the main body of the Bellovaci was and what plans they had formed. They told him that all their men capable of bearing arms, as well as the Ambiani, Aulerci, Caleti, Veliocasses, and Atrebates, were encamped together on some high ground in a wood surrounded by a marsh, and had conveyed all their property into more distant woods. Of the many chiefs who were in favour of rebellion, they said, the people paid most attention to Correus, because they knew that he loathed the very name of Rome. A few days before, Commius had left the camp to get help from the German tribes, who lived quite near by and had unlimited man-power. Finally they explained the plan that had been unanimously approved by the chiefs with the enthusiastic support of the people. If the report that Caesar was coming with only three legions proved to be true, they intended to offer battle, in order to avoid having to fight later on under harder and more un-favourable conditions, when the whole Roman army was in the field. If, however, he brought a larger force, they would remain in the position that they had chosen and by means of ambushes prevent the Romans from getting corn, forage (which at that time of year was scarce and could be found only here and there), and other supplies.

These facts were established by the testimony of a number of prisoners, and the enemy's plan of campaign impressed Caesar as being well conceived and very different from the rash counsels which are characteristic of Barbarian peoples. He therefore decided to do his best to bring them quickly to battle by making them think that they could afford to despise the force he was leading against them. Actually he had three veteran legions of exceptional valour – the 7th, 8th, and 9th – and also the 11th, a legion composed of picked men in the prime of life, who had now seen seven years' service and of whom he had the highest hopes, although they had not yet the same experience or reputation for courage as the others. Summoning his offi-cers, he communicated to them all the information he had received, and told them to encourage the men by passing it on to them. In the hope of enticing the enemy to fight by giving the impression that he had only three legions, he made the three veteran legions march side by side in front, followed by the baggage-train – which even when placed all together was quite small, as is usual in such expeditions – with the 11th legion bringing up the rear. In this way the enemy would be able to see only the number of legions they had declared themselves willing to encounter.

The column came into view earlier than the Gauls had expected. They suddenly caught sight of it advancing with a firm step and formed almost into a hollow square as if for immediate action. In spite of the bold front they were reported to be showing, they did not quit the high ground – whether frightened at the prospect of an engagement, or taken aback by our sudden appearance, or waiting to see what we would do – but merely deployed in front of their camp. Caesar had intended to join battle; but he was surprised to see how strong their forces were, and therefore encamped opposite them on the other side of a deep but not very wide valley. The Roman camp had a twelve-foot rampart with a breastwork of proportionate height, two trenches fifteen feet wide with perpendicular sides, and three-storeyed towers at frequent intervals, joined together by floored galleries protected on the outside by wicker breastworks. Thus, in addition to the double trench, it could be guarded by two rows of defenders – one on the galleries, where they were less exposed on account of the height, and could therefore hurl their missiles with greater confidence and make them carry farther; the other on the actual rampart, where, although nearer the enemy, they were protected by the galleries from falling missiles. The gateways were fitted with doors and flanked with specially high towers. These elaborate defences had two purposes. Caesar hoped they would make the Gauls imagine that he was afraid, and so give them greater confidence. At the same time they would make the camp so strong that it could be defended by a small force, while the rest scoured the country in search of forage and corn.

Frequent skirmishes took place between small groups of men who ran forward into the marshy ground between the camps, and sometimes the marsh was crossed, either by our Gallic and German auxiliaries, who then pursued the enemy vigorously, or by the enemy themselves, who in turn drove our men back some distance. In the course of our daily foraging expeditions it inevitably happened – since the farms from which the hay was obtained were few and far between – that isolated parties were surrounded in places difficult to get out of; and although this only meant the loss of a few servants and animals, it raised foolish hopes in the minds of the Bellovaci, especially when Commius arrived back from his mission to the German tribes[1] with a squadron of horsemen. There were only five hundred of them, but the mere fact that German aid had come was enough to make these natives cock-a-hoop.

As the days went by, the enemy still stayed in their camp, which, protected as it was by the marsh and the strength of its position, obviously could not be stormed without a murderous struggle. To invest it, a larger force was needed. Accordingly, orders were sent to Trebonius to summon with all speed the 13th legion, which was wintering in charge of Titus Sextius among the Bituriges, and having thus made up an army of three legions to join Caesar by forced marches. Meanwhile Caesar used the large number of cavalry which he had called up from the Remi, Lingones, and other tribes, to take turns in escorting the foraging-parties and repelling any sudden attacks made upon them. After doing this duty for some days they grew careless, as generally happens when a routine is continued for any length of time. The Bellovaci discovered where they posted themselves each day, and placed an ambush of picked infantrymen in a spot screened by trees. Next day they sent some of their own cavalry there to decoy our men into the ambush, so that they could be surrounded and attacked. It happened to be the Remi who fell into the trap, as it was their turn of duty that day. Suddenly catching sight of the small party of enemy horsemen, and thinking themselves quite safe because of their superior numbers, they gave chase too eagerly and found themselves encircled by the infantrymen. Alarmed at this they retreated more

1. See above, page 237.

precipitately than is customary in a cavalry action, with the loss of their commander Vertiscus, the chief magistrate of the tribe, who was almost too old to keep his saddle but, like a good Gaul, would not plead age as an excuse for declining the command and insisted on taking part in the fight. This success, involving the death of a principal magistrate and general of the Remi, filled the enemy with pride and excitement, and our men were taught by their misfortune to reconnoitre more carefully before establishing their posts and to use more discretion in pursuing a retreating foe.

Fighting went on daily, within sight of both camps, at places where the marsh was fordable. In one of these encounters the whole of the light infantry which had been brought from Germany to fight among the cavalry went boldly over the marsh, killed the few Gauls who opposed them, and vigorously pursued all the rest. The enemy was panic-stricken. Not only those who were attacked at close quarters or wounded by missiles, but even the reserves posted, as usual, at a distance, fled like cowards, and, dislodged from every piece of high ground where they tried to make a stand, did not stop until they reached their camp. Some were too much ashamed to show their faces in camp, and ran farther still. Their perilous experience filled the whole army of the Bellovaci with dismay; for these Gauls, whom any trifling success made so vainglorious, were just as easily frightened by the slightest reverse.

For several days they still remained in their camp. But when their leaders heard that Trebonius and his legions were close at hand, they were afraid of being blockaded as Vercingetorix was at Alesia, and therefore sent away by night all who were a hindrance – those who were too old or too weak to fight, and those who had no arms – and all their heavy baggage. They were still busy forming up the disorderly train of frightened non-combatants (for Gauls always go with a long procession of wagons, even when they are supposed to be travelling light) when daylight overtook them, and they had to draw up a body of troops in front of the camp to prevent the Romans from pursuing the column and give it time to get some distance away. So long as these troops stood on the defensive Caesar did not think it prudent to attack them, as it would mean advancing up a steep hill; at the same time he wanted to move his legions far enough forward to threaten them and make it dangerous for them to leave their position. The marsh between the two camps was difficult to cross and would hinder a quick pursuit of the enemy. On the other side of it, however, was a hill almost touching that on which the Gauls' camp stood, being separated from it only by a small ravine. Accordingly he laid causeways over the marsh, led the legions across, and hastened to reach a plateau on the hill-top, which was protected on two sides by steep slopes. After re-forming the troops there he advanced to the edge and drew up a battle-line in a place where the closely packed enemy formations would be within range of his artillery.

Confident in the strength of their position, the Gauls were willing to fight if the Romans tried to climb the hill; but they dared not disperse their forces by sending detachments here and there, for fear of impairing their morale, and therefore stayed drawn up where they were. When Caesar saw that they would not budge he measured out ground for a camp, and keeping twenty cohorts ready for action set the rest to work at making the fortifications. When these were complete he drew up the infantry in front of them and placed pickets of cavalry in various spots with their horses ready bridled. The Bellovaci could not spend the night where they were – indeed they could not safely remain much longer. As they saw that the Romans were ready to pursue if they moved, they employed a ruse to get away. They had in the camp a large number of bundles of straw and twigs, which they had been using to sit on. These were passed along from hand to hand and placed in front of their battle-line. Towards evening the word was given to set fire to them all together, so that a curtain of flame suddenly hid their entire army from the Romans, and the natives seized the opportunity to run away as hard as they could. Although the barrier of fire prevented Caesar from actually seeing them go, he guessed that its purpose was to cover their escape and therefore sent some cavalry in pursuit. He also moved the legions forward – with caution, because he feared a trap; the enemy's intention might be to hold their ground and inveigle him into a bad position. Most of the cavalrymen were afraid to enter the dense ring of smoke and fire, and those who were bold enough to attempt it found that they could scarcely see their own horses' heads. They too were suspicious of a trap, and so left the enemy to retire unmolested. This retreat, dictated by fear but executed with the utmost ingenuity, enabled them to reach, without any loss, a very strong position barely ten miles farther on, where they encamped.

From there the Bellovaci kept sending out parties of horse and foot, which by laying ambushes here and there inflicted heavy casualties on the Roman foragers, and these attacks became more and more frequent. Eventually Caesar learnt from a prisoner that Correus had assembled a picked force of six thousand of his bravest infantrymen and a thousand cavalry, with which he intended to lay an ambush at a place where he expected the abundance of corn and hay would attract the Romans. Accordingly, the cavalry which always escorted the Roman foragers was sent there, with some light-armed auxiliary infantry dispersed among its ranks. Caesar himself led out an unusually strong legionary force, with which he approached as near the place as possible.

The Gauls had chosen for their ambush a plain not more

than a square mile in extent, completely enclosed by almost impenetrable woods and a very deep river, and had surrounded it with a cordon. Our men knew what to expect and – being well armed and aware that the legions were coming up behind them – were ready to face any attack. So they rode on to the plain squadron by squadron. Correus thought this was his chance to strike. He came out of hiding, with a small force at first, and charged the nearest units. Our men met his onslaught resolutely and did not crowd together – a mistake frequently made in cavalry engagements through fright: in a tightly packed mass of horsemen losses are inevitable. The squadrons took up separate positions and small groups of the men fought by turns, covering one another's flanks so that the Gauls could not surround them. While Correus' force was still engaged, the rest of the enemy cavalry came out of the woods. Hotly contested fights took place in various parts of the field and continued for a long while without decisive result, until the main body of the enemy's infantry gradually emerged from hiding in battle-formation and forced our cavalry to retreat. The cavalry were quickly supported by the light infantry sent up with them in advance of the legions; the infantrymen dispersed themselves among the squadrons and fought with great steadiness. For some time the battle was even. Eventually it took the usual course of such engagements; the very fact that our troops had survived the initial shock without disaster, though ambushed and taken by surprise, gave them an advantage. Meanwhile the legions were drawing near. Messengers kept arriving, and both sides heard simultaneously that the commander-in-chief was at hand with his troops prepared for action. At this our men fought with redoubled energy, sure of the legions' support in case the battle still dragged on, but determined to win without it if they could, so as to keep all the glory for themselves. The enemy's spirits were dashed and they tried to escape in every direction. Escape was impossible, for they were trapped by the very same obstacles with which they had hoped to entrap the Romans. Demoralized by their defeat, however, and dismayed by the loss of more than half their number, they fled haphazard towards the woods or the river, only to be slaughtered by pursuers following on their heels. But no misfortune could break Correus' resolution. He would neither leave the battle nor take to the woods nor surrender when offered quarter, but fought on heroically, dealing out wounds right and left, until the victorious Romans were provoked by anger to shoot him down.

The battle was only just over when Caesar arrived with the legions. He expected that the news of such a disastrous defeat would make the Gauls abandon their camp, which was said to be only about eight miles from the scene of the carnage. Accordingly, although his passage was obstructed by the river, he got his army across and advanced. Meanwhile a handful of wounded fugitives, whom the woods had protected from destruction, arrived at the enemy's camp with the first news of the disaster. When they heard that everything had gone wrong, that Correus was dead, and their cavalry and the flower of their infantry lost, the Bellovaci and their allies made sure that the Romans must be marching to attack them. A mass meeting was hastily summoned by trumpet-calls, and the soldiers insisted that envoys and hostages must be sent to Caesar. When this was unanimously agreed to, Commius fled to the German tribes from whom he had borrowed reinforcements. The rest dispatched envoys on the spot and begged Caesar to be content with the punishment that they had undergone – a heavier one, they were sure, than a man of his clemency and humanity would ever inflict in cold blood, even upon a foe who had not suffered already. 'Our strength was broken,' they said, 'in the action against your cavalry. We lost many thousands of picked soldiers – indeed, hardly any escaped to tell the tale of the massacre. However, we must be thankful for small mercies at such a time, and the battle has at least brought us one piece of good fortune: Correus, the popular agitator who was responsible for the war, has been killed. While he lived, our senate was always overruled by the ignorant proletariat.' In reply to this appeal Caesar pointed out to the envoys that the Bellovaci had taken part in the general rising of the previous year, and had persisted in their hostility more stubbornly than any of the other tribes, instead of being brought to reason by their surrender. It was very easy of course to lay the blame for their misdeeds at a dead man's door; but no man could be powerful enough, with only the feeble assistance of the populace, to start and carry on a war against the will of the tribal leaders and in the face of opposition from the council and all patriotic citizens. However, he would be content with the punishment that they had already brought on themselves.

Returning to their countrymen at night, the envoys reported Caesar's reply and obtained the required number of hostages. The deputies of the other tribes, who had been waiting to see what success the Bellovaci had, now hastened to make their own submission, to supply the necessary hostages, and to comply with the demands made upon them. Only Commius kept away, being afraid to entrust his life to any man. For the year before, when Caesar was away holding the assizes in northern Italy, Labienus had discovered that Commius was intriguing with various tribes and plotting against Caesar, and decided that it would be no treachery to destroy such a traitor. It was useless to summon him to the camp; he would not have come, and the summons would have put him on his guard. So Labienus sent Volusenus with orders to stage a sham interview and have him put to death. Some centurions specially picked for the purpose went with him. At the interview Volusenus gave the prearranged signal by grasping Commius' hand, but the centurion who made the first sword-thrust failed to dispatch him, only inflicting a severe head wound; either his nerve failed him because he was unused to such work, or Commius' friends were too quick for him. Both sides drew their weapons, but more with the object of getting safely away than of fighting; for the Romans thought that Commius was mortally wounded, and the Gauls, realizing that they had been led into a trap, were afraid that more men might be concealed somewhere. After this experience Commius was said to have resolved never to come again into the presence of any Roman.

§ 2 THE LAST ENCOUNTERS; CAPTURE OF
UXELLODUNUM (51 B.C.)

Now that all the most warlike tribes had been conquered, there was no further prospect of organized resistance anywhere. But as many of the natives were leaving the towns and cultivated lands to avoid living under Roman rule as long as they could, Caesar resolved to send detachments into various parts of the country. He kept the 12th legion with him, and his quaestor Mark Antony. Gaius Fabius was sent with two legions and five cohorts to the extreme west of Gaul, because some of the tribes there were reported to be in arms, and the two legions which Caninius had in the district, being under strength, might not be able to hold them in check. Labienus was summoned to join Caesar, while the 15th legion, which had wintered under Labienus' command, was sent to northern Italy to protect the citizen colonies there from a repetition of the injury done to the people of Trieste the previous year, when a sudden raid by the Barbarians took them by surprise.

Caesar himself set out to lay waste and plunder the territory of Ambiorix the Eburonian, who fled in terror and so could not be forced into submission. Caesar thought that the next best way of obtaining the satisfaction that his honour demanded was to strip the country of inhabitants, cattle, and buildings, so thoroughly that any of the Eburones who had the good fortune to escape would loathe Ambiorix for bringing such calamities upon them, and never allow him to return. Detachments of legionary or auxiliary troops went all over the country, killing or capturing large numbers of the natives, burning the homesteads, and carrying off plunder, until it was completely devastated. Caesar then sent Labienus with two legions against the Treveri – a people who, living so near the German border, were accustomed to fighting every day of their lives; they were nearly as fierce and uncivilized as the Germans themselves, and would never do as they were told unless compelled by armed force.

Meanwhile Caninius received letters and messages from Duratius – always a faithful ally of Rome, although a part of his fellow-countrymen had revolted – telling him that a great crowd of the enemy had assembled in the country of the Pictones. He therefore set out for the town of Lemonum. On approaching it he obtained more exact information from prisoners. Duratius, they said, was besieged in the town by an army of many thousands under Dumnacus, commander of the Andes. Caninius dared not risk an engagement, as his legions were below their proper strength, and therefore took up a strong position and encamped. On learning of the legions' approach, Dumnacus turned his whole force round to face them and tried to storm the camp. After spending several days in this attempt, however, and losing a large number of men without being able to break the defences at any point, he returned to the siege of Lemonum.

Fabius received the submission of a number of tribes and took hostages from them as a guarantee. On the arrival of a dispatch from Caninius reporting what was happening among the Pictones, he set out to rescue Duratius. At this, Dumnacus decided that his position was hopeless; he could not withstand an attack from outside and at the same time keep an eye open for any threatening movement by the garrison of Lemonum. So he hastily retired; his only chance of safety, he thought, was to get his troops across the Loire, which was too wide to cross except by one of the bridges. Fabius had not yet come within sight of his enemy or effected a junction with Caninius. But the information he received from people acquainted with the district led him to expect that the frightened Gauls would take precisely the direction which they actually were taking; so he marched towards the same bridge as Dumnacus was making for. He sent his cavalry ahead of the legions, but told them to be careful not to go too far; they must be able, without tiring their horses, to get back to the camp which they were to share with the legions. These orders were duly carried out. The cavalry came up with the rear of Dumnacus' column and attacked it. The fleeing Gauls were demoralized and hampered by the baggage that they were carrying; many of them were killed, and a quantity of booty was taken. After this success the cavalry made their way back to the camp.

The next night Fabius sent the cavalry out with orders to engage the enemy and delay their march until he came up. The cavalry commander, Quintus Atius Varus, a man of exceptional courage and intelligence, impressed upon his men the importance of following these instructions. On catching up with Dumnacus' column he placed some of his squadrons in convenient positions to act as reserves, and with the rest engaged the enemy's cavalry. The latter joined battle with unusual confidence; for the whole of the Gallic column halted, so that the infantry could come to the support of their cavalry against ours. The fight was hotly contested. Our men regarded the enemy with contempt after beating them the day before; and, knowing that the legions were close behind, they were ashamed to give ground and wanted to finish the battle by themselves. So they struggled with desperate courage against the infantry. As for the enemy, their experience on the previous day led them to assume that our troops would not be reinforced, and they thought they had an opportunity of annihilating our cavalry. As the struggle proved long and hard, Dumnacus drew up his infantry in regular line of battle, so that they could give protection to each squadron of cavalry as need arose. Suddenly the serried ranks of our legions came into view. The sight gave the enemy such a shock that cavalry and infantry alike fled helter-skelter with loud cries of terror, leaving the baggage-train in complete confusion. Our cavalry were now rewarded for their heroic efforts to over-come the enemy's resistance. Beside themselves with joy at their success, they rode forward everywhere with rousing cheers, encircled the retreating Gauls, and killed them with-out ceasing until their horses were exhausted and their right arms tired. More than twelve thousand were slaughtered – some still with their weapons in their hands, while others had thrown them down in their fear – and the whole baggage-train was captured.

After the rout of the Gallic army news was brought that Drappes, a Senonian, and Lucterius, a Cadurcan,[1] were marching towards the Province with a small force – some two thousand at most – collected from the fugitives. Caninius hastened in pursuit of them with two legions, thinking

1. Drappes had been raiding the Roman baggage and supply convoys, ever since the beginning of Vercingetorix's rebellion, with a band of desperadoes assembled from all quarters, including slaves to whom he had promised their liberty, outlaws from various tribes, and bandits. Lucterius had already attempted to invade the Province in the opening stage of the rebellion (see above, pages 181–2).

that it would be a serious disgrace if any damage were done to the Province, or its inhabitants alarmed, by the depredations of these brigands.

Fabius, who by this time had joined Caninius, started with the rest of the army for the territories of the Carnutes and the other tribes which had suffered such heavy losses in the battle with Dumnacus. After their recent defeat, he thought, they would be more inclined to submission; but if they were allowed any respite Dumnacus might induce them to fight again. As things turned out, Fabius was remarkably successful in bringing them quickly to heel. The Carnutes, who though frequently hard put to it had not asked for terms before, now offered hostages and surrendered; and the Aremorican tribes, who live on the Atlantic coast in the extreme west, followed their example, submitting to Fabius' demands directly he appeared with his army. Dumnacus was driven into exile and forced to go skulking alone from place to place until he reached the remotest corner of Gaul.

When Drappes and Lucterius heard that Caninius was close behind them, they realized that it would be certain destruction to enter the Province with a pursuing army at their heels, and that it was no longer possible for them to wander about the country as they pleased committing acts of brigandage. So they halted in the territory of the Cadurci, Lucterius' fellow-countrymen. He had great power over the tribe in the days before the defeat of Vercingetorix, and was still an influential agitator among the ignorant natives. With his own and Drappes' troops he now occupied Uxellodunum, a town of great natural strength which had previously been a dependency of his, and prevailed on its inhabitants to join him.

Caninius went to the place at once to reconnoitre. The town was protected on every side by precipitous rocks, which would be difficult for men carrying arms to scale, even if they met with no resistance. On the other hand, it would not be easy for the Gauls to evacuate it by stealth. He could see that they had a large quantity of heavy baggage, which could not be got away without being open to attack both by his cavalry and by the legions. He formed his troops into three divisions and pitched three camps on very high ground, from which he began to build entrenchments round the town as fast as he could with the limited number of men available.

The townspeople, haunted by the recollection of the tragic events at Alesia, now began to fear a similar fate if they were besieged; Lucterius in particular, who had been through the former siege, kept warning them that they must arrange for a supply of food. The leaders decided unanimously to leave a part of their troops in the town and go out themselves with a lightly equipped force to get in grain. The next night, leaving two thousand armed men inside, Drappes and Lucterius started out with the rest. In a few days they got a large quantity of grain from the country of the Cadurci, partly by voluntary contribution from the inhabitants, partly by forcible requisition. They also made occasional night attacks on Caninius' fortified posts, in view of which he decided not to complete the line of entrenchments for the time being; for he saw that he would be compelled either to leave a part of it unguarded or, by distributing his men among a large number of strong points, to make the individual posts dangerously weak.

Eventually Drappes and Lucterius took up a position about ten miles from the town, intending to carry in their big store of corn a little at a time. They divided the superintendence of this work between them: Drappes stayed to protect the camp with a part of the troops, while Lucterius led the convoy of pack-horses close up to the town. He then placed pickets at various points, and shortly before daybreak attempted to smuggle in the corn by following narrow tracks through the woods. But the noise attracted the attention of the sentries on duty at the Roman camp, and scouts were sent out to see what was happening. Directly he received their report, Caninius summoned the cohorts which were ready armed in the nearest posts and charged the convoy just as day was breaking. Taken by surprise, the Gauls scattered in alarm to seek the protection of their pickets. As soon as the Romans caught sight of men with weapons in their hands they attacked with redoubled fury, giving no quarter to anyone. Lucterius got away with a handful of men, but could not make his way back to the camp.

After this success Caninius learnt from several prisoners, whom he questioned separately in order to corroborate their statements, that a part of the enemy's forces was encamped with Drappes about twelve miles from the scene of the action. Now that one of their two leaders had been forced to take flight, it ought to be easy, he thought, to surprise and overawe the rest of them; it was a lucky chance that none of Lucterius' men, as far as was known, had escaped back to the camp to inform Drappes of their defeat. In any case, Caninius saw no danger in attempting a surprise attack. He therefore sent ahead all his cavalry and the German infantry, who were very fleet of foot. Then he divided one legion between the three camps and led out the other, lightly equipped for action. As he came near the enemy, the scouts sent on in front brought word that according to the usual Gallic custom Drappes had left the high ground and placed his camp on a river bank, and that the Germans and the cavalry had swooped down on it without any warning and attacked. Caninius at once led the infantry forward, drawn up in battle order with their weapons in their hands, and at a given signal they quickly occupied all the surrounding high ground. On seeing the legions' standards the Germans and the cavalry pressed their attack very strongly. The legionaries charged at once from every side, killed or captured all the Gauls, and took a quantity of booty. Drappes himself was among the prisoners. The Romans thus achieved complete success, almost without casualties. Having got rid of his enemy in the open, Caninius returned to the siege of Uxellodunum. Hitherto he had been afraid to complete the investment of the town and distribute his troops among a large number of guard posts. Now he gave orders to push on with the work everywhere, and the next day Fabius' army returned from its expedition against the Carnutes and took over a sector of the siege works.

In the meantime Caesar had left Antony with fifteen cohorts in the territory of the Bellovaci to prevent the Belgae from forming any fresh plans for revolt, and himself visited the tribes in western Gaul. From some he demanded additional hostages, but his main concern was to reassure them and allay their fears. The Carnutes were particularly alarmed because they knew they had been guilty of shedding the first blood at the beginning of the great rebellion.[1] In order to relieve the tribe as a whole from further anxiety, Caesar called on them to deliver up for punishment Gutuater, the person chiefly responsible for the outrage and the principal warmonger. This man went in such fear of his life that he did not let even his fellow-citizens know his whereabouts; but they all made diligent search for him and quickly brought him to the Roman camp. Though Caesar was always averse to harsh punishments, he was forced to execute him in order to satisfy the soldiers, who crowded round and charged Gutuater with responsibility for all the perils and losses they had suffered in the fighting. Accordingly he was flogged to death and his head cut off.

While in the country of the Carnutes Caesar received several dispatches in close succession from Caninius, telling

1. See above, page 180.

him what had happened to Drappes and Lucterius, and with what determination the defenders of Uxellodunum were holding out. Although their numbers were insignificant, Caesar thought they ought to be severely punished for their obstinacy. Otherwise, all the Gauls might suppose that their failure to defeat the Romans was due not to any lack of strength, but to a lack of perseverance, and other tribes which were advantageously situated might follow the example set at Uxellodunum and make a bid for freedom. They all knew that his command was due to expire after one more summer, so that if they could hold out for that time they would have nothing more to fear. Accordingly, leaving his general Quintus Calenus with two legions to follow at normal marching pace, he advanced at top speed with all the cavalry to join Caninius.

His arrival at Uxellodunum was a surprise to everyone. The town was now completely invested, and the Romans were committed to prosecuting the siege at all costs. As he learnt from deserters that the garrison had a large stock of provisions, he decided to try cutting off their water supply. A river flowed along the deep valley that almost surrounded the mountain on which the town stood. There was no way of diverting the water, on account of its position; it ran so low down at the mountain foot that it was impracticable to dig channels which would drain it off in any direction. But the way down to it from the town was so steep and difficult that any opposition on the Romans' part would make it impossible for the defenders to get to the water without the risk of being killed or wounded, or to return safely up the precipitous slope. Accordingly Caesar posted archers and slingers at various points to prevent them from approaching the river, and even trained artillery upon some of the easiest ways down. All the besieged, when they needed water, now had to go to one particular spot right at the foot of the town wall, where a copious spring gushed out. This was on the side of the town which, for a space of about three hundred feet, was not encircled by the river. All our men were anxious to find a way of keeping the enemy away from this spring, but only Caesar saw how it could be done. Opposite the place he advanced a line of mantlets up the slope and began to build a terrace. This involved not only much labour but continual fighting. For the enemy ran down and threw missiles from above at a safe distance, so that our men's determined efforts to ascend the slope cost them many casualties. In spite of this they pushed forward the mantlets and surmounted the difficulties of the terrain by working hard at their task. At the same time they dug mines towards the spring and the rills which fed it; this work involved no danger, since it could be done without the Gauls' suspecting it. The terrace was raised to a height of sixty feet, and a tower of ten storeys placed upon it, not with the object of reaching the level of the walls, which no siege works could possibly have done, but in order to dominate the spring. Artillery was then mounted in the tower and trained on the approach to the spring; and it became so dangerous to go there for water that before long not only the cattle and pack-horses but also the large population of the town were tormented by thirst.

The besieged were dismayed by this calamity. Filling barrels with tallow, pitch, and pieces of lath, they set them on fire and rolled them down on our works, delivering fierce attacks at the same time, so that our soldiers would be forced to protect themselves and unable to extinguish the flames. The mantlets and terrace were immediately set ablaze, because anything thrown down the slope could not miss them, and they were easily ignited by the burning material that lodged upon them. Our men had to fight in a situation of great danger, with the ground against them, but they faced all their difficulties with splendid courage. In their elevated position they were in full view of the rest of the army, and both sides were cheering loudly. Thus every man, in order to prove his mettle before so many witnesses, tried to make himself as conspicuous as he could in risking injury from wounds or burns.

Observing that heavy losses were being sustained, Caesar ordered the cohorts to clamber up the rocks wherever it was practicable, and by raising shouts to give the impression that they were getting a footing on the rampart at various points. By this means the garrison – who could only guess what was happening on other sides of the town – were frightened into recalling their troops from the attack on our works and sending them to man the walls. Relieved from the necessity of fighting, our soldiers soon extinguished the flames in some places, and isolated the parts which were still burning. The townsmen however still resisted obstinately and held out even when numbers had died of thirst, until in the end our mines tapped the rivulets which supplied the spring and diverted them. The sudden drying up of this supply, which had never failed them before, reduced the Gauls to such despair that they did not realize that it was due to the cunning of their enemy, but thought it was the will of supernatural powers, and, yielding to necessity, surrendered.

Caesar saw that his work in Gaul could never be brought to a successful conclusion if similar revolts were allowed to break out constantly in different parts of the country; and his clemency was so well known that no one would think him a cruel man if for once he took severe measures. So he decided to deter all others by making an example of the defenders of Uxellodunum. All who had borne arms had their hands cut off and were then let go, so that everyone might see what punishment was meted out to evildoers. Drappes, on being captured by Caninius,[1] had starved himself to death, either because he could not endure the humiliation

1. See above, page 254.

of being kept in chains or because he feared a still heavier punishment. Lucterius, after his escape from the encounter outside Uxellodunum, had kept continually on the move, because he thought it dangerous to stay long anywhere after earning Caesar's implacable hatred. He was thus compelled to entrust his life to one man after another, and at length came into the power of an Arvernian called Epasnactus, who, being an enthusiastic pro-Roman, without a moment's hesitation put him in chains and took him to Caesar.

Meanwhile Labienus fought a successful cavalry action in the country of the Treveri, inflicting severe casualties upon them and their German allies, who were always ready to help anyone against the Romans. He also captured the chiefs of the Treveri, and with them the only Aeduan chief who was still in arms – Surus, a man of illustrious birth and distinguished courage.

The situation was now everywhere satisfactory. In several years' campaigns nearly all Gaul had been thoroughly conquered. As Caesar had not personally visited Aquitania, however, although it had been partially subdued by Publius Crassus, he set out with two legions to spend the last part of the summer there. He conducted the campaign with his usual speed and success; all the Aquitanian tribes sent envoys and gave hostages. After that he started for Narbonne with an escort of cavalry, leaving his generals to instal the army in winter quarters. Four legions were stationed in Belgic territory under the generals Antony, Trebonius, and Publius Vatinius; two in the country of the Aedui, the most influential tribe in Gaul; two among the Turoni on the frontier of the Carnutes, to hold all the west up to the Atlantic seaboard; the remaining two in the country of the Lemovices, not far from the Arvernian border. In this way no part of Gaul was left without troops. Caesar stayed a few days in the Province, passing quickly from one to

another of the assize towns, settling political disputes and bestowing rewards where they were deserved. He had good
opportunities of learning what attitude each man had
adopted in the general revolt, which the loyal aid rendered
by the Province had enabled him to withstand. On the completion of this business he rejoined the legions quartered
among the Belgae and spent the winter at Nemetocenna.

There he heard how Commius the Atrebatian came to
blows with a party of our cavalry. Antony had reached
his winter quarters and the Atrebates were quiet; but
Commius, ever since he was wounded at his meeting with
Volusenus,[1] had always been ready to act as an agitator
and ringleader in any intrigues or warlike plots that
might be hatched among his fellow-tribesmen. As the
Atrebates were at present submitting to Roman control, he
organized a band of horsemen and supported himself and
his followers by brigandage, intercepting by means of raids
several convoys destined for the Roman camp. Volusenus,
who was attached to Antony's legion for the winter as
cavalry commander, was detailed to pursue Commius'
horsemen – a task for which his outstanding courage fitted
him, and which he undertook all the more willingly because he detested Commius. So he laid ambushes in various
places and made a number of successful attacks on the
horsemen. At length, in a particularly fierce encounter, he
and a few of his men made a determined effort to catch
Commius himself by pursuing him closely. Commius galloped off and drew them some distance away. Then, in his
hatred of Volusenus, he suddenly appealed to his followers
to help him avenge the wound which had been so treacherously inflicted on him, and turning his horse round rode
forward alone and daringly charged his enemy. The others
followed his example, and Volusenus' handful of men
were forced to fly with the Gauls in pursuit. Putting spurs

1. See above, page 247.

to his horse Commius rode close up behind Volusenus, and with his lance couched made a hard thrust clean through his thigh. Seeing their commander wounded, our men drew rein without a moment's hesitation, wheeled round, and repulsed their pursuers. A number of the Gauls were knocked down and wounded by the violence of the charge, and either trampled under the horses' feet in the pursuit or taken prisoner – a fate which Commius escaped by the swiftness of his horse. Thus our horsemen had the best of the fight; but Volusenus was carried back to camp with a wound so severe that it looked as if it might prove fatal. Either Commius was satisfied with his revenge, or else he had lost too many of his followers to be able to pursue the quarrel farther; in any case, he sent to Antony and offered hostages as a guarantee that he would live where he was bidden and do as he was told. His only request was that as a concession to the fear which haunted him he should not be required to come into the presence of any Roman. Antony decided that his fears were justified, and therefore granted his petition and accepted the hostages.

During the winter which he spent in Belgic Gaul Caesar made it his single aim to keep the tribes loyal, and to see that none had any pretext for revolt or any hope of profiting by it. The last thing he wanted was to have to fight a campaign immediately before his departure; for it would mean leaving Gaul in a state of rebellion when the time came to withdraw his army, and all the tribes would be only too willing to take up arms when they could do so without immediate risk. So he made their condition of subjection more tolerable by addressing the tribal governments in complimentary terms, refraining from the imposition of any fresh burdens, and bestowing rich presents upon the principal citizens. By these means it was easy to induce a people exhausted by so many defeats to live at peace.

NOTES

CHAP. I, § I

Page 30. There are several instances in Caesar's narrative of faction
fighting between members of the same family – e.g. Diviciacus
and his brother Dumnorix (Chap. II, § 1), Indutiomarus and his
son-in-law Cingetorix (Chap. V, § 2; Chap. VI, § 3), Vercingetorix and his uncle Gobannitio (Chap. VII, § 1).

Page 31. The rich and powerful corporation of the Druids does
not appear to have played any part as a body in the national resistance to the Romans, though some individuals among them, such
as Diviciacus the Aeduan, exercised considerable political power.

Page 33. The Gallic 'Knights' were noblemen. Most of the Celtic
tribes – though few of the Belgic – had by Caesar's time abandoned monarchy and were generally ruled by oligarchies of these
noblemen, who acted as magistrates and members of the tribal
councils, and surrounded themselves like feudal barons with hosts
of serfs and retainers.

Page 34. Father Dis was the god of death and king of the dark
underworld. Hence the importance of night in the Gauls'
reckoning of time.

CHAP. I, § 2

Page 37. The 'ox shaped like a deer' is apparently the reindeer; but
in reality it has two antlers. The idea that the elk had no joints in
its legs and slept against trees is of course a fairy-tale. As for the
alleged method of catching the animal, it is hard to believe that
Caesar took such a traveller's tale seriously.

CHAP. II, § I

Page 39. The large Celtic tribe of the Helvetii had been for nearly
half a century under constant pressure from the Germans, and was
now confined within the area of modern Switzerland. It was

perhaps the fear of fresh German attacks, after Ariovistus' entry into Gaul, that determined them to seek a new home in western France.

Page 41. The route leading between the Jura and the Rhone is the Pas de l'Ecluse, through which the road from Geneva to Lyons passes.

Page 42. The 'yoke' was made of two spears fixed upright, with a third fastened horizontally across them at such a height that the defeated soldiers, in filing under it, were obliged to stoop in token of submission.

Pages 43-4. Since the route through the territory of the Sequani lay outside the Roman Province, Caesar had, strictly speaking, no right to interfere further. But the danger of which he speaks may have been a real one (although the territory of the Santoni was some 130 miles from the frontier of the Province), and there was precedent for such preventive action on the part of provincial governors.

Of the four legions assigned to Caesar with his provinces (the 7th, 8th, 9th, and 10th) one was already in Transalpine Gaul (p. 42); the other three are those which he now withdrew from their winter quarters at Aquileia. With the two new legions now enrolled (the 11th and 12th) he had in all six with which to oppose the Helvetii.

Page 48. It suits Caesar's purpose to represent Dumnorix as merely an ambitious adventurer. But the facts suggest that he was really the leader of a popular party which opposed, in the national interest, the pro-Roman policy of the Aeduan nobles.

Page 52. A phalanx was a closely packed mass of troops, formed up in considerable depth, and – at any rate in the original form used by the Macedonians – armed with very long pikes, so as to present to an enemy an impenetrable thicket of spearpoints. When this formation was adopted by the Gauls and Germans, the men in the front rank held their shields overlapping one another in front of their bodies.

Page 53. It was the custom in ancient warfare to attack, if possible, the right flank of enemy troops, because on that side they could not easily protect themselves with their shields.

CHAP. II, § 2

Page 63. The slave war referred to was fought in 73–71 B.C. A Thracian gladiator named Spartacus raised a large force and defeated several Roman armies. He was eventually crushed by Crassus, the future triumvir.

Page 66. The plain in which Caesar and Ariovistus were encamped was the plain of Alsace.

Page 72. According to the manuscripts of Caesar's text, the Rhine was 'some five miles' away from the battlefield. But although the site of the battle cannot be certainly identified, none of the possible sites is less than twelve miles from the Rhine. Perhaps the numeral should be XV instead of V.

Page 73. The winter quarters of the legions in the country of the Sequani were presumably at Besançon. The fact that Caesar did not withdraw them to the Province for the winter made it clear for the first time that he intended to attempt the conquest of Gaul. Apart from his personal ambition, it might be urged that the only way of preventing renewed German invasions was to hold the Rhine frontier.

CHAP. II, § 3

Page 74. The two new legions raised in the winter of 58 B.C. were the 13th and 14th. This addition brought Caesar's army up to eight legions, at which strength it remained until 54 B.C.

Page 75. The estimate supplied by the Remi of the Belgic forces was no doubt exaggerated, but even so they must have greatly outnumbered the Romans.

Diviciacus king of the Suessiones was of course a different person from the famous Aeduan of the same name.

Page 77. Numidians were generally employed by the Romans as cavalry. But a later passage in this chapter shows that Caesar used them as light infantry.

CHAP. II, § 4

Page 89. The town defended by the Atuatuci was either at Namur or at Mont Falhize, about midway between Namur and Liège.

Page 91. On the strength no doubt of Caesar's optimistic dispatches to the Senate, it seems to have been thought at Rome that the conquest of Gaul was virtually completed.

CHAP. II, § 5

Page 92. The route which Galba's expedition was intended to open was that through the Great St Bernard pass. Its failure was due to the inadequate size of his force.

CHAP. III, § 1

Page 95. After spending the winter in northern Italy and Illyria, Caesar attended the conference of the triumvirs at Lucca (p. 11) and then immediately returned to Gaul.

There is evidence that as early as 57 B.C. Caesar was planning an expedition to Britain, and it may have been the knowledge of this that provoked the Veneti to revolt. They were the strongest of the maritime tribes of Gaul and carried on a considerable trade with Britain.

Page 100. Caesar's pretext for his savage treatment of the surrendered Veneti is a poor one. The Romans detained by them and their neighbours were not ambassadors but requisition officers. What Caesar really wanted to teach the Gauls was that it was dangerous to rebel against him.

CHAP. III, § 2

Pages 102–3. Caesar says (p. 97) that he wanted to prevent the Aquitanians from sending help to the rebels in Celtic Gaul. As it is improbable that there was any real likelihood of their doing so, his attack on them seems to have been an act of unprovoked aggression. Publius Crassus' conduct of the operation was brilliantly successful.

Lucius Manlius was governor of Transalpine Gaul in 78 B.C.

NOTES

He took part in the war against Sertorius in Spain and was forced to retreat into Aquitania, where the natives attacked and defeated him.

CHAP. III, § 3

Page 106. Although Caesar says that he set out to attack both the Morini and the Menapii, the narrative that follows, taken in conjunction with that describing the operations of the next year in this area (Chap. V, end of § 1), shows that he invaded only the territory of the Morini, who controlled the Channel ports nearest Britain.

CHAP. IV, § 1

Page 112 (footnote). The Meuse does not rise in the Vosges, but on the plateau of Langres. This plateau is in the country of the Lingones; the Vosges are not.

In saying that the Meuse flows into the Rhine, Caesar (or the geographer from whom his information is derived) evidently means that it flows into the Waal, which joins the Rhine not far from Arnhem. The Meuse now meets the Waal only about forty miles from the sea; but the two rivers approach very near each other at the point indicated by Caesar, and may then have been connected by a channel.

Page 114. This episode was discreditable to Caesar. The arrest of the German envoys who came to explain their alleged breach of the truce – which may not have been serious or deliberate – was justly criticized as an infraction of the rule of international law to which Caesar himself had so recently appealed in the case of the Veneti (Chap. III, § 1). His enemy Cato actually proposed that Caesar should be disowned and surrendered to the Germans; but this was no doubt only a political move, and no notice was taken of it.

Page 115. The rendering 'they reached the confluence of the Moselle and the Rhine' depends on an emendation of the text, in which the rivers mentioned are the *Meuse* and the Rhine. That would indicate that the battlefield was in Holland somewhere near the river Waal, in which case the Germans must have retreated a long way north before the engagement. If the emendation is right, they must have advanced south-east through the Ardennes.

In defence of Caesar's cold-blooded massacre of the entire German host it might be argued that, if it was anything like as large as he says it was, its presence in Gaul was a serious menace, and that his drastic action did put an end to German threats to the peace of Gaul.

CHAP. IV, § 2

Page 116. Caesar's bridge was probably near Coblenz.
Page 118. In spite of the elaborate preparations made for this invasion of Germany, it may be that, as Caesar suggests, it was not intended as anything more than a punitive raid and a demonstration of strength. If he ever entertained the idea of a serious attempt to conquer Germany, he was certainly wise in abandoning it.

CHAP. V, § 1

Page 119. Although there was much intercourse between Gaul and Britain, the military aid which Caesar says the Gauls received from the Britons cannot have been the real reason for his invasion. Such assistance could hardly have been of much importance, and in any case the Romans were now in control of the Channel. Probably his main motive was to secure the glory of leading an army to victory in a distant and unknown island, the wealth of which was reputed to be much greater than it really was. The first expedition, which lasted only about three weeks, was intended merely to reconnoitre the country with a view to a more serious invasion the next year.
Pages 120–1. Caesar sailed with the infantry from Boulogne. The cavalry sailed from Ambleteuse, six miles north of Boulogne. The British coast was first reached near Dover. The landing took place between Deal and Walmer Castle.
Page 122. A silver eagle mounted on a pole was the legionary standard.
Page 126. The British war chariots had two wheels and were drawn by two horses. Remains of chariots have been found in British graves. Many more have been found in France; but evidently the mainland Gauls, before the time of Caesar's conquest, had abandoned them in favour of cavalry.

Page 131. The ships built in the country of the Meldi (the neighbourhood of Meaux) sailed first down the Marne, then down the
Seine. On being driven back by a contrary wind they doubtless
returned to the mouth of the Seine.

Page 133. The second invasion of Britain was an ambitious undertaking. The size of the forces employed suggests that Caesar
planned to conquer and occupy at any rate the southern part of
the country. In that case, the failure of the enterprise must be
counted as a serious reverse for him and for the Roman arms.

    The landing must have been made somewhere between Sand-
wich and Deal. The cavalry fight apparently took place on the
banks of the river Stour, not far from Canterbury.

Pages 135–6. The civilization of Britain had many features – including Druidism – in common with that of Gaul, but was less highly
developed. Monarchy was still the usual form of government.

    To say that tin is found 'inland' is an odd way of referring
to the famous tin mines of Cornwall, which had been exploited
for centuries by Carthaginians and Gauls. Caesar – or the authority
upon whom he is relying – apparently did not know what part of
the country it came from. He is also mistaken in implying that
copper was not mined in Britain and that the beech did not grow
there. The iron found 'near the coast' is that obtained from the
ancient mines in Sussex.

    It will be obvious to English readers that the coasts of Britain
are incorrectly oriented in Caesar's description, and their length
over-estimated. The idea that northern Spain lay to the west of
Britain, with Ireland between them, resulted from misconceptions
shared by most ancient geographers. According to their belief, (i)
the coast of Gaul stretched south-west in an approximately straight
line from the Rhine to the Pyrenees; (ii) the south coast of Britain
was roughly parallel to it; (iii) the Pyrenees ran north and south;
(iv) the north coast of Spain ran not west but north-west from
the Pyrenees, and was much nearer Britain than it really is.

    Caesar here calls the Isle of Man 'Mona', although in other
ancient writers the name is always applied to Anglesey.

Page 139. Cassivellaunus' kingdom was in Middlesex and Hertford-
shire. His stronghold was formerly thought to have been Verulamium, near St. Albans. But although Verulamium was certainly
the chief town of his son and successor Tasciovanus, it is probable

THE CONQUEST OF GAUL

that Cassivellaunus' fortress was at Wheathampstead, about five miles N.N.E. of St. Albans.

As no troops were left behind in Britain the Romans retained no real hold upon it. The possession of British hostages may have secured the payment of tribute for the time being; but even that no doubt ceased after Caesar's departure from Gaul.

CHAP. VI, § 1

Page 141. The ill-fated legion placed under Sabinus and Cotta was the 14th. It is not known what legion or legions the five cohorts belonged to.

Pages 144–5. It is surprising to find Sabinus walking so recklessly into the trap set for him by Ambiorix; for in his campaign against the Venelli in 56 B.C. (Chap. III, § 1) he nearly lost his chance of victory by excessive caution, and then saved the situation by employing a similar trick himself.

Page 149. Sabinus' blunder had cost the lives of at least six thousand legionaries. It is said that when Caesar heard the news he let his hair and beard grow in token of mourning, and continued so until the defeat was avenged. The scene of the catastrophe is not mentioned in his account, but a later passage (Chap. VI, § 5) shows that it was at Atuatuca, in Belgium.

CHAP. VI, § 2

Page 149. Caesar claimed that the Nervii were 'almost annihilated' by their defeat in 57 B.C., and the survivors of that defeat said that scarcely five hundred men capable of bearing arms remained (Chap. II, § 4). The following narrative shows that these statements were exaggerations, though doubtless many of those who took part in the attack on Cicero's camp had reached military age since 57 B.C.

The site of Cicero's camp cannot be identified, but it must have been somewhere on or near the Sambre, and cannot have been less than some eighty miles distant from Samarobriva (Amiens), where Caesar was.

Pages 154–5. The narrative shows that Caesar had one legion when he

set out from Samarobriva to relieve Cicero. This must have been
the legion which was wintering (no doubt at Samarobriva) under
Trebonius.

CHAP. VI, § 3

Page 158. For the first time Caesar spent the winter in Gaul. The
three legions with which he went into winter quarters at Samarobriva were (1) Crassus' legion, which Caesar had left at Samarobriva when he set out thence to relieve Cicero; (2) Trebonius'
legion, which Caesar had taken with him to Cicero's camp; (3)
Cicero's legion.

Page 162. From 57 to 54 B.C. Caesar had eight legions. The losses
under Sabinus were perhaps not much more than the full comple-
ment of one legion, which would leave seven. Of the two new
legions now enrolled in northern Italy (in the winter of 54 B.C.),
one took the number of the 14th, destroyed under Sabinus; the
other was numbered the 15th. The legion borrowed from Pompey was the 1st – though apparently Caesar renumbered it afterwards (see note on Chap. VIII, § 1). This reinforcement brought the
number of his legions up to ten.

Pompey held proconsular command as nominal governor of
Spain (Introd. p. 12). In his consulship of 55 B.C. he had been invested with special powers which enabled him to levy troops even
in provinces under the control of other governors.

CHAP. VI, § 4

Page 168. This incursion into Germany had achieved as little as the
former one. Perhaps to distract his readers' attention from its insignificant results, Caesar inserted at this point a long digression
on the customs and institutions of Gaul and Germany, which has
been transferred to Chap. I in this translation in order to avoid
interrupting the narrative.

CHAP. VI, § 5

Page 171. The Scheldt does not now flow into the Meuse, but there is some reason for thinking that these rivers did at one time communicate with each other near their mouths.

Page 175. The two thousand cavalry of the Sugambri must have been accompanied, according to the German custom (pp. 70, 218), by a similar number of infantry, since they regarded with contempt a Roman force which must have considerably exceeded two thousand.

Pages 176–7. Caesar treats Quintus Cicero very tenderly whenever he refers to him in the *Gallic War*, wishing to gratify his brother Marcus Cicero, whose friendship was useful to Caesar. In the present passage he lets him off with a reprimand much less severe than he deserved and mentions all the extenuating circumstances he can think of. Cicero had certainly been incautious and disobedient, and, in a private letter to Marcus, Caesar says so pretty plainly.

Page 178. The 'ancient Roman manner' of execution was by scourging and beheading. By thus setting himself up as a judge over the Gauls, Caesar is quite openly treating them as the inhabitants of a conquered province.

CHAP. VII, § 1

Page 183. Caesar's unexpected march across the Cevennes in midwinter disorganized Vercingetorix's strategical plan, which was to start a widespread revolt in central and western Gaul before Caesar could rejoin his army after his usual winter visit to northern Italy, and at the same time to threaten an invasion of the Province.

CHAP. VII, § 2

Pages 186–7. Vercingetorix, like the good soldier he was, saw now that it was useless either to fight pitched battles or to try holding one fortress after another, and decided on the one strategy that might have been successful – to starve the Roman army by means of a 'scorched earth' policy. But his followers could not see that, to be effective, the work of destruction must be persisted in ruthlessly, and he had no means of compelling them.

CHAP. VII, § 3

Pages 200–1. Excavations carried out in 1861–5 on the instructions of the Emperor Napoleon III revealed remains of the two Roman camps and the double trench connecting them.

Page 203. Caesar had six legions at Gergovia (p. 199). Two of these were placed in the small camp on the hill when it was first occupied (p. 200). But the major part of this garrison was evidently withdrawn later, since in the final stage of the siege the small camp had a garrison only some cohorts strong (pp. 209–10). So Caesar could take approximately four legions to deal with the Aedui, and leave two with Fabius to guard the main camp.

Page 207. It is difficult to believe Caesar's statement that his only objective in this battle was the capture of three half-empty Gallic camps. It seems much more likely that he hoped to take the town by a surprise attack, and sounded the recall only when he saw that this could not be done.

Page 210. This was the only defeat that Caesar himself suffered at the hands of the Gauls. Both he and his troops were to blame – Caesar, for sounding a vital trumpet signal in a place where it was inaudible to most of those whom it was intended to reach; the soldiers, for disobeying the orders of the generals and military tribunes on the spot.

CHAP. VII, § 4

Page 213. Labienus had been sent with four legions against the Parisii and Senones soon after the fall of Avaricum (p. 199).

Page 220. The Eporedorix who had led the Aedui against the Sequani was evidently a different person from the Aeduan of that name mentioned several times earlier in this chapter.

CHAP. VII, § 5

Page 221. The sites of the eight Roman camps, and of five out of the twenty-three redoubts, were discovered by Napoleon III's excavations.

Page 227. The story of the starving Mandubii is made terribly dramatic by what it does *not* say. Of course Caesar had not enough food to relieve them without the risk of running short himself. According to a later historian, he hoped they would be readmitted to the town, and so hasten the time when it must surrender; but they were left outside to die of starvation.

Page 233. So ended the brief but brilliant career of a great patriot. Caesar pays a fine tribute to the qualities of leadership which enabled Vercingetorix to strengthen his hold upon his followers and reanimate them in the hour of defeat (p. 196), but either could not or would not protect him from the fate which Roman custom demanded for a vanquished Barbarian. Six years after his capture Vercingetorix was exhibited at Rome in Caesar's triumph and then executed.

CHAP. VIII, § 1

Page 234. This final chapter is the work of Caesar's friend Aulus Hirtius (Introd. pp. 23-4), who prefaced it with a few modest words of personal explanation. He is quite aware, he says, how inferior his literary effort must appear by the side of Caesar's masterpiece, and it was only the repeated requests of his friends that induced him to undertake it.

Caesar knew that many of the Gallic patriots still refused to accept their defeat as final, and he was anxious to finish off the war at the earliest possible moment. He therefore remained in Gaul and actually spent a large part of the winter in active campaigning. The campaign against the Bituriges started on the 29th of December, 52 B.C., according to the current Roman calendar. But the calendar was in advance of the true seasons, and the date was really about four weeks earlier.

Page 236. This is the first mention of the 6th legion. There is reason for thinking that Caesar had assigned this number to the legion borrowed from Pompey in the winter of 54 B.C. (p. 162), which was called the 1st at the time when Caesar took it over.

CHAP. VIII, § 2

Page 257. The unanimous testimony of his contemporaries proves that Caesar had the reputation of a merciful man, and in the civil war he certainly treated his defeated enemies with remarkable generosity. But in dealing with Barbarians the tradition of Roman warfare knew no mercy, and in the particular case of Uxellodunum there was the additional excuse that the garrison was largely composed of criminals and penniless adventurers who were a continual menace to the peace of Gaul. Such terrorism, too, was common among the Gauls themselves; Vercingetorix thought nothing of punishing lukewarm supporters of the national cause by mutilation or death at the stake.

Page 258. Crassus' campaign in Aquitania took place in 56 B.C. (Chap. III, § 2).

The legions now distributed in winter quarters total ten, and the 15th had already been sent to northern Italy (p. 247). So at this time Caesar had eleven in all, whereas he had only ten in the campaign of 52 B.C. The additional legion was probably the 5th, which he is known to have raised about this time *in Transalpine Gaul*. It was quite exceptional in this period for a legion to be recruited outside Italy, i.e. from non-citizens.

Page 260. Caesar's conciliatory treatment of Gaul as a whole, following on his frightful punishment of the last obstinate rebels, had the desired effect. It was a long time before the Gauls gave much further trouble.

Caesar remained at Nemetocenna until the summer of 50 B.C. Returning there in the early autumn after a visit to northern Italy on political business, he assembled all his legions in the territory of the Treveri, held a review, and took them on some route marches to keep them fit. His last act in Gaul was to distribute them in their stations for the coming winter. One legion was in northern Italy, and in obedience to a senatorial decree Caesar had to surrender two others for a proposed expedition to Parthia, which did not materialize. Of the remaining eight, four were placed under Trebonius among the Belgae – the bravest fighters in Gaul – and four among the Aedui, politically the most influential tribe.

The Gallic war was ended. In less than two months[1] Caesar marched troops across the river Rubicon – the southern boundary of his province of Cisalpine Gaul – and invaded Italy. In his own words, 'the die was cast'. The civil war had begun.

1. On the 10th of January, 49 B.C., by the Roman calendar (actually about the 22nd of November, 50 B.C.).

GLOSSARY

(The references are to chapters and sections of the Translation,
and to sections of the Introduction.)

ACCO (VI 3, 5; VII 1). A chief of the Senones.

ADMAGETOBRIGA (II 2). The site of a battle between Ariovistus
and the Gauls in 61 B.C. It cannot be identified, but was probably
in Alsace (then part of the territory of the Sequani).

AEDUI (I 1; II 1–4; V 2; VI 3; VII 1–5; VIII 2). A large tribe living in
central France, between the Loire and the Saône; see Introd. 3, 5.

AGEDINCUM (VI 5; VII 1, 4). A town of the Senones about 65 miles
S.E. of Paris, on the site of Sens (derived from *Senones*).

ALESIA (VII 5; VIII 1, 2). A stronghold of the Mandubii on the
plateau of Mont Auxois, about 30 miles N.W. of Dijon.

ALLOBROGES (II 1, 2, 5; VII 4). A powerful tribe whose territory lay
between the Rhone, the Isère, and the lake of Geneva, and formed
the northernmost part of the Roman province of Transalpine
Gaul; see Introd. 3.

AMBIANI (II 3, 4; VII 5; VIII 1). A Belgic tribe living on the Somme
in the neighbourhood of Samarobriva (i.e. Amiens – derived from
Ambiani).

AMBIORIX (VI 1–5; VIII 2). Joint king of the Eburones with Catuvolcus.

ANDES (II 4; III 1; VII 1; VIII 2). A tribe living N. of the lower Loire,
in Anjou (derived from *Andes*).

ANTONY, MARK (Marcus Antonius: VII 5; VIII 1, 2). Served under
Caesar in Gaul as general (52 B.C.) and as quaestor (51 B.C.), and in
the civil war. Some time after Caesar's death, Antony, Octavian
(the future emperor Augustus), and Marcus Aemilius Lepidus controlled the Roman world as the 'Second Triumvirate'. Later,
hostilities broke out between Octavian and Antony, who after
40 B.C. fell under the influence of Cleopatra. In 31 B.C. he was defeated by Octavian at the battle of Actium, and in 30 committed suicide in Egypt.

AQUILEIA (II 1). A town at the head of the Adriatic in the province
of Cisalpine Gaul.

AQUITANI (I 1; III 2). A group of tribes speaking Spanish dialects
and living in AQUITANIA (III 1, 2; VII 2; VIII 2), the S.W. corner
of France between the Garonne and the Pyrenees.

AREMORICAN TRIBES (VI 3; VII 5; VIII 2). A group of tribes living in Normandy and Brittany.

ARIOVISTUS (I 1; II 2; IV 2; VI 1, 3). King of the German tribe of the Suebi; see Introd. 3.

ARTILLERY. Machines resembling huge crossbows or catapults. They derived power from the recoil of tightly twisted gut or horsehair and discharged either stones or feathered javelins.

ARVERNI (II 2; VII 1, 3–5; VIII 2). A powerful tribe living in south central France, in the district of the Auvergne mountains; see Introd. 3.

ATREBATES (II 3, 4; V 1; VI 2; VII 5; VIII 1–2). A Belgic tribe living in N. France in the neighbourhood of Arras.

ATRIUS, QUINTUS (V 2). A Roman officer.

ATUATUCA (VI 5). A fortress of the Eburones (not of the Atuatuci, in spite of its name); perhaps Tongres in E. Belgium, 12 miles N.N.W. of Liège.

ATUATUCI (II 3, 4; VI 1–3, 5). A tribe living in S.E. Belgium, principally on the left bank of the Meuse.

AULERCI (II 4; III 1,3; VII 1, 5; VIII 1). A group of tribes living between the lower Seine and the lower Loire.

AVARICUM (VII 1–3). The chief town of the Bituriges, on the site of Bourges (derived from *Bituriges*), 60 miles S.S.E. of Orleans.

BACULUS, PUBLIUS SEXTIUS (II 4, 5; VI 5). A chief centurion.

BASILUS, LUCIUS MINUCIUS (VI 5; VII 5). A Roman officer.

BELGAE (I 1; II 3, 4; III 1; V 1; VI 1; VIII 1, 2). One of the main divisions of the Gallic tribes, inhabiting N. France, Belgium, S. Holland, and the part of Germany lying W. of the Rhine; see Introd. 3.

BELLOVACI (II 3, 4; VI 2; VII 4, 5; VIII 1, 2). A powerful Belgic tribe, inhabiting, however, a comparatively small area in N. France – the district around Beauvais (derived from *Bellovaci*).

BIBRACTE (II 1; VII 4, 5; VIII 1). The chief town of the Aedui, on Mont Beuvray (12 miles W. of Autun).

BIBRAX (II 3). A town of the Remi a little N. of the Aisne, between Laon and Rheims.

BITURIGES (II 1; VII 1, 2, 5; VIII 1). A tribe living in west central France, in the neighbourhood of Avaricum (i.e. Bourges – derived from *Bituriges*).

BOII (II 1; VII 1, 2, 5). A Celtic tribe which migrated westwards with the Helvetii and was afterwards settled in central France, probably between the Loire and the Allier.

BRATUSPANTIUM (II 4). A stronghold of the Bellovaci, probably between Amiens and Beauvais.

BRUTUS, DECIMUS JUNIUS (III 1; VII 1, 5). Served under Caesar in the Gallic and civil wars, but was one of his murderers. After Caesar's death occupied Cisalpine Gaul; besieged by Antony in Modena until relieved by Octavian and the consuls of 43 B.C., one of whom was Aulus Hirtius, author of the eighth book of the *Gallic War*. Killed by Antony's order later in the same year.

CADURCI (VII 1, 4, 5; VIII 2). A tribe inhabiting a district in S.W. France roughly corresponding to the Dept. of the Lot.

CAESAR, LUCIUS JULIUS (VII 4). A distant relative of Gaius Julius Caesar, and one of his generals in the later Gallic campaigns; consul 64 B.C.

CALENUS, QUINTUS FUFIUS (VIII 2). One of Caesar's generals.

CAMULOGENUS (VII 4). A leader belonging to the tribe of the Aulerci.

CANINIUS (Gaius Caninius Rebilus: VII 5; VIII 2). One of Caesar's generals.

CANTABRI (III 2). A tribe living on the N. coast of Spain.

CARNUTES (I 1; II 4; VI 1, 3, 5; VII 1, 5; VIII 1, 2). A tribe living S.W. of Paris between the Seine and the Loire.

CASSIVELLAUNUS (V 2). Leader of the Britons in Caesar's second invasion.

CATUVOLCUS (VI 1, 5). Joint king of the Eburones with Ambiorix.

CAVARILLUS (VII 4). An Aeduan nobleman.

CAVARINUS (VI 3). King of the Senones.

CELTILLUS (VII 1). Father of Vercingetorix.

CENABUM (VII 1, 2; VIII 1). A town of the Carnutes on the site of Orleans.

CENTURION. See Introd. 4.

CHERUSCI (VI 4.). A German tribe, probably living between the Elbe and the Weser.

CICERO, QUINTUS TULLIUS (VI 1–3, 5; VII 5). Younger brother of Marcus Tullius Cicero the orator. Served under Caesar 54–52 B.C., but on Pompey's side in the civil war; put to death, like his brother, by Antony in 43 B.C.

CIMBRI (II 2–4; VII 5). See Introd. 3.

CINGETORIX (V 2; VI 3). A chief of the Treveri, rival of his father-in-law Indutiomarus.

CINGETORIX (V 2). One of four kings of Kent.

GLOSSARY

CISALPINE PROVINCE (VII 1). The province of Cisalpine Gaul; see Introd. 1.

CLODIUS (Publius Clodius Pulcher: VII 1). A profligate Roman patrician, the bitter enemy of Marcus Cicero. Used by Caesar as a tool for his own purposes; assassinated in January, 52 B.C. by Milo, a rival political gangster.

COHORT. See Introd. 4.

COMMIUS (V 1, 2; VI 3; VII 5; VIII 1, 2). King of the Atrebates.

CONSUL. The two annually elected consuls were the chief executive magistrates of the Roman Republic, and commanded its armies in Italy. After their year of office, which was known by their names, they normally held provincial governorships as proconsuls; see Introd. 1.

CONVICTOLITAVIS (VII 3, 4). A magistrate of the Aedui.

CORREUS (VIII 1). A leader of the Bellovaci.

COTTA, LUCIUS AURUNCULEIUS (II 3; V 1; VI 1, 2, 5). One of Caesar's generals.

CRASSUS, MARCUS LICINIUS (II 1; IV 1). A member of the 'First Triumvirate'; see Introd. 1.

CRASSUS, MARCUS LICINIUS (VI 1–3). Elder son of Crassus the triumvir; quaestor 54 B.C.; served in Gaul 54–53 B.C.

CRASSUS, PUBLIUS LICINIUS (II, 2, 4; III 1, 2; VIII 2). Younger son of Crassus the triumvir; served as one of Caesar's officers during the first campaigns.

CRITOGNATUS (VII 5). An Arvernian nobleman.

DECETIA (VII 3). A town of the Aedui on the Loire – on the site of Decize, about 20 miles S.E. of Nevers.

DIVICIACUS (I 1; II 1–4; VII 3). A pro-Roman Aeduan, brother of Dumnorix.

DIVICIACUS (II 3). A king of the Suessiones about 100 B.C.

DIVICO (II 1). A leader of the Helvetii.

DRAPPES (VIII 2). A leader of the Senones.

DUMNACUS (VIII 2). A leader of the Andes.

DUMNORIX (II 1; V 2). An anti-Roman Aeduan, brother of Diviciacus.

DURATIUS (VIII 2). A pro-Roman leader of the Pictones.

DUROCORTORUM (VI 5). A town of the Remi on the site of Rheims (derived from Remi).

EBURONES (II 3; IV 1; VI 1–3, 5). A Belgic tribe inhabiting a large

277

THE CONQUEST OF GAUL

area W. of the lower Rhine, on both banks of the Meuse, including part of E. Belgium and a strip of W. Germany.

EPOREDORIX (VII 3–5). An Aeduan nobleman.

EPOREDORIX (VII 4, p. 220). Another Aeduan nobleman.

ERATOSTHENES (I 2). A Greek scholar of the 3rd century B.C., head of the library at Alexandria; a man of great and varied learning, especially in mathematics and geography. He calculated the circumference of the earth to within some 200 miles of the correct figure.

FABIUS, GAIUS (VI 1–3; VII 3, 5; VIII 1, 2). One of Caesar's generals.

FABIUS, LUCIUS (VII 3). A centurion.

FABIUS MAXIMUS, QUINTUS (II 2). Consul 121 B.C.; conqueror of the Arverni.

GALBA (II 3, 4). King of the Suessiones.

GALBA, SERVIUS SULPICIUS (II 5). One of Caesar's generals.

GERGOVIA (VII 1, 3, 4). A stronghold of the Arverni on a plateau 1,200 feet high at the N. end of the Auvergne mountains, about four miles S. of Clermont-Ferrand.

GORGOBINA (VII 1). A town of the Boii in central France, near Nevers.

GUTUATER (VII 1; VIII 2). A leader of the Carnutes.

HARUDES (II 2). A German tribe living probably in the neighbourhood of Hamburg.

HELVETII (I 2; II 1, 2; IV 1; VII 5). A large tribe living in Switzerland.

HELVII (VII 1, 4). A tribe living in the province of Transalpine Gaul, at the N. end of the Cevennes.

HERCYNIAN FOREST (I 2). A huge tract of forest in central Europe, said to extend from the source of the Danube to Bohemia.

ICCIUS (II 3). A leader of the Remi.

ILLYRIA (II 4; III 1; V 2). A district on the east of the Adriatic; see Introd. 1.

INDUTIOMARUS (V 2; VI 1, 3). A chief of the Treveri, rival of his son-in-law Cingetorix.

ITIUS. See PORTUS ITIUS.

LABIENUS, TITUS (II 1–4; III 1; V 1, 2; VI 1–3, 5; VII 3–5; VIII 1, 2). The ablest of Caesar's generals in the Gallic war; fought against Caesar in the civil war, and died in the final campaign (45 B.C.).

GLOSSARY

LEGION. See Introd. 4.

LEMONUM (VIII 2). A town of the Pictones on the site of Poitiers (derived from *Pictones*).

LEMOVICES (VII 1, 5; VIII 2). A tribe occupying the province of Limousin (derived from *Lemovices*), W. of the Auvergne mountains.

LEXOVII (III 1, 3; VII 5). A tribe occupying the coast of Normandy in the neighbourhood of Caen and Lisieux (derived from *Lexovii*).

LINGONES (II 1, 2; IV 1; VI 5; VII 1, 4; VIII 1). A tribe living in central France in the neighbourhood of Langres and Dijon.

LISCUS (II 1). An Aeduan magistrate.

LITAVICCUS (VII 3, 4). An Aeduan nobleman.

LUCTERIUS (VII 1; VIII 2). A leader of the Cadurci.

LUTETIA (VI 3; VII 4). A town of the Parisii – the nucleus of Paris, situated on the Ile de la Cité in the Seine.

MANDUBII (VII 5). A tribe living in central France, N.W. of Dijon.

MANDUBRACIUS (V 2). A chief of the Trinovantes.

MANLIUS, LUCIUS (III 2). See pages 264–5.

MANTLETS. Stout wooden sheds, usually some 16 feet long and some 8 feet wide, mounted on wheels. They were placed end to end in a line, and were used especially to protect soldiers engaged in bringing up material for the construction of a siege terrace.

MARIUS, GAIUS (II 2). A democratic leader, seven times consul between 107 and 86 B.C. A great soldier (see Introd. 3), and reorganizer of the Roman army, which he converted from a citizen militia into a professional army.

MARK ANTONY. See ANTONY.

MELDI (V 2). A tribe living on the Marne near Meaux (25 miles E. of Paris).

MENAPII (II 3; III 1, 3; IV 1; V 1; VI 3–5). A Belgic tribe living mainly in S. Holland.

METLOSEDUM (VII 4). A town of the Senones standing on an island in the Seine, near the site of Melun (25 miles S.S.E. of Paris).

MILITARY TRIBUNE. See Introd. 4.

MORINI (II 3; III 1, 3; V 1; VI 1; VII 5). A tribe living on the coast of Belgium and N. France approximately between Zeebrugge and Boulogne.

NANTUATES (II 5). A tribe living in S.W. Switzerland on the upper Rhone, in the neighbourhood of St. Maurice.

NEMETOCENNA (VIII 2). A town of the Atrebates on the site of Arras.

NERVII (II 3, 4; VI 1–3; VII 5). A powerful Belgic tribe living E. of the Scheldt in central Belgium.

NITIOBROGES (VII 1–3, 5). A tribe living in S.W. France between the rivers Dordogne and Garonne.

NOREIA (II 1). A town in the Austrian province of Styria, on the site of Neumarkt.

NORICAN (II 2). A native of Noricum (part of Austria).

NOVIODUNUM (II 4). A fortress of the Suessiones, just over 2 miles N.W. of Soissons.

NOVIODUNUM (VII 1, 2). A town of the Bituriges in central France, probably near the site of Neuvy-sur-Barangeon (18 miles N.N.W. of Bourges).

NOVIODUNUM (VII 4). A town of the Aedui on the Loire, probably on the site of Nevers.

NUMIDIAN (II 3, 4). A native of Numidia (Algeria).

OCELUM (II 1). A town on the N.W. border of Italy, probably Avigliana on the S. bank of the Dora Riparia (about 18 miles W. of Turin).

OCTODURUS (II 5). A town of the Veragri situated near Martigny in S.W. Switzerland.

ORGETORIX (II 1). A Helvetian nobleman.

OSISMI (II 4; III 1; VII 5). A tribe living in Brittany in the neighbourhood of Brest.

PARISII (VI 3; VII 1, 3–5). A tribe living in the neighbourhood of Lutetia, a town on the site of Paris.

PEDIUS, QUINTUS (II 3). One of Caesar's generals.

PICTONES (III 1; VII 1, 5; VIII 2). A tribe living on the W. coast of France, on the S. bank of the Loire. The town of Lemonum (i.e. Poitiers – derived from Pictones) was in their territory.

PISO, LUCIUS CALPURNIUS (II 1). Consul 112 B.C.; killed in battle with the Helvetii (107 B.C.).

PISO, LUCIUS CALPURNIUS (II 1). Consul 58 B.C.; grandson of the above mentioned Piso, and father of Caesar's wife Calpurnia.

PISO (IV 1). An Aquitanian nobleman.

PLANCUS, LUCIUS MUNATIUS (VI 1). One of Caesar's generals.

POMPEY (Gnaeus Pompeius Magnus: IV 1; VI 3; VII 1). See Introd. 1.

POMPEIUS, GNAEUS (VI 1). An interpreter employed by Sabinus.

PORTUS ITIUS (V 2). Probably the harbour of Boulogne (possibly Wissant, 11 miles N. of Boulogne).

PROVINCE, THE. The province of Transalpine Gaul; see Introd. 1.

GLOSSARY

QUAESTOR. The quaestorship was the magistracy which was held
first by Romans entering on a political career. Twenty quaestors
were elected annually in Caesar's time. Some of these were employed in Italy, mainly on financial duties. The rest were attached
to generals in the field or to provincial governors. Normally they
acted as paymasters, receivers of revenue, etc., but they were sometimes employed on military duties. In 54 B.C. Caesar had two
quaestors serving under him – an exceptional arrangement.

REGINUS, GAIUS ANTISTIUS (VI 3; VII 5). One of Caesar's generals.
REMI (I 1; II 3, 4; III 1; V 2; VI 1, 3, 5; VII 4, 5; VIII 1). A powerful
Belgic tribe living on both sides of the Aisne, in the neighbour-
hood of Rheims (derived from *Remi*).
ROMAN KNIGHT (III 1; VI 1, 5; VII 1, 4). See Introd. 1.
ROSCIUS, LUCIUS (VI 1, 3). Served in Gaul as quaestor in 54 B.C.
RUTENI (II 2; VII 1, 4, 5). A tribe living in S. France, partly in the
Roman Province, partly just N. of it.

SABINUS, QUINTUS TITURIUS (II 3; III 1; V 1; VI 1–3, 5). One of
Caesar's generals.
SAMAROBRIVA (VI 1–3). A town of the Ambiani on the site of
Amiens (derived from *Ambiani*).
SANTONI (II 1; III 1; VII 5). A tribe of W. France living near the
river Charente; the town of Saintes derives its name from *Santoni*.
SEDUNI (II 5; III 1). A tribe living in S.W. Switzerland on the upper
Rhone; the town of Sion derives its name from *Seduni*.
SEMPRONIUS RUTILUS, MARCUS (VII 5). One of Caesar's officers.
SENATE. See Introd. 1.
SENONES (II 3; VI 3, 5; VII 1, 3–5). A tribe living S.E. of Paris in the
neighbourhood of Agedincum (i.e. Sens, derived from *Senones*).
SEQUANI (I 1; II 1, 2; IV 1; VII 4, 5). A tribe living in E. France be-
tween the river Saône and the Vosges and Jura mountains.
SERTORIUS, QUINTUS (III 2). A supporter of the Roman demo-
crats who in 80 B.C. put himself at the head of revolting Spanish
tribes, and with the help of Roman exiles defied the Senate's
generals (including Pompey) for eight years, until he was
assassinated by one of his own officers.
SEXTIUS, TITUS (VI 3; VII 3, 5; VIII 1). One of Caesar's generals.
SIEGE TERRACE. A terrace consisting of logs piled in layers, en-
closing a core of earth and rubble. It was begun at some distance
from the wall of the place under siege and gradually advanced
towards it, the length of the terrace being usually at right angles

to the wall. Wooden towers several storeys high were erected on the terrace, and artillery and snipers placed in them.

SILANUS, MARCUS JUNIUS (VI 3). One of Caesar's generals.

SOTIATES (III 2). A tribe of S.W. France living in the neighbourhood of Sos (derived from *Sotiates*), in the Dept. of the Lot-et-Garonne.

SUEBI (II 2; IV 1, 2; VI 4). A powerful German people who for about a century before Caesar's time had been gradually expanding south-westwards from their home in N. Germany.

SUESSIONES (II 3, 4; VIII 1). A Belgic tribe living in the Dept. of the Aisne, in the neighbourhood of Soissons (derived from *Suessiones*).

SUGAMBRI (IV 2; VI 5). A German tribe living on the E. bank of the Rhine between the rivers Ruhr and Sieg (derived from *Sugambri*).

SULLA, LUCIUS CORNELIUS (II 1). See Introd. 1.

SULPICIUS RUFUS, PUBLIUS (V 1; VII 5). One of Caesar's generals.

TARUSATES (III 2). A tribe of Aquitania.

TASGETIUS (VI 1). A nobleman of the Carnutes.

TENCTHERI (IV 1, 2; VI 3, 5). A German tribe which, with the Usipetes, invaded Gaul in 55 B.C.

TEUTONI (II 2–4; VII 5). See Introd. 3.

TREBONIUS, GAIUS (V 2; VI 1, 5; VII 1, 5; VIII 1, 2). One of Caesar's generals.

TREBONIUS, GAIUS (VI 5). A Roman Knight serving in Gaul.

TREVERI (II 2, 4; III 1; IV 1; V 2; VI 1–5; VII 4; VIII 2). A tribe living W. of the Rhine in S.E. Belgium, Luxemburg, and part of Rhenish Prussia; the town of Treves preserves their name.

TRINOVANTES (V 2). A tribe living in Essex; their chief town was Camulodunum, on the site of Colchester.

TURONI (II 4; VII 1, 5; VIII 2). A tribe living on the banks of the Loire near Tours (derived from *Turoni*).

UBII (IV 1, 2; VI 4). A German tribe living on the E. bank of the Rhine between the rivers Sieg and Main.

USIPETES (IV 1, 2; VI 5). See **TENCTHERI**.

UXELLODUNUM (VIII 2). A stronghold of the Cadurci in S.W. France, probably the hill called Puy d'Issolu, near Vayrac in the Dept. of the Lot.

VALERIUS CABURUS, GAIUS (II 2; VII 4). A prominent man of the Helvii, father of **GAIUS VALERIUS PROCILLUS** (II 2) and **GAIUS VALERIUS DOMNOTAURUS** (VII 4).

GLOSSARY

VALERIUS FLACCUS, GAIUS (II 2). Governor of the province of Transalpine Gaul in 83 B.C.

VALERIUS TROUCILLUS, GAIUS (II 1). A prominent man of the province of Transalpine Gaul.

VATINIUS, PUBLIUS (VIII 2). One of Caesar's generals.

VELLAUNODUNUM (VII 1, 2). A town of the Senones in central France – probably Montargis, between Orleans and Sens.

VENELLI (II 4; III 1; VII 5). A tribe living on the coast of Normandy in the neighbourhood of Cherbourg.

VENETI (II 4; III 1; VII 5). A tribe living in the Dept. of the Morbihan in Brittany.

VERAGRI (II 5). A tribe living in S.W. Switzerland on the upper Rhone, near Martigny.

VERCASSIVELLAUNUS (VII 5). A leader of the Arverni, cousin to Vercingetorix.

VERCINGETORIX (VII 1–5). An Arvernian, commander-in-chief of the revolt of 52 B.C.

VERTICO (VI 2). A Nervian deserter employed by Cicero during the siege of his camp.

VERTISCUS (VIII 1). A chief magistrate and cavalry commander of the Remi.

VIRIDOMARUS (VII 3–5). A leader of the Aedui.

VIRIDOVIX (III 1). A leader of the Venelli.

VIROMANDUI (II 3, 4). A tribe living on the upper Somme near St Quentin.

VOCATES (III 2). A tribe of Aquitania.

VOLCAE (I 2; VII 1, 4) Tribes living on the coast between the Pyrenees and the Rhone.

VOLUSENUS QUADRATUS, GAIUS (II 5; V 1; VI 5; VIII 1, 2). A military tribune; commander of Caesar's cavalry in the later campaigns.

MORE ABOUT PENGUINS
AND PELICANS

Penguinews, which appears every month, contains details of all the new books issued by Penguins as they are published. From time to time it is supplemented by *Penguins in Print*, which is our complete list of almost 5,000 titles.

A specimen copy of *Penguinews* will be sent to you free on request. Please write to Dept EP, Penguin Books Ltd, Harmondsworth, Middlesex, for your copy.

In the U.S.A.: For a complete list of books available from Penguin in the United States write to Dept CS, Penguin Books, 625 Madison Avenue, New York, New York 10022.

In Canada: For a complete list of books available from Penguin in Canada write to Penguin Books Canada Ltd, 2801 John Street, Markham, Ontario L3R 1B4.

VIRGIL, CATULLUS AND CICERO IN THE PENGUIN CLASSICS

VIRGIL
THE AENEID
Translated by W. F. Jackson Knight

CATULLUS
POEMS
Translated by Peter Whigham

CICERO
THE NATURE OF THE GODS
Translated by Horace C. P. McGregor

CICERO
MURDER TRIALS
Translated by Michael Grant

CICERO
ON THE GOOD LIFE
Translated by Michael Grant

CICERO
SELECTED POLITICAL SPEECHES
Translated by Michael Grant

CICERO
SELECTED WORKS
Translated by Michael Grant

THE PENGUIN CLASSICS

Some Recent and Forthcoming Volumes